ALSO BY LISA ZEIDNER

Customs

Talking Cure (Poems)

ALEXANDRA FREED

ALEXANDRA FREED

A NOVEL BY

LISA ZEIDNER

4803

ALFRED A. KNOPF   NEW YORK   1983

Library of Congress Cataloging in Publication Data

Zeidner, Lisa.   Alexandra Freed.

I. Title.
PS3576.E37Z78   1983   813'.54   82-48735
ISBN 0-394-52750-X

Manufactured in the United States of America

FIRST EDITION

The author thanks the Rutgers Research Council for its help, and is
also grateful to Alice Quinn for her invaluable editorial assistance.

Grateful acknowledgment is made to the following for permission to
reprint from previously published material:

Alfred A. Knopf, Inc.: Excerpt from *The Magic Mountain* by Thomas
Mann, translated by H. T. Lowe-Porter. Copyright 1927 and
renewed 1955 by Alfred A. Knopf, Inc., Copyright 1952 by Thomas
Mann. Reprinted by permission of Alfred A. Knopf, Inc.

Princeton University Press: From *The I Ching or Book of Changes*. The
Richard Wilhelm translation rendered into English by Cary F.
Baynes. Bollingen Series XIX. Copyright 1950 © 1967 by Princeton
University Press. Copyright © renewed 1977 by Princeton University
Press. Excerpts reprinted by permission of Princeton
University Press.

For Russell and Merrie

She began to talk about how fascinating it was to cough. It was a solid satisfaction, when you felt a tickling come in your chest, deep down, and grow and grow, to reach down after it, and get at it, so to say. Sneezing was much the same thing. You kept on wanting to sneeze until you simply couldn't stand it any longer; you looked as if you were tipsy; you drew a couple of breaths; then out it came, and you forgot everything else in the bliss of the sensation. Sometimes the explosion repeated itself two or three times. That was the sort of pleasure life gave you free of charge.

—THOMAS MANN, *The Magic Mountain*

ONE

1

Everyone everywhere has always felt trapped in one way or another, and I was no exception. Each year would add another bar to my cage until I shriveled up and died, probably of lung cancer. But I'd die happy. I wore a pearl-buttoned sweater in heliotrope cashmere which I'd bought that afternoon to allay my anxiety about being unemployed. Despite national and personal recession, I was afraid of no ball this world could serve me.

In 1979 I was twenty-nine. It was the end of a decade and the beginning of middle age, because it's in the Freed genes to die young, or at least we say it is. A Freed likes to say I told you so; a Freed doesn't like to be surprised, least of all by bad news.

But on Halloween, my future had been superseded by immediate pleasures. My best friend Pat had sent her daughter off with a neighbor so we could get drunk on the steps of Pat's house, dispense candy to children in ghoul regalia, and banter, as was our wont. Stacey, who had been our friend since she broke up Pat's marriage, had joined us for the spectacle with camera and tripod; in lieu of original costumes, she was working on the moon, which was an interesting notch off full.

"Moon's been done," I said.

Stacey, who had devoted most of her time since she modeled baby powder at age one to proving that her thought was deeper than her tan, aimed the camera at Pat and me. "I'll put it on automatic," she announced, "and sit between you," but a couple in love was passing. Their bodies were intertwined, and it took them a long time to walk past us. Next we were interrupted by blond twins dressed as Satan and angel with missing teeth—they were too cute to photograph.

It was Trash Night. Usually I could rant about Philadelphia trash collection for as long as my New York friends went on about subways. But the moon, the costumes, the wine, the weightless feeling you get from not smoking, and the howl of watchdogs as doorbells rang lent atmosphere to Pat's neighborhood. With a positive outlook, the curbed garbage could smell like roasted chestnuts or, better yet, like truffles. Soon in southwestern France where I'd never been, old peasants with leashed pigs would harvest most of the world's crop of the fungus. The pigs would sniff soil until they detected the delicacy; they'd be beaten off with sticks and pulled away, fed small potatoes as compensation. In this manner, a truffle farmer might yield two dozen a day of the two hundred and fifty tons of "black diamond" demanded annually by the world's great chefs at a price of a hundred dollars a kilo, dearer than caviar. I felt sorry for the pigs. Like me, they grunted their lives away in search of satisfactions they never got. Worse yet, they hadn't the consolation of self-pity—sweet in moderation but, like chocolates or figs, nauseating in excess. Being single and aimless at almost thirty was not cause for suicide, especially when my presence served to make such a pretty study in contrasts with my friends on the steps: Stacey with her long blonde hair, her face sultry and vague as a daguerreotype; Pat radiating simple health (lit, she liked to joke, from within); me between them, shorter than both, the genes of my Russian ancestors bestowing my face, on good days, with the gloomy angularity sometimes called striking. Stacey set the camera and dashed for the steps.

"*Little Women*," I suggested as the flash went off.

"Someday," Stacey said crossly, "I'm going to get a picture of you when your mouth isn't moving."

"I quit smoking. That's a start."

"Shut up, Alex!"

Stacey set the camera again and rejoined us to pose with glasses of wine and with the self-righteous, slightly self-mocking melancholy of women without men. In her best photographs, Stacey's women, though modern in dress and posture, get an old-fashioned interiority, an aura of being resigned to imprisonment in their lives and thoughts. But that's not how the picture came out, because a man materialized from the alley to the left of Pat's house and walked directly in front of the camera in time for the flash.

"Hey!" Stacey said.

The man had a strong chin, a bony nose, and eyes that suggested some depth. He wore a tweed jacket and a bright red scarf. I noticed the scarf first. It wasn't cold enough for a scarf. The day had been windless, cloudless, flatly lit—more like a movie set of Indian summer than real weather. The red scarf was even more percussive against the man's auburn hair, or at least I thought it was auburn. Its color seemed to wink on and off, like the iridescent Jesuses found at Woolworth's—a color especially hard to pin down in the dusk, which, a split second after his trespass into our composition, got visibly darker, then lighter again, as the streetlights were ignited by whatever invisible power sees to such things. This quick series of changes must have been startlingly unnatural for me to have noticed it at all, absorbed as I was with the man. His attention, in turn, was fully on the sky: Stacey's "hey" made him freeze an expression appropriate to the suspicion that God had decided to speak to him.

"Walter!" Pat said.

Only then did he turn to us.

"Pat?" the man said.

Pat and the man laughed and embraced.

"I hardly recognized you without your beard," Pat said. "It's been years. Why are you here?"

"On my way to a costume party. Where's Preston?"

"We're divorced."

"Us too," Walter said grimly.

"I didn't even know you got married."

"Neither did my wife. Introduce me to your friends."

"Walter Danner, Stacey Easterlin," Pat said. Before she could say my name, I offered "Alexandra Freed," very solemnly. Walter shook Stacey's hand, dipped his head toward me, and said "Alex," equally solemnly.

"What a small world," Pat said.

"Just a small town," Walter corrected.

"I agree," I said. "The other day in Chinatown, I found myself in the Happy Paradise seated next to my gynecologist."

Pat rolled her eyes at me and explained, "Walter and Preston were roommates for ten seconds in—Christ—1968."

Walter sat. "I hate to do this, Stacey, but I'm sure you were at Frank Something's New Year's party in 1977. Somebody tried to jump out the window. You wore a black dress with a train. You're a photographer, right? Arts Academy."

"You have a good memory," Stacey admitted.

"Photographer was just a clever guess," Pat noted.

"And you?" Walter said, turning to me.

The question of my occupation, though inevitable, had come up too fast for my taste. "A friend of mine in Portland," I said, "did a dissertation which proved that in any town of a hundred thousand people, there's a forty percent chance that you've shared a lover or an occupation with anyone of the opposite sex you meet."

"You made up the statistic," Pat said, pouring Walter some wine in her glass.

"Ad-libbed it, but the dissertation's real."

"What do you do, Alex?"

"I used to do PR with Pat," I said, defeated.

"She's now the best-educated person on welfare, to make a long story short," Stacey announced.

"Unemployment," I snapped. "There *is* a difference."

Walter groaned. "Career guilt?"

"That's what my brother says," I told him. "He says our vocational confusions are entirely decorative, as compulsory for young ladies as white gloves used to be."

Walter Danner's laugh came from deep in his throat. I could have said more, but I'd been meaning to revise my flirting techniques—a little less of performer, a little more of attentive audience. I liked Walter's auburn mustache; I liked how he sat, inclining like a lizard in sun toward each of us as we spoke, his shoulders tight with a tension that suggested sexual energy. He was a thirty-one-year-old architect and real estate developer who, for the half hour before Stacey packed her equipment and left to meet the mathematician she'd recently taken up with, spoke to all three of us with democratic appreciation. That in itself should have made me suspicious. Instead, I was glad to see Stacey leave. With just three of us, I thought, we had a better chance of getting down to the gritty business of the soul. But since one of my current and perpetual projects was to stop trotting out my soul for show-and-tell too soon, I sat quietly as Pat told Walter about her recent killing in silver options, and about a deal that might interest him.

"There's an old man across the street who has lived there for forty years, never comes out, on Halloweens he lights his place up and scares the kids to death with his bad teeth and smell. I've gotten him groceries during storms, commiserated with him about the neighborhood, so he confided in me when he found out he's got terminal cancer. Now that he's admitted to himself he might die, he wants to go somewhere warm at once, with cash. I want to remove the furniture for him and renovate. The thing is, the poor guy needs medical funds and has a garage out back with a Packard he has driven maybe fifteen times—must be worth twenty grand alone. The house is in bad enough shape that I think I can buy him out for twenty-five, thirty thousand. I wouldn't be ripping him off, because he needs the money fast and the market's bad. What do you think, Walter?"

I thought it was odd for Pat, who had never got anything easily in her life, to discuss large sums of money so casually. She had gone from playing charwoman to six boorish brothers and an alcoholic father to supporting an eternal graduate student, who reinforced her only in her fear that she was stupid because she'd never read Proust and still got teary at midnight mass. Pat didn't have time for self-pity, between working full time and raising a daughter, yet in her calm there was something more enduring than in the accomplishments of my more ambitious friends. Pat, of course, resented me casting her as earth mother, just as Stacey resented being cast as California girl. If Pat had patience to reupholster a couch or rewire a lamp, it was only because she couldn't afford new ones, couldn't concentrate on anything more intellectually demanding, and had no one to help her. Her "calm," she said, was as painful an entrapment as my chattiness. Still I admired her strength. I had no time for people who didn't admire Pat.

"I hope he's stupid as well as cancerous," Walter said, "because otherwise he'd never sell for twenty-five thousand on this block, no matter what kind of shape the place is in. If he will, snap it up and get a loan for a contractor. I think you'll find do-it-yourself renovation work to be more back-breaking and nerve-racking than you imagine."

Before he could expand, Pat's daughter Nessie (the name Vanessa was the ex-husband's idea) arrived with one tired adult and a troupe of costumed children. Nessie was dressed as a large West Philadelphia rodent. I wouldn't have guessed from the mottled gray bathmats pinned to her clothes, unless forewarned.

"Eek, a rat," I exclaimed.

"Mom told you," Nessie accused. "No one could tell." And she burst into tears as her mother waved goodbye to adults and children. I took the child into my lap and helped her to sort her candy between snuffles.

"A child!" Walter said. "I can't believe this. When did you and Preston produce this beauty?"

"A moment of forgetfulness in 1973," Pat said. "Come on, Ness. We're going upstairs."

The child clung to my neck and screamed. "She's tired," Pat apologized. "Ness, be unpredictable and skip the whole performance."

"*I* could tell you were a rat," I offered.

"Liar!"

"In acting," Pat said, "the point is never costume. I already explained that. If you promise to go to bed afterwards, I'll let you subject Walter and Aunt Alex to your Stanislavski version of a rat."

Nessie sprang from my lap, scattering Zappos and Holy Smokes everywhere, to do a jazz-dance rendition of a rat. During her performance, I rebagged candy, and Pat slumped into the posture of a large bass player watching intently as the drummer slips into a solo—Pat does vicious, flawless imitations. Her impression of me smoking imperiously, wiggling my foot, and leaning forward on a tiny college desk to make a fatuous point about an obscure tribe's childbirth practices had once made one of my lovers laugh so hard he'd spilled a mug of coffee all over my freshly painted kitchen wall. I'd never been able to remove the stain.

While I picked up candy and watched Pat and Vanessa, my eye was a fish-eye lens revealing that Walter was watching *me*. Whether he would have chosen me if Pat hadn't had a daughter and if bewitching Stacey hadn't left were questions I was willing to forestall for the pleasure that sensing him watch afforded— the pleasure of a store detective witnessing a theft in an empty aisle on his video set. When Pat scooped up her child, I felt the awe of a petless person when someone lifts a cat by the loose skin on its neck and makes the animal go limp. The pleasures of the evening could go on without wine. But when Pat asked us to wait until she put Vanessa to bed, I objected.

"I can't," I said. "I have to get home. I can't stand another moment awake without a cigarette."

Though I didn't have to get home, I'd just watched Walter hitch up his pants and felt a flutter of lust. Even the sight of his wrist coming out of his shirt-cuff, airbrushed with reddish-blond hair, was enough to induce in me the telegraphic memory of sex. I'd made a promise to myself: in the new decade, I'd sleep with no more men I didn't know. I'd endured three months of abstinence so I could go into 1980 with a clean slate, and I wasn't about to blow it now.

"Stay awhile," Walter said.

"Yes, do," Pat said, but from the way she distractedly curled a part of her growing-out bangs around her finger I knew she was tired and wanted to be alone.

"I'd need a cigarette," I said. "The wine, you know. Also, I've got to prepare for a hangover."

"In that case, you promised Nessie a bedtime story."

"I did? I did!"

"I'll wait here for you," Walter said, "and drive you to your car, or home."

In Vanessa's bedroom, while the child was choosing pajamas as a stalling tactic, Pat took me by the shoulders to say: "Listen up. You'd be better off with Rasputin. Walter is completely deranged. I don't use the term lightly."

"Give me a for instance of deranged."

"At one party, he took three different girls into the bathroom and screwed them on the floor, one after another."

"That's not deranged. It's undergraduate. Maybe he grew up."

"I doubt it."

"But Pat, your taste and my taste have never skipped hand in hand."

"True. I've developed a taste for humans and you still like selfish sadists. Don't put yourself through this again. I'm not going to stand by and let you get involved with a diagnosed madman."

"If he's that weird, don't you think I'll figure it out?"

"No."

"Ye of little faith!"

"Don't come crying to me in the morning," Pat warned.

Nessie was naked by then, suddenly as mute and dazed as a new puppy. A drunken flash: Pat was jealous, not of Walter in particular, but of the possibility of romance. I understood. We spent a good part of our time convincing each other that we were pretty and smart enough to deserve love. I thanked Pat for dinner, told her that my life would be empty without her, and took the steps of my surrogate home as gleeful as a teen on a first date.

"Alone at last," Walter said. "Where do you live?"

"What about your party?" I asked.

"Skip it."

"What's your costume?"

He took a tie from his pocket and held it up for me to see. "I was going to wear a tie and jacket and go as someone else," he said, "or go as a Republican—except it's really cheating, because I wear ties and jackets all the time."

"Are you a Republican?" I said.

As answer he mock-punched me in the arm.

We walked to his car, a 1971 Cortina (impossible, I knew, to get parts for). In the car we talked about car maintenance and how hard it is to meet people in Philadelphia ("There are no public spaces here," Walter said, "or in any American city"). When we determined that we frequented many of the same restaurants and bars, we got too excited, laughed, and fell into a reverent hush.

At a light Walter said, "Pat's a good woman."

"One of the finest."

"Maybe too good. In college she was so worried she'd never be more than a housewife she used to overcompensate—she used to act like those Joan Crawford types in forties films."

"She's still alive. Don't talk about her in the past tense."

"Hey, no offense."

"Pat could do anything. I'd be a passenger with her in a two-seater plane even if she'd never flown before. I also think she would make a terrific actress."

Walter laughed. "If I ever need a press agent, I'll hire you. What did Pat say about me upstairs?"

"Nothing."

"She told you to watch out for me, didn't she? I was pretty wild when she knew me. Now I'm just a working man. Up at dawn, income taxes. Anyhow, when I'm nervous I tend to revert to class clown. Usually I'm a nice guy."

"I never trust people who announce their own kindness."

"I like you, Alex."

"I'm glad."

"I'm not jumping the gun. Good things are going to happen. I can tell. Something's clicked. Hasn't it for you?"

"I just realized how much I drank," I replied, but what had clicked—as Walter pulled into a parking space two blocks from my apartment and we got out—was the memory of how nice it is to walk with a man you hadn't seen naked yet, especially an employed man who likes old movies. It would be hard not to make love if he touched me lightly on the small of the back, but I'd resist. My head was almost empty except for the piano-player rendition of a thirties tune called "Stop! Look! Listen!" We had reached the little park near my apartment. High on wine and willpower, I stopped for a moment to breathe deeply, to throw my head back and see stars, of which there were a good splattering.

"Kiss me," Walter said.

I could smell his cologne. "I'd like to, but I can't."

"Are you otherwise committed?"

"It's not that."

"Are you gay?"

"Why, yes. You guessed it."

"I didn't think so." He grabbed my neck, moved me closer, and kissed me hard, the red mustache surprising my lip.

"Gee," I said, pulling away.

"It'll get better."

"It's fine. I just have a new rule about screwing on a first date."

Walter put his hands in his pockets, hurt. "Did I say I wanted to screw? I just want to kiss you. Let's kiss under those trees, okay?"

"In front of all those people?" I objected, gesturing grandly to the empty park.

"Why not?"

I bounced on my heels and laughed, began to walk toward the trees like John Wayne all set for the draw, but Walter, who was strutting behind me, didn't notice. He was comically serious about this kiss. I myself was looking forward to it. "Shoot," I said.

"Are you sure you wouldn't rather sit?"

"Can't you kiss and stand at the same time?"

"Sure," he said, and he did, for what might have been a minute, until (even drunker than I thought) I lost my balance and fell down. Walter, laughing, sat on me.

"Hey," I said.

I tried to sit up with him straddling my belly. Walter looked puzzled. He dipped his head to kiss me.

"I'm for longer courtships," I said. "In slightly warmer weather and in slightly older clothes that didn't need to be dry-cleaned, I'd be more obliging. Under the circumstances, however, I'd appreciate being restored to an upright position."

Walter began to fumble with my skirt.

"I mean it, Walter!"

But I didn't quite mean it yet, and I didn't pursue the plea, because Walter was doing something so curious that I just watched, mesmerized. What he accomplished was a move that landed him down still on top of me, but facing the other way, so that I could see only his flat tweed back, with my shoes peering out on the other end. He took off my pumps carefully, placed them beside my purse, and began to *roll down* my pantyhose. He turned the pantyhose right side out, folded them in half, rolled them up, and placed them on top of my purse—all of this efficiently as a chef mass-producing crêpes.

"Don't worry about my pantyhose," I said. "Worry about my immortal soul." And I pulled his hair, screaming, my scream too high-pitched, like the scream on a tape recorder.

Walter about-faced to bottle the scream with another kiss, holding my arms over my head with his arms. "Do you believe this?" I asked his teeth.

From the smell I decided that we were in ginkgo trees. I wondered what kind of landscape architect would plant ginkgoes in a park—unless the stink was from trees on a neighboring block. Pat was right as usual. I stopped thinking of Walter as a potential lover and husband and conjured all the folk wisdom I'd heard about dealing with rapists. A street-wise friend from St. Louis once told me that unless you have a black belt in karate, running is the best self-defense. But even if my reflexes had rallied after the wine, it was too late to run. I knew that I should vomit or act crazy. Acting crazy sounded easier. I thought of reciting "George Who Played with a Dangerous Toy and Suffered a Catastrophe of Considerable Dimensions," a children's poem I knew by heart and used to do at top speed in tandem with my brother. Walter, however, had already unzipped his pants. Both Walter and I looked at Walter's barely erect penis. Maybe there was still time to talk him into civility.

"This may surprise you," I said tremulously, "but rape is against the law. Also, you're hurting my arms."

"I'm sorry," Walter whispered, rubbing against me.

"Then stop."

"I know it's an imposition, but I'll be most grateful."

"What is this, a tea party? That's my underwear you're removing. Given the importance of my body, I think I should get a last cigarette. I think I should get to call my family and put my affairs in order, make a will so the government doesn't inherit my Cuisinart. Could you please sit up a minute so I can flash my life before my eyes?"

Walter spat on his hand and wet my labia. I didn't close my legs. I couldn't the way I was positioned; besides, my instinctive reaction to fear was talk. "Is life-flashing appropriate in such situations?" I asked him. "I mean, should I start from birth chronologically, or maybe I should work for a montage effect of crucial moments?"

"This is lovemaking," Walter said, "not a seminar in post-modernism."

"Lovemaking?" I gulped. "Oh, brother!"

I was apparently being raped at around eleven o'clock on a Wednesday by a handsome young Caucasian who dropped terms like post-modernism. He was doing his best to hold my arms down with one hand while working himself up to an erection with the other. "Where are the gangs of teenaged boys with large radios when you need them?" I asked him, but he didn't answer. Maybe someone would see us from an upstairs window on Pine Street and call the police, though it was possible that the trees covered us from view. My scream had been more full-bodied than it might have been if I hadn't quit smoking, but there was no response; maybe someone hearing it assumed it was a trick-or-treat prank. It was such a nice night, it was Halloween—why weren't there more people out? There were always people out. My pumps sat near my purse, upon which my pantyhose rested; my underpants dangled off one foot and I was lying in the dirt in a sixty-dollar sweater. Once Walter got going, maybe he'd let go of my hands; if someone passed, I'd scream again.

"Are you sure you don't want to reconsider?" I asked.

"I wish you were wetter," Walter accused. "Here we go."

I'd never been raped before, but I was by no means a virgin, and I could tell from Walter's languid thrusts that he planned to be at this for a while.

I had a headache, my stomach hurt, and I had just lost respect for yet another man.

2

The first lie that I ever told, or at least the first lie that I remember having told, had to do with the neighbor's dog, which was run over one summer dusk when I was six or seven.

My brother Theo, our baby-sitter, and I were on the front lawn when it happened. The baby-sitter naturally tried to get us into the house, but we wanted to watch. That summer, I'd seen two dead squirrels, a mauled-over bird, and a dead opossum in my neighborhood, not to mention the worms and slugs that atrophied in our carport when it rained. The opossum was particularly disgusting, because the older kids ran over it with their bikes for several days until it was a pink and brown mass textured by flies and tire tracks, scarily abstract, like a Francis Bacon painting.

I might have got a better look at the opossum if it hadn't chosen to die so close to the retarded girl's house. The girl was about twenty, with breasts as big as my mother's. She wore her waist-length hair in braids and she rode a tricycle. I spent as little time as possible on this girl's block. I wanted to reduce the block in my head to something as insignificant as a crack in the sidewalk or a weed in the median strip, but, like the run-over dog, it took up a great deal of space in my brain.

The bloody poodle whimpered and twitched. The neighbors and Theo cried. The baby-sitter, who would get pregnant and drop out of high school a year later, comforted Theo. We didn't eat supper. I saw the green car speed off. That evening, my parents let me tell this story to the police, although it was past my bedtime. In my flannel pajamas I told the police everything I remembered: the green station wagon; the driver's face, round and red as Santa's (he was probably drunk); how he'd thrown back his head and laughed.

This wasn't a lie exactly. It's only that later I couldn't quite remember if the car had been green rather than blue or gray. Was the driver a red-faced blond, and was he really laughing, not coughing or sneezing?

Since that incident, I had tried to be more careful to say only what I could prove. But even sworn to empiricism, I found I couldn't help exaggerating. Once, in college, as I was walking to a Salvation Army center, an old man had called to me and mumbled something. I told him gently that I hadn't heard. I thought he was sick. I was willing to help. But the old man repeated: "Suck my cock." I stormed off, badly shaken. That evening I told dinner guests that I'd been held up at gunpoint near the Salvation Army, that I'd merely tossed my head and walked away. I told this story two or three times over the years, until I could only selectively remember if it had happened that way or not. I exaggerated to give my stories authority and charm, because I regretted being forever fated to the blandness of suburbia.

Like most women of my generation, I had a mental list of lovers whose names I counted like sheep on sleepless nights. By 1979, when I was ashamed rather than proud of my sexual history, I counted men as wolves. Pat claims that no relationship that ends can end well, but over each of the hopelessly inappropriate males I'd suffered the usual withdrawal symptoms: irrepressibly haunting memories of their hands, walks, kisses; mistrust of every attractive woman they might prefer; and what I had dubbed "the red Volkswagen syndrome," after my first boyfriend, who had one—the ability of the sight of a car to stop the heart at the prospect of a possible glimpse of the ex-object. For a month or so, I'd see Volkswagens, and later, Hondas or Toyotas everywhere. Then I would somehow recover. Victor, who looked so good in his beige jacket; or Jim, with his timid, lopsided smile, would simply be added to my list. I would tell blithe stories about these men in the context of a friend's heartache.

But sometimes I couldn't remember the last names of men early on my list; sometimes I couldn't remember if I'd actually made love to these men or just fooled around with them; perhaps they fell during the time when I had no birth control and merely performed fellatio with the grim altruism of a nurse at the front. If I'd slept with them once or performed fellatio, should they be on my list? I would vow to remember better. Perhaps if I paid more attention, I could even take my own experiences more seriously. But often things simply weren't clear.

Once I was in a matinée on Market Street alone. The theatre wasn't crowded. In the middle of the film, a man sat down beside me in the otherwise empty row. I didn't change seats. The man didn't bother me. Maybe he was just lonely. I continued watching the show. Soon I noticed an odd smell. The man nudged me, and I looked down to find that he was masturbating. Before changing seats, I went to the back of the theatre and told the usher indignantly: "Sir, there's a man masturbating in here, and it's ruining my concentration." I had vowed to get a gun, and since the incident at the theatre I had been mentally shooting everyone who bothered me: men hooting from cars, rude bank clerks, happy couples smoking menthol cigarettes on billboards. I didn't want to kill anyone, of course. I was a liberal, entirely for gun control. My victims never died or even fell over backward. They merely froze, like the last shot before the credits in a movie.

As a rule I had trouble concentrating. Everything made me think about sex. I would try to jog, notice small blue flowers by the side of the track, hear the splotcha-splotcha of my feet as I leaped over a puddle near the bleachers, and fantasize about marrying a blind rock star who would be moved by such sounds; almost immediately I'd tire of jogging and want to be at home listening to Motown. At the symphony, I understood the music in terms of the continually shifting balance of power between men and women. The violin (female) had her say at the beginning of the symphony, but when the woman got too plaintive, the voice of the (male) cello, which had been a strong undercurrent throughout, began to dominate. Soon the movement of so many bows in unison, the contrast of black tuxedos and red velvet curtains, would soothe me to sleep. In graduate school, I would watch my professors' hands and wonder how they were in bed. The real work of anthropology didn't interest me. I hated learning languages and I hated fieldwork—traveling threw me out of whack. I simply liked the idea of being a strong, smart, versatile woman like Margaret Mead. "In Mundugumor," Mead wrote, "people copulated in gardens belonging to someone else, just to spoil their yams. Lovemaking was accompanied by scratching and biting, and people committed suicide by getting into a temper tantrum and drifting down the river in a canoe to get captured and eaten by the next tribe." Such anecdotes kept me from worrying about what I would do with my life.

In the eight years since I graduated from Swarthmore, I had worked as a museum curator aide, an anthropology graduate student, a waitress, a teacher of English to foreign students, a rare-book librarian, and, most recently, a public-relations copywriter. I had campaigned for a Democratic senator and helped write the subtitles for a Japanese film. The average length of my jobs was nine months, sadly parallel to the frame of an academic year. Nine months also seemed the limit of most of my relationships with men and of most of my hobbies, from obsessive cello practice to cooking classes. In defending me, my friends often tried to pawn my short attention span off as "range," but I had no delusions of being a Renaissance woman. On the contrary, I knew I was a dilettante. The degree to which this bothered me varied with the weather, the phases of the moon, my love life, and my debts. A long time ago, I had pledged to kill myself on my thirtieth birthday if I hadn't yet, as my parents would say, "accomplished something." Now, with my thirtieth birthday due in five months, I'd saved some money and, with Pat's help, got myself officially fired from the PR job in order to collect unemployment while I made some decisions about my future. No more half-lit, cognac-fueled conversations about how the Koreans have no word or concept for zero!

I by no means intended to find myself. Myselfness was, in fact, something that I'd had quite enough of. I didn't believe I had depths waiting to be tapped, secrets rich as oil that, once dredged up, would lighten my load, float me to happiness and wealth. I could say without embarrassment or defensiveness that I was all pretty much on the surface. By this I didn't mean to say that I was superficial—although with the Freed pressure to perform I worried about that. I could take an idea and get it so tangled up in all parts of my being that it wound through my sleep, seeped into my showers and my lovemaking. It was my strongest conviction that all human thought and activity comes down to just about the same thing. Everything brings you up against the self, and you push harder, trying to get somewhere else. Then you get somewhere else and are homesick for the self, so you head back inside again. If this was true, then there wasn't much difference between a devoted punk rocker and a nuclear physicist. Dig a tunnel to China and you wind up in your own backyard, wondering where you put the barbecue coals.

Life was a picnic for me, a conventional—and not entirely satisfying—way to pass the time. True, I wasn't a slave dying for the pyramids, or a slave of capitalism who only had energy to mow the lawn and watch the news. I had no speech defects, I had miraculously avoided herpes, my parents had never beaten me, I had never been kidnapped or caught in an earthquake, and not only did I never go hungry, but I had an electric coffeemaker, a food processor, and the wherewithal to concoct a midnight chocolate mousse, if I so chose. I could choose, but where was I? More often than not, I was eating a ham sandwich on a damp square of ground some miles from my apartment, watching young men scull on the river, and thinking how much better life would be if it were spent in France. Would France make me wave at policemen, not be as prone to colds and hangovers, quit smoking, be more productive or not mind being less? If I lived in France, could I avoid a life in which my car loan was rejected and I backed away reciting Yeats to myself through gritted teeth? While being raped, would I at least have the good sense to be completely devastated?

It was October 31st and I was, indeed, getting raped. It was a pleasant night in Fitler Square in Philadelphia, a city where I'd lived for the past eight years; a city where one minute you're at a friend's and the next minute you're being raped in ginkgoes, a children's poem lodged in your brain as stubbornly as a twig in your side.

One thing was sure. I refused to lose 1980 to a rape, especially to a rape like this, which more closely resembled bad sex: Walter fell out of me every eight or nine thrusts and spent most of his time—when he wasn't holding down my arms and bottling my screams—fumbling with his penis. My lawyer friend Vivian West would probably want to use my trauma to further a feminist cause. But I didn't feel so much violated as determined not to let the rape become an issue. I was too strident a fan of trauma. The last thing I needed was another issue. I needed simple days that built slowly to a sense of purpose, because I had no idea what I was going to do with my life, and as far as problems go, that seemed sufficient.

"The heart thinks constantly," the *I Ching* counsels. "This cannot be changed, but the movements of the heart—that is, a man's thoughts—should restrict themselves to the immediate situation. All thinking that goes beyond the immediate situation only makes the heart sore." I couldn't help thinking ahead to how a rape would affect me. I wasn't going to work for a rape crisis center, turn lesbian, or search for a sweet fellow who would settle for holding my hand until I worked out my loathing of male genitalia. I would go to the police, put this idiot on my list as my thirty-fourth fuck, and forget about it. *The moral is that little boys should not be given dangerous toys.* At this time of month, I didn't even have to worry about getting pregnant.

3

"Oh, well," Walter sighed.

He rolled off me, stroked sweaty hair from his forehead, and lay down next to me, on his back, face to the stars.

"That it?" I snapped.

Walter moaned.

I pulled up my underpants, pulled down my skirt, picked twigs from my sweater, and put on my shoes. "May I go now?"

"I didn't come," Walter said.

"Pardon?"

"*I didn't come.*"

I laughed.

"It isn't funny," Walter informed me.

"Only I would get an impotent rapist."

"I'm not a rapist! And I'm *not* impotent."

"You're not?" I leered.

The palms of his hands covered his eyes, and his mouth was open. He was breathing hard. "What is this—I'm supposed to comfort you?" I said. "Listen, you affront to mankind, you pathetic specimen of all things vile, I'll be running along now, as soon as I locate my purse, which you must have kicked somewhere in your soggy heat."

"I'm a bastard," he said.

I was standing over him, my arms crossed, my purse against my side, completely wiped out by indignation, tempted to kick him or otherwise express myself. He lifted his hand from his eyes. His pants were still unzipped, his forlorn penis on his stomach; he was pouting.

"I'm sorry," he said. "I'd like to say 'I don't know what came over me,' and I don't, but I know it's lame. Partly I thought you wanted it."

"I led you on!"

"Why don't we go to the police together? No kidding. I'll confess."

"I'll get you legally," I said. In a spontaneous gesture of magnanimity, black humor, and confusion, I offered Walter my hand. Rather than shake it, he used it to lift himself up off the ground. So now we were both standing. He was much taller, and he squinted at me so intently that I remembered I'd better get home as quickly as possible—this man, though impotent, was nonetheless dangerous. "My lawyer will call your lawyer," I said.

I wasn't lingering. The whole exchange before I began my brisk getaway had taken perhaps half a minute.

"Don't leave," Walter said. "Let me explain!"

I only got about five steps from him before he grabbed my arm, raised it to his mouth, kissed it near the wrist, and planted an overly cinematic kiss on my neck. "You're shivering," he said. In one gesture he removed his jacket, threw it over my shoulders, and began to lead me toward a park bench.

I shook off his arm.

"No way," I snapped. "You don't get sexual services and

psychotherapy in one free shot. That's expecting a bit much for beginner's luck."

I let his jacket fall off my shoulders to the ground. Walter's face twisted into deep pain as he picked it up. His arms fell limply to his sides. "Please," he whined. He replaced the jacket on me tenderly as if to say, See? There's nothing to fear.

"Do you want me kicked out of the International Sisterhood?" I asked him.

"Please."

"Kicked out of the Universal Order of Sane People?"

"I won't tell anyone you were nice. We'll tell the police you bit and kicked."

"I did bite and kick!"

He showed me a tooth mark on his arm and grinned. "Please."

I sat. Perhaps I was in shock.

Walter Danner, wearing a beige shirt with a thin brown stripe, sat beside me, smiling. He took my hand, placed both his hand and mine on his thigh, and began to trace the outline of my fingers.

"You're kind and brave," he noted.

"I've developed such a sweet tooth for the 'unusual' that I've lost all perspective."

"You haven't," Walter told me. "Don't say that. Give me a chance. It's a nice night; you must admit we were getting along at Pat's. Relax. Pretend we've just met."

"If there's one thing I hate above all other things," I said, "it's men instructing me to relax."

4

By the time he was ten, Walter Danner told me, he had lived in eight houses, all in suburban Philadelphia. His mother was looking for a house that didn't smell. Their first house really did smell for a while. Two hamsters that Walter and his sister Judy had let out of the cage hid to die. This was in summer, before air conditioning. The smell was bad, but Margaret Danner continued to smell hamsters long after they'd been exhumed. She smelled hamster from the farthest corner of the backyard, over hot dogs and honeysuckle, a full year later.

She smelled it on her husband too, no doubt. Walter's father soon left for more temperate climates and less finicky women (Walter fought to keep the stuffed alligator Jacob sent from Key Biscayne).

After the divorce, Margaret Danner and her children moved to a fine old house that agreed with her for half a year, until she began to smell something "disconcerting." They went through a long series of maids, each bringing an untenable smell of her own. After that, the Danners moved once a year into smaller and smaller spaces. Mrs. Danner owned a real estate firm and had access to houses with the freshest paint, the most recent pipes and wood. The chewed teddy bears went, the old boots and mason jars. Her eighth house was as sparse as an infirmary.

Surprisingly, Margaret Danner wasn't fastidious. She didn't mind reaching into a turkey for gizzards; she didn't scrub the bottom of her copper pots with a special cleanser. In fact, she gave off an intense smell of her own, which Walter had always associated with chicken *paprikás* in a Hungarian kitchen—why Hungarian he didn't know, for Margaret was Greek, as feisty and outspoken as his father Jacob's German blood made him reserved. Her skin was dusty olive, her hair a deep auburn. She was robust and energetic. One of Walter's fondest memories was of his father, after cutting ivy from the chimney, reaching into Margaret's cleavage, ostensibly to check for bees escaped from their nests. His hand plunged into the expanse like a bird into clouds and her laugh was annoyed but affectionate.

Margaret wasn't crazy, Walter said. Crazy doesn't mean much these days anyway, with everyone vying for the most epic idiosyncrasy. Margaret saw no ghosts, was possessed by no demons. She simply had a very good nose.

A month before the press revealed that a nearby factory was dumping toxic wastes into the river, Margaret smelled something alkaline in her drinking water and refused even to wash her face with it. After her heart attack, she insisted that she smelled smoke through the respirator. The nurse said that was impossible, but as it turned out the respirator had a tiny leak in its control and smoke was, indeed, creeping in from the Nurses' Lounge. Margaret could tell Pepsi and Coke apart by the scent of the sugar level. Once, at a party, she amused the guests by blindfolding herself and smelling the difference between the candy coatings on M & M's.

Big smells didn't bother her. She worked blithely in her kitchen right after the exterminator sprayed. She could abide the bad breath of old drunks, the cacophony of perfume and cigarette smoke during intermission at the symphony. What bothered her were the smells dim enough to be ambiguous—what she called soul smells. (Walter's, she said, was like cashews—"not bad, just a little briny"; Judy Danner smelled like potting soil.) Margaret's least favorite smells were chemical—envelope glue, the plastic in which new shirts are wrapped. Walter didn't imagine that his mother was fussy about sex; she might have even liked the malty smell of sperm. If she stopped making love with Jacob Danner, it was probably because she was too busy at work to have more children, and couldn't put up with the rubbery or chemical smells of the available contraceptive methods.

It was the pace and anxiety of real estate work, not the oppression of smells, that did Margaret Danner in. She believed in housing. She was moral about it. Mrs. Danner talked prospective buyers out of houses with unevenly laid floorboards or bad water pressure. Whole wings of her condominiums remained empty because they had views of billboards. She was popular with customers, but not with banks, and she had to work so hard to keep her company going that she was bound to have heart problems.

After her heart attack, Mrs. Danner stopped drinking and smoking but kept working at the same pace—a pace aggravated by the divorce and by her frequent moves. She liked nothing better than the confusion of applications, deadlines, and payments. Perhaps the sureness of her nose made her a little too sure of her judgment, for once she was convinced of a truth, she held to it stubbornly. She was often cranky, and the divorce made her bitter. She never forgave Jacob. "There is no more despicable type of character," she would say (quoting William James, for she was well read; she read quickly, underlining in felt-tip), "than that of the sickly sentimentalist who welters in a sea of emotion and sensibility, but is incapable of performing a single manly concrete act." Jacob Danner's firmest act had been leaving his wife. That didn't keep her from believing that while he was noodling with his art (he made an adequate living as a free-lance artist), *she* was out making money and dealing with people.

Margaret Danner had no patience with tears and indecision. If the house smelled, you cleaned it. If that didn't work, you moved. When her business was faltering (it was still worth a good deal), she spoke of selling it and going to law school. She could have done it too, between moves and dinners, between her "good reads" and her dates with various acceptable men, who were never, however, acceptable enough to marry.

It was from Margaret that Walter acquired a taste for strong women. By strong, Walter didn't mean muscle-bound. Nor did he mean the desexualized, stoical objectivity that so often passes for strength. Margaret, like Walter's ex-wife, cried easily, aroused easily. She wasn't a bully. Walter admired determination, especially in the face of adversity.

Mrs. Danner had a stroke. She survived, but lost the use of her right arm—she couldn't write clearly, certainly couldn't return to work. She sold her business and bought a Bala Cynwyd condominium. She would spend her life scrubbing and preventing odors, reading fanatically, and attending dinner parties, where she could be counted upon to rail against marriage, hospital administration, Philadelphia legislation, and the black comedy of her own health.

The stroke occurred when Walter was sixteen, his sister twenty-one. Judy Danner was engaged to be married, and had plans to move to Washington (where her fiancé was working on the Hill) to study psychology. Walter could have got by at sixteen emotionally as well as financially if Margaret would only have given access to his trust fund. He could select cuts of meat and balance a checkbook; he could cook and make love. But Margaret refused to give him any money until he finished high school. Jacob Danner, who had found it hard to free-lance without his Philadelphia connections, had recently returned to the city. With Margaret's grudging permission, Walter moved in with his father to a Rittenhouse Square apartment, visited his mother weekly, and looked forward to leaving the city for college.

Jacob Danner didn't have his wife's emotional depth, Walter told me, but he was kind to Walter for the years they lived together. Jacob made an elegant dinner companion once he got over his urge to treat his son like an android simply because at sixteen the boy knew when it was advantageous to itemize on your tax return. Walter's maturity was useful for impressing Jacob's dates (mostly waitresses who aspired to something else, though Jacob had recently overcome the fear of professional women instilled by Margaret and dated a stockbroker). Jacob in turn impressed Walter's dates, who found him attentive and suave. They were impressed that Walter was allowed to entertain girls in his bedroom if he behaved discreetly; they liked the fact that Walter called his father Jacob, not Dad, and were amazed that when Walter got home from school, he always had a drink with his father.

After Margaret, Jacob had developed a strong mistrust of conflict. He was quite content to earn money, spend it on himself, and have time left for creative work. He loved art and he loved his children. Walter never begrudged his father ordinary happiness.

One day, in his last year of high school, Walter had stepped off the bus from school and was walking quickly, already three-quarters of the way across the intersection. He just had time to notice the blur of red Volkswagen before he was under it. He managed to push against the hood in such a way as to keep at least part of his balance, and he wasn't crushed, though he suffered torn ligaments in his ankle and years of muscle problems.

It took him three days to "regain consciousness." The phrase—like "Do not pass Go, do not collect $200" on the game board—had always amused him. The date of the accident was April 15, 1965. Walter remembers it because Jacob was in a sour mood about taxes. Walter was mainly concerned about where he'd go to college to avoid the draft, but the accident decided that for him.

He was so dizzy, his migraine and back pains so severe, that it took him a month to realize he couldn't smell anything. Several specialists confirmed that the accident had destroyed his olfactory sense and his taste, and they confessed that they couldn't do much about it.

In the past fourteen years, Walter had gained a little weight in search of something that had a taste, thus going from scrawny to trim. Mushrooms sautéed in butter did nothing for him. Charcoaled steak tasted like turkey. There was only a slight textural difference between borscht and bouillon; a eucalyptus cough drop barely cleared his nose. If he threw a live match into the trash, he had to wait for smoke to know fire.

Walter realized he was lucky—he would much rather not smell or taste his food than not be able to lift a fork to his mouth. There was no logic to explain why he'd lost his smell rather than his arm. Margaret was still struggling for use of her writing hand. Walter couldn't help feeling, however, that there was a super-literary justice at work. Though his mother smelled everything and he smelled nothing, mother and son were identically smell-obsessed. Walter had inherited the family bugbear.

Like Margaret, Walter was most concerned with the tiny smells, the tiny signs. He missed raked leaves, the interesting fungal smell of women. He missed Sunday mornings most of all: the coffee, the bacon, the hasty smell of fresh newsprint that makes the new week distinct from the last.

Since the accident released Walter from the draft, he was free to decide what to do with his life. First he chose the University of Pennsylvania, his "safety school," and told Jacob he'd remain at home—most of the country's olfactory specialists were in Philadelphia, and they were costly enough that Walter was willing to save money by commuting. The accident affected his career choice as well. He'd always been drawn toward math and science; now those professions seemed unsensory. He started college as an English major, but Walter shared his father's distaste for random talk, and English majors talked far too much. He decided he preferred the architects. Walter loved the distance between the way a building seemed in his head and the way it looked axonometrically rendered. He loved the distance between the renderings and the way the buildings looked in the world, the contrast between sensuous ideas and solid structures. As an architect, he was the perfect synthesis of his father's art and his mother's real estate. After suing the narcoleptic driver of the car that hit him, Walter had enough capital by the time he finished his M.A. to start his own firm. He bought lots from the city development authority and put up his own buildings in parts of town that hadn't yet become fashionable. Soon he got interested in renovation as well, and began to buy property in Washington Square West and Society Hill. He was happy. Then he met Judy.

Judy Gold was a classmate of Walter's sister Judy Danner Stark at George Washington University, and Walter met her in 1971 while visiting his sister in D.C.

Judy Gold was two years older than Walter. She grew up in Maryland, where her father was a small-business man. She was short, solid, perky, and hardworking. Her main goal was to get out of Washington (she claimed it was a sterile city) and thus out of her parents' grip. Walter was the one-way ticket. He was reserved, articulate, handsome, sympathetic with ambitious women, and employed. They were married in June, 1972, when Judy finished her dissertation; and she moved with him to Philadelphia, where the problems were almost immediate.

Judy's parents didn't like Walter, if for no other reason than that he was raised in anti-Semitic Philadelphia suburbs and had German blood. Walter's father couldn't stand Judy, who was far too much like Margaret Danner. Walter didn't care much for the Golds, who struck him as pretentious and overbearing; and Judy detested Jacob Danner, who struck her as pretentious and self-absorbed. Judy didn't like her job, and she hated Philadelphia, which she thought was a toy city. She also wanted Walter to make more money. She had a strict notion of dedication and progress. She didn't want him to spend five months making one slum dwelling magnificent; she wanted him to get his name on the masthead of a major firm and build a shopping mall. She claimed that Walter didn't take any risks, that he'd been cowed by his mother into unadventurousness. Walter couldn't buy this. His mother, after all, was the most adventurous person he knew; and his real estate speculations were more daring than they would be if he were employed by someone else. Since he and Judy couldn't resolve these disagreements, they gave up talking and spent more time in bed. There they remained relatively happy until 1976, when Judy met a Jewish psychiatrist in New York whose accomplishments seemed more impressive to her than Walter's and whose anxieties and aspirations more closely matched her own. Within a month, she'd left Walter and relocated; four months later, she was divorced and ready to remarry.

Margaret Danner knew about Judy's intention to divorce her son before he did. Despite Walter's pleas, Margaret wouldn't try to talk Judy out of leaving. In fact, she maintained that she could understand why Walter made an inadequate husband for Judy. Walter was furious. He and his mother suffered a serious split, which had only recently mended. Margaret remained recalcitrant on the subject of Judy Gold; but her health was worse, and Walter felt guilty about deserting her in what might turn out to be her last years.

Since 1976, Walter said, he hadn't been able to have an orgasm with a woman.

He'd tried twenty women, in relationships of varying intensity, but with all of them he'd get numb and sore and find himself thinking about Judy.

Seeing a therapist didn't make any sense—it was a psychologist, after all, who had introduced the problem. Anyway, a therapist would surely tell Walter, as Judy Gold and Judy Stark had done, that he was fixated on his mother. He was not fixated on his mother; he was fixated on Judy Gold. And it was not a transference. Walter was simply hopelessly monogamous. While it was probably true that he was monogamous in reaction to his father's distaste for commitment and his mother's thirst for change, the fact remained that he was, *at that moment*, unable to come, and he didn't want to spend five hours a week talking about how his mother threw out his slobbered-up teddy bear.

The rape was meant to be a correctional step, an electric jolt to unblock him. He had hoped that a flagrantly misogynistic gesture would compensate for being too courtly, for loving women too much. He committed the rape in the same spirit that one of the Three Stooges hits another Stooge over the head, because that Stooge had been acting strangely since the last hit on the head. He committed a rape with the same thoughtless desperation that makes people kick broken TVs. But it hadn't worked.

Later, Walter would jokingly lament the fact that he hadn't chosen to rape a nice blonde with high cheekbones and a small red mouth—like Stacey, for instance. But he'd chosen me, and now, he said, I was stuck with him.

5

Walter Danner and I had been sitting in Fitler Square for well over an hour.

I was still surprised that there were so few people out. One couple had passed, deep in conversation. Several young women had passed walking close to each other, all dressed in leotards and purple balloons (a bunch of grapes?). A young lawyer had passed, with a lawyer's briefcase and lawyer's shoes, eyes to the ground, anxious to be home.

As Walter talked, I found myself adopting the slightly defeated posture of women who realize they're not as young as they used to be, but are confident they're the best at something—dulcimer, calligraphy, lemon meringue. I turned on the bench to face him. He looked straight ahead, so I had over an hour to study his profile. He had a good nose and a tight, muscular mouth. His large-jointed hands were slightly too small for his body; he probably cracked his knuckles. One of his arms rested along the back of the bench, not touching my shoulder. The other hand stayed on his thigh.

Around one-thirty in the morning, a policeman passed.

Walter's speech had been winding down, but when he saw the policeman, he stopped talking and turned to me sharply. I'd already determined that there was no way to convince an officer that this man with his arm around me, whose jacket I was wearing, was a rapist. At that point, I had to admit to myself that I had no desire to turn Walter Danner in. If anything, I was even afraid that the officer might ask us to leave the park. But the officer merely nodded slightly and winked at me, as if he were the understanding uncle of a fifteen-year-old off to her first prom. Walter ran his fingers through my hair, a gesture that never fails to buckle me. A small, satisfied sound came from my mouth; I watched Walter's eyes open for a second and glaze, as if he'd recognized the sound, then shut it out.

I'd had to go to the bathroom for at least a half hour, and at that point I couldn't say which was worse, the pressure to pee or the pressure to say something that would remind Walter, and myself, how preposterous it was for us to be talking at all. The combined pressures made me want a cigarette very badly, and I breathed sharply, in lieu of one.

"You're probably a latent homosexual," I said.

"Judy tried that too. If I'm latent, I'm very, very latent."

"Impotence is very common in divorced men, and in men who lack confidence because of overbearing mothers."

"She's overbearing all right. I was raised by matriarchy."

Matriarchy: now there was an invitation to a more general

conversation, but I didn't take it up. I certainly didn't need another man who could turn any conversation back to himself. I was wondering how long it would take him to notice that he'd raped me and was now giving a curriculum vitae without bothering to find out my birthplace or age. Also, the alcohol was now more in my bladder than in my bloodstream, and I was beginning to remind myself that I was in a park in the middle of the night hearing the life story of a rapist.

"I'm from D.C. suburbs, you know," I said. "Maybe Judy and I went to high school together."

"You're also Jewish, but you're more flexible than she is. You have a much quieter, more internal sense of self. I can tell from the way you make love."

"You call that making love?"

"You know how you sort of grind downwards to take me in, rather than pushing upwards?"

"I have an inverted uterus."

"I should have guessed."

"An inverted uterus, Casanova, has very little to do with an 'internal sense of self.' Besides, I was trying to push you *out*."

"You weren't concentrating, because you didn't think you'd come without any foreplay, but you weren't suffering much. You didn't keep your arms stiff at your sides either; you threw them over your head—"

"You were holding them there!"

"If we'd been in a bed, you'd have gripped the headboard to anchor yourself, and you'd have liked it if I held your hands there. Judy liked that too. But your movements are much looser than Judy's and you have much more control over your vaginal muscles."

I caught myself listening to Walter too attentively, as you actually harken to a fortune cookie the second it cracks apart; perversely, I was almost flattered that he had paid attention to my reaction. My interest in Walter's analysis was my family's fault. We have two maxims that we live by, that we believe in fiercely:

Know what you're doing, and why.
Don't examine yourself too much.

A Freed to the end, I embrace both dictums, am only occasionally aware of how hopelessly they clash. I'm proud to understand my reactions down to the mille-emotion, ashamed that I bother to examine the workings of my mind in such detail. Obsessive self-examination explained why I had allowed myself to listen to Walter in the first place.

When he mentioned Judy again, I had already decided against him. The only thing I needed less than a self-involved man was a self-involved man still smarting from involvement with another woman. I'd played the supporting role in that scenario one too many times.

"You're angry," Walter observed.

"It's overmuch analysis for six minutes of unaffectionate sex foisted on me under the preposterous theory that every woman adores a Fascist."

"You're not angry about that. You're angry because I talked so much about myself and then, rather than switch the subject to you, I talked about Judy. I'm sorry."

"Listen, shithead, I didn't make an appointment for you to ruin my new sweater, then tell me how your mother didn't love you and your wife didn't understand you."

"Low blow. But fair."

"I'm going."

"Tell me when I can see you again."

"In court."

"You're not going to pretend," Walter said, "that you don't find me attractive. So, great sexual prowess I don't have right at this minute, but I can do other things and anyway we can just be friends."

"He wants to be friends," I said.

"Why are you speaking about me in the third person?"

"We're speaking in shock to the powers above."

"Ain't no powers above."

"That may well be," I said, "given this evening."

"Here's my card."

Walter drew the card from a wallet he took from the back pocket of his pants. The card announced Danner Associates, his address, and a phone number in thin gold letters.

"You expect me to call you?" I gasped. "First it's the Fitler Square therapist and now I'm invited to play Dial-a-Rapist. I can't believe that I endured this. I'm a disappointment to my parents, a jack-of-all-trades and mistress to none, and now I'm chatting with a rapist."

"Enough with the rapist stuff. What's your brother's name?"

"Theo," I said, startled.

He shook his head. "Alexandra and Theodore. No wonder you're so warped." He reached into the inside pocket of his jacket—I flinched as his hand grazed my breast—to draw out a thin brown appointment book. "I'll cook dinner. How's next Friday? That'll give you a week to think more kindly of me. Friday at seven okay? I can pick you up."

I stood, shifting on one foot, because I really had to go to the bathroom.

"You think you won't see me," Walter said, "but you know you will. Wouldn't it be easier if you just got used to the idea of a short and unusual courtship? You would have wanted to make love anyway. So now the worst is over."

"You *are* crazy," I said, meaning it fully for the first time. And I walked away.

"My jacket," Walter called.

I took off the jacket. Walter jogged toward me and claimed it. "I'll call soon, Alex," he said.

Mortified that he knew my name, I turned back to see if he was following me. He wasn't. He was bobbing diagonally across the square, and unless my ears were deceiving me, he was whistling "My Favorite Things."

He was crazy, but I'd been crazier to listen. Among my resolutions was a promise not to find any more madmen "interesting." In the morning I'd get an unlisted number.

The phone was ringing when I got home.

It was my brother Theo checking in from Boston. "How's unemployment?" he asked.

"Don't scold me now. I had enough last night from Mom and Dad. How are you?"

"Fine. You?"

"Fine. Pam?" I asked automatically.

"It's the end of the line for us."

"Why?"

"She calls me selfish, I call her demanding, and she storms out, returning to storm out again. You know the routine."

"But what's new?"

"The frustration's mounting is all. Her objections are, on the one hand, that I hold all the cards—make all the rules, as it were—and that she therefore has to do all the bending; and on the other hand, that I demand she be stronger, more self-sufficient, won't let her have needs. 'I'll never be an Alex for you,' she once said, and she was right. I want Pam to be stronger, but more like those china cups in the ads—'A Strong Elegance,' it says—strong and delicate at once. A good trick. To tell you the truth I like her best when she's coming, because only then do I get the feeling that she's completely forgotten about me, that she's totally her own at least for the moment, yet at the same time I know I'm instrumental. Is that sexist?"

"Yes."

"But only during sex can Pam feel her way through things *aesthetically*. She asks me to come over in such a plaintive way. It's too easy for me to say that she's turning toward me with a greedy eye toward security and support. She is, but I'm bitter because she'll never admit that *she's faltering*. I may be an unreasonable, self-righteous prick, but even if I were a saint, Pam wouldn't be happy with me. She wants to be more like you or like—well, more like someone else. Alex?"

"Yes?"

"Say something."

"I guess it'll be hard for you. You've been seeing her for a long time."

"That's all you have to say when I spill my guts on my love life which I so rarely discuss?"

"How seriously are you two on the rocks? I hate to say anything nasty in case she becomes my sister-in-law and you never invite me to dinner with my nieces and nephews because I'd insulted her. Anyhow, I like Pam. I always have. I just don't think she's right for you."

"Why not?"

"I don't know. The obvious."

"What happened, Alex, did you get a lobotomy along with your walking papers?"

"I guess I'm not in the mood to talk about relationships. Tell me how psychohistory is."

"After all the shit I listened to about Victor and Edgar and Ken and Jim and the whole cast of thugs, I finally get up the courage to speak to you about a woman I've seen for three years and you're 'not in the mood to talk about relationships'?"

"*Tu quoque.*"

"Up yours too."

"I'm sorry, Theo. I really am. But I'm not smoking, I'm hung over, my head feels like the San Andreas fault, and I have to pee. Can I call you tomorrow?"

"What's wrong with you, anyhow?"

I didn't want to tell him about the rape. I didn't even know if I wanted to tell Pat Graci. For years I'd told Pat everything— even done things I knew I shouldn't because I thought they'd make good stories. But I wasn't sure I wanted to hear her say she told me so, and Pat was generally more sympathetic with my bad men-patterns than my brother, so I said, "I'll be fine. I'll call tomorrow."

"You better, or the next time Mom and Dad complain about what a lazy, self-centered bitch you are, I'm not going to defend you."

"Cute."

"Good luck with your headache."

The apartment was quiet then, and dark—I'd been pacing and had neglected to turn on the lights.

I lived alone. I had no pets. I took a luxurious piss, then walked through my rooms, wanting a cigarette, turning on lights, then turning them off again. I stood in front of the full-length mirror in my bedroom to examine the damage to my sweater. It wasn't critical—the ground under the ginkgoes, unlike Walter Danner, had been hard.

I was too tired to shower. I was tired, my limbs were sore, and I was disoriented—the kind of disorientation that makes you take the cream from the refrigerator, pour cream into your coffee, put the mug of coffee back into the refrigerator, and bring the carton of cream to your reading chair. I undressed slowly in front of the mirror. The only damage to my body was a twig scratch near my waist. My body wasn't bad: long in the limb, narrow in the waist, the nipples dark and large, the pubic hair in a neat dark triangle. The problem was that in my bare feet I only stood five four. I had always wanted to be taller.

I brushed my hair and lit a candle. Still standing in front of the mirror, I wet a finger and swirled it over one nipple. I opened the door that the mirror was on the back of and positioned the mirror so I could see it from the bed.

Then I did something that I have never done before or since.

I turned off the light. Furiously surprised with myself and ashamed—but too surprised to be much ashamed—I masturbated sitting up, with my eyes open.

6

Even in winter, I never sleep under the covers because I hate making beds. I sleep on my back in heavy nightgowns and socks with one foot dangling over the side, and witnesses confirm that I do not move once I'm asleep, though I often talk between snores—once I said "To the left," and once I said, "The Civil War!" I woke at one in the afternoon on Thursday, the first of November, to the doorbell.

"It's Walt," a voice said over the intercom. "Are you awake?"

"Go away or I'll call the police."

Walter rang three more times. I didn't answer. I pressed "Listen" to make sure he was gone.

"That you listening?" Walter said. "I've got to see my electrician. I've left you some things down here. I'll come back later. Don't panic. Well, goodbye."

I crouch-walked over to the window and tried to look over the ledge, raising myself higher slowly until I could see the opposite curb. Walter—in the same jacket, his hair much redder in daylight—stood across the street, in front of his Cortina, waving sheepishly. He got into the car and drove off.

I went into the kitchen for an anger-dispelling cigarette before I remembered I didn't smoke.

Day twelve.

I paced, still not awake, deciding.

Walter had interrupted my favorite recurrent dream, the one in which I met a man in library stacks, at World Fairs, and in the back seats of Packards to engage in vivid domesto-sexual activities. He usually made love to me from behind on the floor of a breezy sunporch, with irises in a wine bottle on a table and a tastefully framed Vermeer reproduction. Ass in air, I was propped up on both elbows to read a book as the man entered me from behind, kneading my waist. The book was in Chinese and bound in red; the rug was bright yellow, and in between thrusts I read a Shanghai dime-store novel about a tempestuous love affair that began in front of the Great Wall, the only man-made object visible from the moon. "Did you come yet?" the man always asked. Invariably I said no, then came in a cheerful spectrum that included the yellow rug, the purple irises in the green wine bottle, the Oriental sheen of the man's hair, the steady roar of waves from an ocean outside, the smell of dead fish from that ocean, and the amusing smell of contraceptive jelly, for I have a strong practical side, and in dreams this concrete I almost never forget about birth control.

When I wake from this dream, I'm usually less sad about losing the man than about forgetting how to read Chinese. My brother says that this is a dream of intellectual guilt. He claims I worry that I've long ago traded my brain for my clit. No matter. A rapist was harassing me. He might well be dangerous. He might have driven around the corner and come right back, which was too bad, because I had to go downstairs for my mail.

I always got the mail just after my shower and just before my first cup of coffee. If I slept late and was sure the mail would be in, I would get it before I got dressed: I'd open the mailbox so fast that anyone passing wouldn't have time to notice I was in my nightgown. If there was nothing important, I'd dress slowly, trying to restructure my day to exclude mail. If there was some-thing juicy, I'd position the letter near an empty mug and dress quickly as the coffee brewed, savoring the letter as I used to savor my first cigarette, holding off the pleasure, not even allow-ing myself to think of mail, thinking instead about what I'd do with my day if it was disappointing. It rarely was. I correspond with about fifteen friends across the country; I'm also on the lists of almost a hundred galleries and charitable institutions, and I'm usually waiting to hear about one job or another. That year I had already been offered three jobs I didn't take: one in PR in Hano-ver, New Hampshire; one in a New York gallery; and one at a prep school in Maine. I needed to maintain the Freed illusion of

"keeping options open." I'd applied for jobs that I couldn't possi-
bly get, and some that I wouldn't want even if I could get them,
simply to keep my mailbox full and my soul full of hope. One of
the reasons I hated working nine to five was that it fouled up my
mail ritual. I often dreamed of bottomless mailboxes swarming
with mail—chains of letters so long they'd rival the trail one
person's nerves would make when wrapped around the globe.

Now, because of Walter Danner, I couldn't check my mail.
That wasn't fair! I was not going to let a sexually depraved man
rearrange the comforting routine I'd spent years perfecting. So,
in a ten-year-old pink nightgown with a constellation of cigarette
burns across the front, I went downstairs for my mail.

I heard the yelping before I rounded the stairs.

In the entrance hall of my building, in front of the mailboxes,
was a basket containing a Doberman puppy.

The puppy sat unhappily in the basket, which was tied to a
large gift box. Tied to the puppy's neck with a pink bow was a
legal-sized envelope addressed to Alexandra, the name underlined four times. The dog's ears had been straightened and its
tail amputated so recently that there were still scabs around the
removed stitches. The minute it saw me, the puppy stopped
yelping and wagged its stump, waiting to be picked up. I got my
mail, put it in my teeth, picked up the basket and the box, and
carried them upstairs. Then I untied the ribbon from the puppy
and—not even looking at my real mail, with the puppy investigating my naked feet—read Walter Danner's letter.

Alex dear:

I'm a steady person. Every morning I get up at eight, get
dressed, and get to work. The tweed jacket you saw me in
I've had since my senior year in high school—I'm cheap, or
so I'm told, so please interpret these gifts not as bribes but as
a breakthrough for me. I'm grateful to you for letting me give
them. It's a male puppy, in case you can't tell, and in several
months he'll protect you better than your fingernails in

Fitler Square. Remember, if you don't want him, we can take him back.

I want you to understand that I'm serious about the possibilities for us, despite what you undoubtedly consider an inauspicious start. I'm so basically plodding that I always think if I do something fast, things'll work out for me. Maybe this is leftover adolescence. Maybe it's because (living with my mother, then Jacob) I pretty much missed both childhood and the sixties. Anyway, I'm always prodding myself to just live, and that's what you saw an attempt at last night. I realize it's going to be hard for you to accept me, but I'm willing to work extra hard to help you do it.

You may object that I don't know you well enough to include you in my schemes. You're right, but I know you well enough to know I want to know you better. I like your self-control, I like your irreverence and self-irony, I like your body (sorry), but most of all I'm touched by how shy you are to admit you connect.

I don't care what you *do*. You could be an heiress, you could be a baker or a candlestick maker or a Marxist philosopher. Whatever you do is fine by me, including doing nothing.

Which isn't to say I don't care. I just want us to defy the résumé crap and move right into each other's lives. By that I don't mean anything mystical. I don't want to share your heartbeat and your Karma. Nor do I want to share your TV dinners and your menstrual cramps. Your whole manner indicates that you like living alone. So do I. I think we'll get along precisely because we both respect distances.

"What?" you're now exclaiming, in your inimitable voice (its mix of smoothness and excitement was in my head all night). "A rapist who respects distances?" On this you are going to have to take my word and trust me. *You are not besieged.* Much as I want to be your lover and/or friend and/or confidant, I'll respect your wishes. You are neither hostage nor victim. When I come with your alternate present, tell me what you want. If you tell me to leave you alone, I will.

I was up all night thinking what to write down, and this morning I was up early to get the dog and the rest of the presents (things in the box are self-explanatory), so I'm as ragged as a man can get. It'll be worse later in the day unless I get a second wind, so be gentle with me. The puppy, incidentally, is supposed to be housebroken.

Yours (I hope!),

WALT

Walter Danner's handwriting was small, sloppy, uneven, and crammed right up to the margins of the page, but his signature was an architect's—four tidy square draftsman's letters. An amateur graphologist, I knew that his cursive indicated a diligent effort at control hampered by a confused response to assailing influences. He was torn between trying to give me what he thought I wanted (the "heartbeat and Karma" riff a bad attempt to mimic my speech) and telling me to shut up and take what I deserved. Walter was a pathetic wreck at best, a sociopath at worst. His good logic and occasional charm only made me feel more afraid— and thus, alas, more intrigued, for I was not easy to intimidate. I read the letter again, still undecided about whether or not to call the police.

The puppy, meanwhile, had been investigating the apartment, and was now at my feet again, looking up at me with a blend of love, anxiety, supplication, and contempt. No doubt about it, this was a precious puppy, if you happened to like Dobermans. I didn't. In fact, I didn't like dogs at all. The puppy wagged at me. I got it a dish of water, which it finished. I got it another. "Nice Fred," I said, petting it a bit. It squirmed around in bliss—it was as soppy as Walter Danner.

I opened the box.

The box was too deep for the sweater that I found underneath the tissue paper—a duplicate, in yellow cashmere, of the sweater I'd worn during the rape. I wondered how Walter had found it. Pinned to the label of the sweater was a note, in the same manic print: "Purple looks good on you but purple is quickly going to be OUT." Under that sweater was more tissue paper and another sweater, a thick pullover in bright green, and another note— "You'll look better in this." Under *that* sweater was more tissue-paper. At the bottom of the box was a wrapped pair of black-seamed pantyhose and a black leather dog leash.

The puppy had watched me open the box with considerable attention. It whimpered, then raised a leg to spray a tiny bouquet of piss onto my wall.

"Thanks," I said, attacking the wall with a paper towel. "Go sit by the door."

The dog didn't move. The phone rang. It was Vivian West, on the end of her lunch break, eating a sandwich at her desk and wondering, given the tightness of her schedule and the trouble we'd lately been having connecting, whether she might write me in for dinner on the following Friday.

"Friday's Stacey's show," I reminded her.

"That's right. Then I'll see you there."

"Listen, Vivian, I need your advice. I got raped last night—"

"Jesus."

"My sentiments exactly. I was going home from Pat's and this guy—an old acquaintance of hers, he'd passed her house on the way to a party—got me in Fitler Square."

"Black?"

"Quite white. An architect."

"What'd he do, give you a calling card?"

"As a matter of fact, he did. This is a problem. I did talk to him at Pat's and accept a ride home; I was drunk and stunned and after the rape—"

"You didn't enjoy it, did you?"

"Of course not. It was cold. He wasn't really even hard. But afterwards I let him 'explain' for an hour or so, and though I told him to leave me alone when he was done, he came over this morning to give me a Doberman puppy and some sweaters; I wouldn't let him in, so he left everything on the doorstep and now he says he's coming back to—get this—discuss our relationship."

"How did he find your apartment?"

"I guess he looked me up in the phone book. A police officer passed us in the park and I didn't scream, though I screamed during the rape. So do I tell the police my rapist was a handsome, unarmed man I'd chatted with at a friend's, that a medical examination wouldn't show any damage, that he's giving me gifts and writing me love letters—"

"You're making this up."

"Woe, I am not."

"Is he handsome by normal standards, or just by Freed standards?"

"He certainly doesn't look criminal. In this letter, he says that I can tell him what I want. 'You are not besieged,' he says, and I quote: 'When I come with your alternate present, tell me what you want.' "

"So what's your problem? Get the alternate present, then tell him to kiss off."

"Vivian!"

"Sorry. It's just so funny. He sounds perfect for you. Maybe he's aggressive enough to stand up to you."

"Fuck you."

Vivian apologized again. "Maybe he'll just go away."

"You're telling me to let it go? What if he doesn't go away?"

"Then call me back. I haven't done much rape, but Sal will know. I'll see her later this afternoon."

"And if he kills me?"

Vivian and I arranged a time for Vivian to call. If I didn't answer the phone, or if the line was dead, then Vivian would call the police. After I got done scolding her for her shoddy feminism and her lack of understanding of a mind in shock, I dressed quickly, made coffee, read my mail (bills, ads, an announcement for Stacey's show, and a postcard from Theo confirming he'd be in Philadelphia for Thanksgiving), and watched the puppy case my apartment. I threw an *I Ching* and opened the book, hoping for better advice than I'd got from Vivian.

I have a spot in my heart for Chinese mysticism, and basically agree with the Book of Changes' definition of the superior man. Since I could always hope for a clear statement from the *I Ching*, I expected, on the subject of the rapist, to be told something like

"Now is the time to pursue lawsuits." I got the hexagram P'i, "Standstill," which instructed:

> Evil people do not further
> The perseverance of the superior man.
> The great departs; the small approaches. . . .
> Thus the superior man falls back upon his inner worth
> In order to escape the difficulties.
> He does not permit himself to be honored with revenue.

That made sense. I certainly didn't intend to accept sweaters and dogs from a rapist. I was perfectly willing to "hide my worth and withdraw into seclusion"; that was the whole point of my unemployment. Certainly I could make Walter Danner accept my rejection.

But why was I throwing *I Ching*s rather than calling the police, when what I had on hand was a rapist and not the boy next door?

The Doberman, who had settled onto the mat in front of the sink, looked my way forlornly.

I was tempted to put the dog in its basket, the sweaters and stocking-stuffers into their box, and both basket and box in the foyer with a note telling Walter thanks but definitely no thanks, then go hide for a couple of days. But it was my apartment and Walter would probably read avoidance as courtship anyway.

Besides, what I needed was a cigarette.

Take a walk, I told myself, look at the pretty trees, breathe real air. But as I decided to walk I felt the ghost of Alex Freed gliding into the store for a fresh pack.

I got my jacket and took the phone off the hook in case Vivian tried to call. The Doberman was ready at the door, its tail stump a metronome. "You're staying," I said. The puppy decried the injustice. It took a solid five minutes to close the door to the apartment without hitting puppy paw or puppy nose. I took the stairs quickly. I knew it would be lovely out; I knew I'd last a block before I bought cigarettes, and while I was prepared to be disappointed in myself, I was also very happy.

At the door to the building I encountered Walter Danner.

He was tired but radiant. In his hand he held a fur coat. "Hello," he said. "Where's the dog?"

"Upstairs, and I'm so anxious to get rid of him I'm even glad to see you."

"Your lease says no pets?"

"I hate dogs. And for political reasons I don't wear mink."

"Sable. Don't feel guilty. It's a used coat—belonged to my Aunt Hattie. These animals have been dead for twenty, thirty years, and they died of natural causes. See? The lining's torn."

"I think we need to get some things straight. I will not permit myself to be honored with revenue."

"That what your horoscope told you?"

"Please go away."

"You look like you want me to stay."

"You promised you'd leave me alone if I told you to."

Walter squeezed past me and sat on the bottom step near the mailboxes, the coat over his lap, his shoulders hunched. "You mean it?"

"I mean it."

"You're not being coy?"

"Certainly not."

"Then why do you look like you want me?"

"Perhaps you're misinterpreting the look. Let me level with you. You're very pretty. You're an architect. I've always liked architects and pretty men. You can speak. I like men who can speak. You're a romantic. I like romantics. I just spoke with my counsel. She said you sound perfect for me."

"I am."

"I like spontaneity," I continued, beginning to pace in the narrow foyer. "I'm drawn despite myself to big, desperate gestures. So here you are, the singing telegram. I don't trust it. I'm twenty-nine and single. Although I cherish my friends and they cherish me, I spend most of my time alone. I have to learn to live with that—"

"And you're stronger for it."

"Maybe. Much as heart and mind balk at the prospect, I believe that I'm alone. I intend to stop titillating myself with bourgeois dreams of happy husbands and little courtyard gardens in major cities. You understand that the rape fantasy is the fullest expression of a longing for middle-class family life. You said it yourself—don't interrupt!—you committed rape because you're a hopeless family man. I don't believe that these violent swings move one toward the golden mean. Anyway, 'normality' is not what I want—sanity yes, order yes, but I want my stability to *glimmer*. What's wrong with my life now is that its order is stale, despite my efforts not to trap myself into anything unproductive. Thus the golden mean is only gold-plated—it rots in the rain."

"What is this, Marxist Love Comix?"

"You offer yourself to me as if you could change my life. Vanity of the proposition aside, I don't believe that anything external will change my life now. Dating a rapist, no matter how he goes on about 'respecting distances'—"

"I knew you'd get me for that."

"—is bound to be a wretched effort to deny my life. Your letter attempts to convince me that the rape need not be the monolithic or mythic center of any relationship between us; that our being together could be sensible and meaningful, all in the course of exalted daily life. The problem is I don't love daily life. I'm still trying to free myself—"

"No pun intended?"

"I have to either love my life or get up the strength to change it. You wouldn't represent a major change. While it's true that you're trying to tempt me with two hard lines, brute force and romance (which are not, again, really opposites but two sides of the same coin, manifestations of the same longing), you're not much different from most of the men I've been seeing—"

"Don't count on that."

"Things would shine for a while. Then they'd tarnish. It's that simple. I'd be left feeling guilty for not seeing more clearly from the onset. To ward off self-castigation, I'd blame you. Easy enough—you're a rapist. You'd undergo the same process of rationalization and we'd wind up with an ugly rain dance that feels tribal and primal and true but is in fact mostly ornamental. There's really no point."

"Did you spend the morning writing this speech? I'm flattered."

"As for you. You can't smell and you can't come, so you assume that what you need is a flood to the senses. You're trying to plan randomness. You want to program spontaneity. Even if I were willing, I'm not plucky or lusty enough for such play. I don't think any conscious woman is. You claim to want a conscious woman, but a conscious woman would never play these games. So, you see, I can't cooperate."

Toward the end of this speech, I'd begun to notice the puppy yipping upstairs; Walter Danner watched me pace, his green eyes (in daylight quite green) almost the color of the sweater he'd given me.

"Whew," he said.

"Fair? Clear?"

"Sure clear you're a talker."

"Talkers are no great doers."

"Why do you back off? Aren't you used to people being kind to you?"

"Since you ask, no, and that's precisely why I back off."

"But don't you see that your backing off fulfills the prophecy?"

"Walt, I've made my case. Just respect my wishes."

"You called me Walt! Admit you're softening."

"Come upstairs and retrieve your dog," I said.

I was softening. This, too, was a pattern. I would often announce to men that I no longer intended to see them, then feel so proud and exorcised that I'd jump right into their laps. Therefore no one ever believed that I meant what I said. I could be in positive apoplexies of disappointment and people still wouldn't take me seriously. If I were ever to call a friend at four in the morning and say I'd just swallowed fifty Valiums and a fifth of Scotch, I'd probably hear "Sleep well. See you at the party." I didn't intend to let people like Vivian chuckle when I got raped anymore. No matter how inviting Walter's mustached mouth and kind smile, no matter how well he argued—and the truth is I like a good fight—I wouldn't visibly soften.

As soon as he got up from the landing with the coat over his arm and followed me eagerly upstairs, I realized that Walter would take being admitted into my apartment as the first step in the weakening of my resolve. The puppy virtually attacked us as we entered.

"Hi, Sport," Walter said.

"Something smells funny in here," I said. I went in search of the smell. Walter followed at a slower pace, inspecting my apartment much as the puppy had.

"Shit!" I called from the bedroom. "Literally. Damn dog. Bring some paper towels, will you?"

"Either they lied or he's just nervous," Walter said, bringing the towels, his eyes to the ceiling. "Shame they dropped the ceiling in here."

"Bring some wet, please."

The puppy stood whimpering by the bed. Walter came back with wet towels. As I mopped, holding my breath, Walter stood on my bed on tiptoe, investigating the ceiling.

"Cardboard," he scoffed. "Do you hear every sound from upstairs?"

"The upstairs people work all the time and only hole up to make love and sleep."

"You hear them make love?"

"In Sensurround."

"How much you pay here?"

"No wonder your wife left you. I'm mopping shit and you're studying architecture. Drop this in the toilet, will you?"

"Sorry," Walter said, carrying the towels away with less revulsion than I would have.

"You're lucky to face south," he called. "I can't stand dark apartments. Say, do you have a plunger?"

Walter had dropped all the paper towels into the toilet at once. I stormed into the bathroom and handed him the plunger. "Thanks," I snapped.

"Don't get hysterical."

I sat at the kitchen table wringing my hands because there is almost nothing that distresses me more than malfunctioning machinery. The toilet gurgled and roared; the Doberman joined me for comfort. "Get out of my sight," I told it, "if you value your little life."

"There," Walter said. "That wasn't so bad, was it?"

He examined the kitchen: the glass canisters of flour and pasta; the pots, pans, and wok hanging from a space-saving rod; the Francis Bacon print from a show in Paris; the clean stove with a copper teapot. Then he looked at his letter and the gift box on the table. "You don't like the dog?" he asked, washing his hands, drying them on his pants. "Do you like the sweaters?"

"I like the sweaters very much."

"Keep the sweaters and the coat; I'll keep the dog. He's a high-class number. Want to see his tattoo?"

Walter squatted and turned the reluctant Doberman onto its back. The puppy flailed like a capsized insect as Walter searched for the mark, which was branded near one of the dog's hind legs. He held the puppy still for me to see, then released it. The dog headed for safety in the living room. "Control your bowels," I called. "Don't knock anything over." Walter sat down across from me at the table, pushing the box aside so he had room for his elbows.

"They brand them because dog theft is so high," he said. "Personally I think Dobermans are much maligned. They're very lovable and highly trainable. Notice how he sat in his basket until you came for him."

"What are you going to call it?"

"Don't know yet." Walter looked at his watch, then leaned across toward me. "Admit something."

"Is this not blinking of the eyes, this unnatural widening of the eyes, meant to be the next step in the seduction of Alexandra Freed?"

"Admit that in a short period of time we've gotten close."

"Here we go."

"Admit we've cut corners and avoided the usual first-date vaudeville."

"What's this stress on speed? The only Rome you can build in a day is a playing-card castle that tumbles if you cough—"

"I agree, but don't change the subject. Admit you find me interesting."

" 'Interesting' is a curious contemporary adjective. Its etymology is 'between being'—neither indifferent nor involved. Interest presumes a certain degree of detachment. An interesting thing is something you dissect under a microscope, without passion."

"Passion I can't demand yet. I'm asking for a simple vote of confidence."

"If I vote, will you leave me alone?"

"Aloneness guaranteed."

I raised my right hand.

"And admit—"

"You promised!"

"Admit you don't really think you won't see me again."

I considered. "You're right, but I'm hoping."

Walter grinned and stood.

"Hoping I *won't*," I clarified.

"I've got a settlement at four." He whistled. The Doberman high-tailed into the kitchen, its nails sharp on the tiles. "Nice dog. Good boy. Ask Alex if she'll walk us to the car."

"She will, because she hasn't been outside all day and she's just about to break all promises to herself by buying cigarettes."

"She'll hate herself in the morning."

Walter made a silent-movie gesture, the defenseless orphan pushing away the evil landlord—*but I* can't *pay the rent!* The Doberman—unleashed, trying to follow us, not sure of the steps— flinched. "Don't do it," Walter said. He put his arm around me and squeezed my shoulder fraternally. I hadn't been held in months. "Seriously," he said. "How long have you lasted?"

"This is day twelve. I'm miserable."

"Hang in there. By a year from now, the cravings will only come about once a month."

The Cortina was parked in front of my building. As we got to the door of the building, Walter removed his arm from my shoulder and lifted the puppy. I stood on the curb, my hands in my back pockets, as he unlocked the car door with one hand, got in, and put the puppy down on the passenger seat.

"You got a ticket," I said.

Walter groaned. I took the ticket off the windshield and handed it to him through the window. Walter looked like a working man in a hurry. He had already started the car.

"Thanks for the memories and the sweaters," I said.

He smiled broadly. Whatever else, the smile was fine. "See you," he said.

I bought a pack of cigarettes and walked home quickly, presumably because the jacket I was wearing wasn't warm enough, but really because I wanted to smoke.

At the kitchen table I lit a cigarette tentatively. My hand, as I studied the cigarette, felt numb—I couldn't quite remember which hand I smoked with. I took a deep drag and stretched my legs. I got an ashtray from the cabinet where I'd hidden them and poured myself fresh coffee. Let them send a bomb off and turn the planet into cockroach food, so long as they leave us cigarettes and coffee.

The kitchen soon stank of smoke, which hurt my eyes and almost obscured Walter Danner's cologne—he'd been wearing too much, a sure sign of a man who dresses hastily and has no olfactory sense.

After the cigarette, I got up and felt the curious distance between my feet and the floor that not enough oxygen to the bloodstream produces. I opened the kitchen window, washed the ashtray, thrust one cigarette into the back of the cabinet, ran water over the rest of the pack, and threw the pack in the trash. "Bad Alex," I said. "You're slipping, Freed."

In the bedroom, which still smelled of dog-blunder, I opened another window—eradicating Walter, airing the whole episode out of my life—and noticed that the phone was still off the hook. I had never replaced the receiver when I'd planned to get cigarettes, almost two hours before. I called Vivian at her office.

"Thank God you're alive," she said. "Pat said that if it was Walter she wouldn't put it past him. She knows him from college. Once, in their freshman year, they were in a Pancake House for Sunday brunch—this was when Pat had just met Preston. Walter told a bad joke, and when nobody laughed, he picked up one of those things of strawberry syrup and began to pour it, completely straight-faced, over his head. Are you hurt? I called and called. Pat didn't think it was serious, but then she's so excited about the house deal if you told her you'd been shot and killed she'd probably say 'How lovely.' I thought your architect had busted into your apartment and cut you up into a zillion pieces. I didn't know whether to come over myself or get some guys from the office to come with me or what. I was just about to call the police."

T W O

7

Dear Theo,

Of course a book on China sounds interesting. Need you ask that of your greatest fan, of a closet Taoist to boot? Timely too, not only for the world but for you—it'll pass the time you're used to spending with Pam. Just think, you won't have to justify your workaholism to anyone. You can get up at six, mime a Buddhist trance, throw papers on your floor, and forget to eat until bedtime—I'm glad I'm not around.

But don't complain to me about having too much to do, because I'm in the opposite boat.

Without a job and without cigarettes, life has no rhythm. "Weekend" loses all meaning. The time passes painlessly enough, although I feel an occasional aching guilt for not making better use of my expensively won thinking time. I'll notice it's 10 p.m. and shudder a bit: if I were working, I'd have to start thinking about bedtime; if I were a waitress, I'd be gearing up for the after-movie rush. At 2 a.m., I'll find that I've been sitting on the edge of my bed for a half hour, wondering sporadically if it's time to put on my nightgown; I'll wish I had a seminar paper due the next morning so I had an excuse to stay up all night, producing a page per twelve minutes and cigarette on my rusty typewriter. Or at three in the afternoon, I'll remember being seventeen and a senior in high school, just getting out of classes on April 15th, running home in the hopes of a fat envelope with a university letterhead—*We want you! Come to us.* In retrospect, I can think of no sweeter suspense than the wait for college acceptances. In those days, I felt a great tenderness toward every mailman; the sight of a mailbox produced biological changes in me.

Is this sufficing as an explanation to your question about how
I spend my time? Not in memories exactly, but in sensations,
like scars that call attention to themselves in damp weather.
When the sensations collide with the craving for a cigarette, I
can feel positive spasms of self-loathing, but spasms don't last
long, and I'm often convinced that I'm thinking more clearly, or
at least tracing a clearer topology of the limits of my thought. In
better moments, I feel no guilt. Still, I can't help waiting for
something to give.

I began this letter after returning Theo's call. I hadn't slept
very well since the rape. In the following two nights I'd had two
nightmares. Both were set on South Street, two blocks from my
apartment. That part of South was black and poor. You never
walked there alone. Most of the buildings were condemned; the
air itself seemed dispossessed and pee-stained. Once, driving home
from a party at Pat's, my car windows rolled up, I'd witnessed
an arrest in that neighborhood. The police who led the apparent
addict to the paddy wagon were gentle and preoccupied; the
addict didn't resist. The whole scene was so slowly picturesque
that I felt as if I were viewing it underwater, through a time
warp, riding past it as gingerly as an archaeologist would treat
the ancient remains of a sunken galleon. Indeed, the South Street
of the dreams belonged more to ancient Greece or to the crowded
marketplaces of Jerusalem than it did to Philadelphia. Although
nothing overtly awful happened to me in the dreams (in one, a
toothless old woman shouted that she wanted curtains, she had
to have curtains), my feeling was one of being distinctly out of
my league. The skin that divided me from complete confusion
was as thin as the two narrow streets that divided my fashionable
neighborhood from the ghetto.

I, too, needed a curtain. There were things I couldn't presently confront. I didn't intend, however, for my calm to be a
façade, as the city's was. I had often compared the prettiest parts
of Philadelphia—especially Society Hill, on the other end of
town—to Treblinka. The whole of quaint downtown Philadel-

phia, in fact, seemed to me an elaborate movie set designed to hide the city's basic squalor. I lived in the part of town I liked best. Fitler Square was residential, but not ritzy; it was reserved, but not stuffy. If I was to feel safe anywhere, it was here. But I didn't feel safe. After the dreams, I was actually scared.

Meanwhile I talk apocalypse. There's a glum satisfaction in believing it's a watershed period for the country and for my friends. You're about to make definitive claims about the Chinese. My friend Vivian is about to win a pivotal case about eyewitness testimony for Philadelphia blacks. (A sister at a suburban nunnery sees a black man in her study. He flees. The nun gives a description of a medium-height black male in jeans and a white T-shirt, and within minutes the police pick up a tall black male in a health food store in a shopping mall twenty miles away. The guy has just picked up his girlfriend from work. Not only is he tall, but he's wearing a maroon mesh T-shirt and an armload of silver bracelets which he never removes. They throw him in jail with a $9,000 bail. I can just see Vivian, looking as if she just stepped out of a documentary about high life in Saint-Tropez, asking the nun, "Sister Smedley, do you think all black people look alike?") Pat is about to buy a house. As if that isn't enough, yesterday she was winding up a campaign for a chemical company when a journalist calls her and starts hitting her up for information for an exposé. She has drinks with him, thinks she may fall in love with him, and any minute she's going to be eroding the system from within. Another friend has a show this weekend. A guy who was with me at Penn is finally defending his dissertation on Iran. All of his predictions are about to come true. Though this renders his document obsolete, he's walking around like a man who has just made a hole in one.

I'm playing Bach. I can tell you who died this week, who's getting married. Last week I had Halloween with Pat and Vanessa, and the week before that I went to a party with English majors— the kind of people who, when bored, say that their lives have "pacing problems." The party was at the house of Preston, Pat's ex-husband. He's living with a very dull girl who fancies herself an artist. She had made a mural for their bathroom wall. The mural is of a bathroom, and where the bathroom window should be, she has cut the canvas out so there's a real bathroom window. "Why don't you paste a little square in the center of the window," I suggested, "depicting a photograph of this bathroom, with a photograph pasted on its window?" She squinted thought-fully—too vain for glasses and contacts mess up her eye makeup, you know the story—and said she feared that might be a little derivative. *Derivative!* I tell no lies.

Typing barred sounds from the street. Unfortunately, I was superstitious. I embraced the domino theory of disaster. Light-ning usually strikes twice in the same place. After you're mugged, you have to get fortified for an even worse indignity. Now that I'd been raped, I was prepared for pyromaniacs, burglars with stockings over their faces, murderers who liked to decapitate their victims. The news reported what seemed a disproportion-ately high number of fires, rapes, burglaries, and murders. I wished that my phone number were unlisted, but I didn't change it, because the prospect of my friends not being able to reach me was much more harrowing than the threat of an obscene phone call from Walter.

It wasn't the nightmares that scared me, or even the prospect of nightmares ("All you have to fear is fear itself," my father used to tell me—for years I thought he'd made it up). It was the prospect of those seconds after my eyes adjusted to the dark and my mind began to shadow the back of my lids with images. Those are the seconds in which, after a day of ice-skating, your body lusciously skates, in which mind melts into body like Cinderella's foot into its slipper. Usually I cherish that time. It is, after all, when you most appreciate living alone. But now I felt too out of control.

My mind was blank, except for fear. Turning on the light didn't help; closing the shades tighter didn't help either. All I could do was wait rigidly for sleep and chastise myself for being a coward. I was no more grown-up now than I'd been at ten, when my father took Theo and me to a Hitchcock film and had to drag both of us up from under our seats.

Suddenly I was afraid of sleeping alone. I was up typing a chatty letter to my brother because I was scared of the dark. Several times I'd caught myself wanting to call Walter Danner.

The English-major party made me happy I don't know too many writers and painters anymore. A nice reminder because lately I've missed being hip. Remember how hip I used to be? I got to be an apostate for *Hiroshima Mon Amour* and Philip Glass before anyone else had even heard of them; I felt so special I could almost rationalize being an underachiever. Do the Chinese have these problems? One thing I've got to hand to hip people is that they're useful when you're bored. You ask them for dinner and they break into an imitation of a Tanduri psychiatrist at a state mental hospital in Kentucky. They keep the imitation up past dessert, and just as you're ready to kill they inform you that *Romp in Tanzania* is on. This movie is so bad you can't tell if it's supposed to be a comedy, but they're mesmerized as you haven't been since you watched "Star Trek" after school at age ten with a big glass of Mountain Dew (no ice) and a Yoo-Hoo. When the movie's over, they turn grave and tell you all about the sixteen-year-old they impregnated, or how the doctor who was supposed to help their mother over her Valium addiction turns out to be a mass-murderer who can get pachinko machines wholesale. By the time they leave, your boredom seems a blessing.

My friends here are all earnest and straightforward. Instead of being relieved, I sometimes feel, rather petulantly, that I'd go farther if I didn't live in this provincial town where mostly everyone is complacent. But—here's the rub—what if I'm just a loquacious, neurotic airhead? What if I die having contributed nothing to this rapidly deteriorating planet?

True to my resolution, I didn't discuss the rape. I brushed off Vivian and Pat's concern. I would not be treated like a cripple. Insomnia was not a terminal illness, and the knowledge that a rape had triggered it filled me with the sweet consolation that fear was permissible—the sense you have when you're exhausted and discover you're running a fever.

Every night at 1 a.m., my upstairs neighbors made love.

They were working late that week, and hard work appeared to give them an enormous appetite for lovemaking. The woman's moans were loud, even, and melodious. She moaned in harmony with the bed banging the wall, in the offbeats, in between her husband's strokes. The man only made noise when he came; then there was the same drawn-out, sonorous *oh*, each time at exactly the same pitch.

Knowing other people made love so often made me want to be making love myself, rather than writing to my brother. I didn't consider the noise an intrusion, but a soothing and dependable reminder that life did, indeed, go on.

> Needless to say, Connie and Phil are calling once a week to ask if you've found the Jewish girl of your dreams yet, if you're eating right, if I've finished my dissertation. They remain convinced that I've not only started, but have nothing left to do but some dainty adjustments to the footnotes.
>
> I'm going to love seeing you for Thanksgiving in a setting where we don't both immediately have to regress, bemoaning bedtime and refusing to make our beds.

Though my dreams were littered with armed men, I felt—in some sense I didn't yet understand and might never understand—that I was unassailable, that I was bound to my life like moss to a rock, that nothing could ever separate me from myself. "How can you ask others to love you if you don't love yourself?" my family used to say. I may not exactly have loved myself, but I didn't want to be anyone else. Even then, I was content to be stuck with myself as I was stuck with my family.

> It'll be bliss, in short. When will you hear about the grant, and how's learning Chinese? Please remember to pack some clean clothes as well as the eternal hieroglyphic index cards. When

you get here, I'll talk to you about Pam so much you'll be sorry
you ever brought her up.

Love,

Alex

It was three before I finished the letter. As I got into bed, I
realized that my neighbors hadn't made love. I imagined I'd scared
them off with my typing, but they'd waited for me to get into
bed, as my parents used to do.

As soon as they began, I found myself able to think about
happy moments of community: good days at the Chesapeake
Bay; my lover Greg from my junior year of college, in an olive
corduroy jacket, putting his arm around me outside a car—clearly,
simply wanting me; another lover and I naked in very bright
afternoon light, in the attic room he kept at his mother's house in
Jenkintown, our eyes open the whole time, hardly blinking. That
night, almost asleep, I truly believed that the couple upstairs
made love for me, to remind me how good after all it is to be
alive.

8

Pat Graci and I stood arm in arm, in some of the good clothes we
never got to wear anywhere, before a large photograph of a thigh.

"I'm about to overdose on goose bumps," I announced.

"Champagne should make you more charitable," Pat said.
"That's my thigh."

"I like photographs," I said, "but are they art? Cameras—like
straightedges, vibrators, crossword puzzle dictionaries—have
always struck me as cheating."

"Cheating's okay if you get the right answer."

"Finding the truth's no hot shakes if it flies into your eye."

"Spare me."

"But, Pat, this one of a wrist is called 'Occam's Razor.' Stacey thinks she can get two hundred bucks for that joke in poor taste. Aren't you embarrassed for her?"

"She'll hear you," Pat warned.

"I don't care. It makes me sad. Remember when all three of us were moping one time about the future of America—"

"*You* were. I was moping about Preston, and Stacey, I believe, was moping about being stuck with two manic-depressives on the Fourth of July."

"And she took those pictures."

"They were great. What's your problem, Alex?"

"My problem in a nutshell: what's Stacey doing showing pretentious art in a pretentious place like this?"

Across the room, Stacey Easterlin was encircled by admirers like Scarlett before the war. Flushed with pride, her face was a sexual pink. Like sex, I thought, success is not to be trusted.

"Let the girl have some fun," Pat said.

"I'm irritated," I retorted too loudly, "by this contemporary tic of isolating one aspect of the world—a thigh, a stuffy dinner party against a beige interior—writting it larger than life, boring us to death, and waving 'reality' in our faces. Boredom and claustrophobia aren't reality."

"I'd suggest you come to the office with me someday if you hadn't come for a year."

"Ten months was sufficient. Anyway, I'm not asking that art be pleasant. I'm just saying it's a lot easier to paint a flaking wall black than to spackle it and give it three coats. Despair and irony are kid's stuff. Conviction costs more, and so does happiness. Happiness can't be duplicated in laboratory tests. That's why in the movies they always have to condense the good times into vignettes—fruit-picking, prancing to the ocean."

"I think Stacey wanted to take some pretty shots of skin—and you know what? They're pretty."

"You're so sweet and supportive."

"You're jealous. You want to be the birthday girl. You want to jump from Stacey's cake with pasties on."

"Hah! For them? I wouldn't make art for them if you paid me. They all have the same round pink glasses. It's disheartening."

"Except for Frank," Pat laughed.

"Is that the mathematician?" Vivian West asked, joining us before the thigh, from which we hadn't budged—anyone watching may have assumed that we'd been debating the photograph's merits, which in a sense was true.

Vivian is precisely the kind of black woman whites find fetching. Her cheekbones are high, her nose is aquiline, her eyes so large and liquid that even when she's cruel she has a hurt, naïve expression. Her rump is high and tight; her nipples startle her silk shirts. Vivian made me feel pale, flaccid, and gawky.

"Yes, it is. Poor guy," Pat said.

"He feels left out," Vivian said.

"I like him better than anyone here," I said. "Go talk to him, someone."

"He's even more out of it than he looks," Vivian said, dragging on her cigarette.

"Give me that," I said.

"I thought you quit." She offered me her pack.

"I did. Take another for yourself; I don't want the pleasure of lighting one—ah!"

Within seconds, the cigarette had misted my consciousness enough to suffuse everyone in the room in a gentler light, a halo of sincerity and importance.

"Mathematicians aren't nerds," I said. "Mathematicians need an anti-defamation league. Real math captures something of the precision and flow of Oriental culture. Have you ever watched a Japanese man at an abacus? The brain waves almost dance. In fact, I've always thought that as far as cerebral activities go, math is the most aesthetically complex. Watching Baryshnikov on television once, I was trying to understand what it'd be like to have that kind of sense of your body, rather than just to live in your head—to control space rather than just to tumble along your own synapses."

"This is about math?" Vivian asked.

"That cigarette's going to burn your hand," Pat observed.

"I probably wouldn't have noticed, so happy am I to smoke it. Aren't you glad Stacey found this normal man to get her away from that awful crowd she's been zooming around with?"

"You've only met him once for ten seconds," Pat said.

"At least he doesn't wear zippered neon leather or tease his hair. So sad to watch what in Nottingham was an at least quasi-energetic political statement become stylized high fashion."

"It always happens that way," Vivian said. "Remember when patches were to cover holes in your pants?"

"No," I grinned. "Before my time."

"I don't know," Pat said. "I sort of like the zippers."

"Shit," I said.

I cursed because Walter Danner had just entered the gallery.

I saw him right away and he saw me, but he looked at Vivian. Vivian is almost six feet tall, taller in her shoes; she was wearing purple pants belted with a pink suede contraption and a wheat-colored blouse that opened tantalizingly along the buttons.

Walter colored and headed toward Stacey. I was wearing one of the sweaters he'd given me. For some reason, he was the only male present wearing a tie. The jacket slung over his shoulder was—I could tell even from that distance—of the softest ecru cashmere, and though he carried no briefcase, he looked like a man who loved his work, breezing by from the office after a particularly rewarding day. His auburn hair, his paleness were transformed by his confidence into distinctions; though he wasn't the tallest man in the room, he was the most attractive.

"What," I said, "do you imagine he's doing here?"

"That's your rapist?" Vivian asked. "A *redhead?*"

"I meant to tell you," Pat said. "He called me this afternoon to discuss you."

"You meant to tell me? Christ, Graci."

"He feels very bad about what happened."

"You're going to defend him?"

"No, and I hardly gave him any information. I didn't tell him about the show, either. Stacey told him. He called Stacey too."

"Shades of 'General Hospital,' " Vivian said. "You didn't tell me he was a looker. I'm going to check him out."

"Give me a cigarette first." I lit it furiously and watched Vivian head toward Walter, watched Stacey's mathematician head that way too—Walter was attracting a small crowd of his own.

"I tried to call you," Pat continued, "and so did Stacey, but you were out buying more things you can't afford. Walter put us in an awkward position. You've been so quiet about it that I had no idea how you'd want me to respond, but by not responding I think Walter assumed I was withholding something. It wouldn't have done any good if Stacey told you he'd be here anyway— you wouldn't have missed the opening for him. You're much better off now, because Viv and Stace and I can spirit you off."

I tried to curl my lip.

"Hey," Pat said. "Did I ask you to get involved with him?"

"Yes, yes, you told me so. Now go talk to him about your house and let me finish admiring these photographs so I can get out of here."

"You're too old for this," Pat admonished, starting off.

"Pat? What did he say?"

"He thinks he could love you," she said, sighing.

"Like Stalin loved the Czar," I said, and Pat and I exchanged a reconciliatory roll of eyes.

Across the room, a woman Walter apparently knew was leaning toward him, whispering (one of the women with whom he'd failed to have an erection?). I walked to the pictures of Pat, Stacey, and me, which I'd been saving for last.

The huge pictures were buried in a side room, where they took up all the wall space. They were the best things in the show, and I felt furious that Stacey had given up doing candids for this silliness of dismembered body parts.

In the first photograph that Stacey took on Halloween, Pat and Stacey have identical expressions, eyes and mouths wry; the similarity is highlighted by how different their features are and by the preposterously grinning jack-o'-lantern on the ledge behind them. Their jeans blend into the steps and the night. On the right side of the photograph, I'm all purple sweater, gesture, and open mouth. The purple creates a fuzzy contrast with the orange of the pumpkin, and my stockings (why had I dressed up for Halloween at Pat's?) snare the streetlight to sparkle in a vertical glow. I look as if I'm having a stagy seizure, and the best thing is that neither Pat nor Stacey is noticing. Their indifference seems sexy, posed, and there's something terribly private about their faces—a feeling of the calm before the storm, the second a woman's body arches before an orgasm.

In the second photo, Pat and Stacey are blocked by Walter walking in front of them, but their faces peer around opposite sides of his shoulder to register two shades in a spectrum of surprise, from Pat's first recognition of him to Stacey's anger. I don't look surprised at all. I look determined, in fact, not to be surprised. But there's a softness to my face, a patient expectation, almost like the solicitude of parent for child. Walter's back is to the camera, making his face the unknown variable, merely the catalyst for our reactions. Stacey has cropped the photograph to highlight its technical miracle: the comet of color starting with Walter's scarf, melting into my sweater, melting into the pumpkin. Red, purple, orange—the only colors in the photograph, as abrupt and final as the last few intervals of a Beethoven symphony, and what's so eerie, so fortuitous, is that the most artificial thing in the picture is also the least planned.

"Amazing," Walter said. He'd taken advantage of my concentration to sneak up on me. "I just bought them both. You started again," he added, pointing to my cigarette.

"Being raped weakened my resolve."

Walter didn't have to redden; he was already quite red. "I'm sorry," he said. "I've been trying to think of a way to apologize."

"Stop trying."

He nodded gravely. The nod was familiar from the first time

he'd said my name at Pat's. Across the room, Vivian, Stacey, and Pat chatted conspiratorially, standing together like models—swaybacked, legs spread. They weren't talking about me. There were other things in all their lives.

"Alex," Walter said, "sometimes things aren't so black and white. Sometimes they're not clear cut. I just want to talk to you."

"Everyone wants to talk to me these days. To me or about me. I'm a hit."

"Don't worry. You have good friends who won't gossip behind your back."

Champagne, cigarettes, and random sexual energy all at once joined forces to make me want to massage Walter's back. I considered whether he and I could belong together in some way that logic couldn't touch, and decided not. I needed him to keep wanting me. Maybe Pat was right. Maybe, an elder child, I couldn't endure Stacey getting so much attention, couldn't resist switching Walter's focus to me. Maybe I just wanted out of the gallery. In any case I said, "Let's go, then," and watched Walter's face light as we went to congratulate Stacey.

Stacey gave me a look that meant Poor girl, you're not mining your potential—a cross between leer and pout that did curious things to her lips. Stacey and I had not been getting along lately, though neither of us had admitted it yet. Maybe I was imagining this—imagining, too, that she had classified Pat and me as earnest but unaccomplished feminists. We had made a good support group at one stage of her evolution, but now she had outgrown us. It hurt me to attribute such thoughts to her, though I was also aware that I wasn't alone in them—at galleries, as in the kitchens of restaurants, tension circulates. I asked Vivian if I could bum a couple of cigarettes. She gave me a whole pack from her purse, triumphant that I'd quit quitting.

"I haven't, you know," I told her.

"What?" she said.

"One assumes," Pat said, "that you know what you're doing,"

and I left before I could disagree with her, confident that her good opinion of me, which had just dropped sharply, could be regained at a later date.

Walter steered me out of the gallery with his arm around me in the same fraternal way he had done when we left my apartment the last time we saw each other. His gesture was so utterly familiar that I had a strong false impression of having known him for a long time. Outside he turned me toward him timidly and kissed me between the eyes, on the bridge of my nose. I put my thumbs to his temples and pressed them in a circular motion, as if he had a headache—when we reached the Cortina he thanked me, and told me he had. That was the only thing that got said in the ten minutes we drove, other than his remarking that Vivian West seemed very nice. I felt curiously at peace, though I had no idea where I was going.

9

According to my father, people's orbits are as fixed as those of planets. If you observe people scientifically in their environments, you can know them thoroughly enough not to be shocked by even their most uncharacteristic acts. Though I'd argued with Phil Freed on this point, joked that a meteorology of personality was bound to be as unreliable as a weather report, I basically agreed. My father and I wanted a mathematics of the soul—not, alas, a higher math but addition, subtraction, straightforward as checkbook balancing. No doubt the craving for certainty is defensive, desperate: when we're unsure is precisely when we pose as objective. Given how much I doubted Walter Danner, it's not surprising that I entered his turf with my highest-decibel bravura of deductive faculties.

Walter lived in the North Liberties, a part of town mainly inhabited by deserted warehouses and Hopperesque diners. In seven or eight years, Walter told me, the area would be swanky; then he would move somewhere else.

"The dog," I said, somewhat winded, as Walter opened the door to his third-floor apartment and the Doberman jumped on him. "I'd entirely forgotten. He has grown."

I held my breath in the dark hallway until Walter turned on the lights and led me into the living room, where he took off my coat, turned on more lights, and went to replace the dog's newspaper on the floor in the kitchen. The Doberman stayed with me in the living room, happy recognition in its tail stump. Walter ran some water in the kitchen, then passed me, smiling, as he went back into the hall, where I could hear him fooling in a closet.

The two-story living room was perhaps too much as I'd imagined a young architect's apartment: sparse, with blond wood floors, an exposed brick wall, a celestial skylit ceiling, and large windows. A complicated series of beams over an imposing Art Deco couch in royal-blue velvet supported a jungle of plants in lush variants of green, their leaves casting interesting shadows over the butternut table and the large framed Palladio exercise from freshman architecture class that, among the antique furniture, had a look of artifact. There were periodicals stacked under the coffee table—design magazines, last Sunday's comics, a *New York Review* opened to the personals. The Doberman tugged on my pantsleg. In one of the windows, I saw that a clump of hair had escaped from my part and was sticking up stupidly.

"Watch the dog," Walter said, emerging barefoot from the hallway in a T-shirt and chino pants with the hem down in one leg (his house outfit, apparently), carrying two snifters and a bottle of Armagnac. I was shocked to see how big his feet were, how pale. "He's in the aimless chewing stage. Ate one of my shoes this morning."

"Have you named him yet?"

"He answers to Sport. Did you see the bedroom?"

The bedroom was bounded on three sides by enormous picture windows, almost the entire length of the walls. One window overlooked the city and its lights. A second scanned the roofs of the warehouses, their outlines indistinct, black on deeper black, like an Ad Reinhardt painting. The Delaware River and the Ben Franklin Bridge appeared in the window in front of the bed, stately and just the right angle off center.

"What do you think?" Walter asked.

"A little city heaven."

"Not so little." He turned on lights. The huge room was bare except for the large bed on the floor, a drafting table, and a wall of filing cabinets. The bed was covered with an elaborate hand-made quilt.

"You're just the kind of man," I told him, "who would have a quilt from an old girlfriend."

"You'll be sorry to hear that my mother made it for me in physical therapy after the stroke. Here's something." He led me back to the living room, where he pointed to a closet so finely joined to the wall that its outlines barely showed. He pressed the wall of the closet near the door with his foot; the wall rotated slowly to reveal a ceiling-high bookshelf crammed with books.

"I've never approved of using books for decorative purposes," he explained.

"Oh, I don't know. The bright new spines, the cracked and venerable spines—books are pretty."

"But then company sits around inspecting your titles," Walter said, swinging the door shut before I could inspect his. "Something tacky about that, like leaving out your bowling trophies or your pay stubs."

"Meanwhile, company inspects your books anyway, with the closet as an added attraction."

"You devil. Some cheese? I have St. André, chèvre, some gjetost, I think."

I followed Walter and the dog into the kitchen. "Cuisinart pans," I noted, patting the Doberman, whose head brushed my hand. Walter set up a cheese tray with the seriousness of a Japanese flower-arranger. He had a fine selection of spices, arranged alphabetically from the allspice to the turmeric; when he opened the refrigerator, I saw that it was full of fresh fruits and vegetables.

"I'm going to put a skylight in the kitchen," he said, leading me back to the couch, "and grow herbs. Someday. Believe it or not, I've been here for three years and I just recently finished painting. One of the frustrations of this business is that you make ten houses for someone else before you have time to attend to your own. Also, as my business grows I have less and less room. Unless I annex the second floor or move, I'm going to have to do something about storage."

"Where are the bedroom closets?"

"In the hall. I hate closets."

"Isn't room for them anyway, with all the windows."

"The bedroom gets so bright in the summer you don't even need an alarm. You wake up completely refreshed, like you've slept in the woods."

"Must be a bitch to air-condition."

"Actually, the insulation's top-notch."

"I'd love a study in the grand old style: the cushy reading chair, the bookshelf with a ladder for the loftier editions, an ottoman, an ornate secretary desk with lots of cubbyholes for paper clips and rubber bands and stamps."

"No bearskin rug?"

"Oriental. To give you an idea of how middle-class my fantasies are, there's usually a picture on the desk of the spouse and kids."

His shrug told me that I hadn't complimented his apartment enough. Clearly he was very invested in its elegance, its efficiency. He sat on the part of the couch arranged to get maximum sound from the expensive stereo equipment (presently tuned to FM jazz), and though he was aware of my presence, a stronger metabolic part of him had sunk into the meditative state that sitting in that particular position with his feet up produced: his eyes followed the lines of the walls and ceilings, savoring details to the rhythm of the jazz.

"I'm a smoker again," I announced. "Do you have an ashtray?"

He didn't, so he brought me a saucer, using the trip to the kitchen as a pretext for dumping the dead leaves he'd collected idly as we sat.

"Would you rather do architecture from scratch than renovation?" I asked, and he perked up.

"The priorities are different," he said. "The trick of renovation is to transform the space while making only what changes are necessary. New construction is actually simpler. People think renovation is surface work, but the cliché that form follows function is no joke—it's hard to learn a language without knowing how its verbs are conjugated."

"But aren't a lot of the details just the equivalent of menu-talk, to mix a metaphor?"

"Not at all. The chances of someone who doesn't understand architecture making sane decisions about trim are about as good as the chances of someone who had never touched a keyboard sitting down to play—just adequately, mind you—the Chopin Ballades. Do you know what trim's for?"

"Decoration," I said.

"Exactly wrong. You'll wash the floors and you won't want to splash on the walls—here molding is a mediator. You'll bang your furniture against the walls unless they're guarded. Floors and walls expand and contract at different rates; a space must be left to allow for this. Unfortunately the crack is unsightly. It collects hard-to-clean dirt and provides a home for roaches. Molding resolves these problems. Architects glorify moldings. The gargoyles at the corners of buildings are more functional than decorative. They cover globs of nails, caulking, steel plates. They're not meant as an excuse. They're placed there precisely so we'll recognize the importance of the juncture. Obviously gargoyles aren't the essence of building, but when you ask an architect to talk about a street or, on a larger scale, a city, that's what you hear."

I nodded. I was thinking of a story about my brother. Theo hadn't spoken a word or walked until he was three, and my parents had been crippled with worry that he had brain damage. Connie and a friend were in the kitchen while Theo crawled around under the table. Connie was saying that she didn't know what to do. She discussed the inadequacy of the experts they'd taken Theo to for tests in hearing, autism, intelligence. Theo emerged from under the table, stood shakily, and declared: "I'm fine. Please don't worry." Those were his first words—not Mama, not Dadda, but "I'm fine. Please don't worry." Theo claims that he remembers making a decision to walk and talk. He had practiced in his room and felt secretly exultant. He had been watching from his vantage point on the floor as my parents screamed at me, beat up on me, criticized me, and he had opted for a low profile. Only the threat of their sending him away, which is what he remembers hearing that afternoon under the table, made him speak up. Connie often says that even if she dies of a heart attack, she'll never come closer to one than she did the day Theo first stood and talked. That's how I felt during Walter's pedantic speech, which seemed jarringly out-of-character until I remembered that his ex-wife had been disparaging of his renovation work. He was on the defensive.

So I said, "I'm impressed," and felt immediately resentful as Walter grinned: any husband-catching manual will suggest that males like nothing better than a captive audience. I reached for a cigarette to punctuate my irritated concurrence with the old sentiment, but Walter stopped my hand with his hand, steered me toward him, and kissed me. I held my hands over his ears and kissed back. The dog barked a reproach.

It's harder to kiss strangers than to screw them. Genitals, like hearts or lungs, are almost all alike, whereas mouths, closer to the eyes, the brain, are more personal. I had imagined that Walter would kiss (once we got down to it) with a jazz-improvisation-style balance between passion and playfulness, but I was wrong: this kiss was just as aggressive as the one in Fitler Square. It was a kiss like a house tour; Walter was the broker, pointing out the unique features and capabilities of his mouth. I found myself thinking, Form and content, and imagining both form and content as identical gold ingots on opposite sides of Justice's scale; I also thought about my high-school English teacher and first idol, who told us that although he loved his wife, there were at least half a million other women he might have loved. Indulging in such thoughts, I let myself enjoy the sensation of being outside of normal time until Walter rose abruptly and changed the radio station to something baroque. I lit a cigarette, waiting to see what change in mood the change in music mandated.

"Put your head in my lap," Walter commanded.

I did, although it was hard to smoke.

For the length of the cigarette the room was entirely quiet, except for the suction of my inhaling, Walter's shirt-sleeve brushing the couch as he stroked my hair, and the Albinoni in the background.

I got up to crush out the cigarette, he to dim the lights; then I returned to his lap, which smelled—I'd put my finger on it— of fabric softener. For twenty minutes in his lap, my thoughts on the brink of sleep were architect's thoughts. The plane of his lap seemed to be a sharp line, the tightrope separating tenderness from passion. Walter must have been falling asleep himself, for his thigh twitched the way it does when you're trying to wing your body to sleep and part of someone else's body is pinning you down. The twitch startled me. I shifted. Walter moaned and pressed my head into his lap, trapping my hand between his legs. I got the hand back and, half asleep, unzipped his pants.

"Don't," Walter said.

His penis was as soft and hot as the forehead of a sick child. I nuzzled it. The dog, roused by speech and movement, stretched and tried to get its nose between Walter's legs. I pushed the dog away and put my mouth to Walter Danner's penis.

"Alex," he said.

Except that his voice seemed to come from a great distance, the way the voice of a dead relative will sometimes ricochet through your head, then spin out into orbit. I pulled the pants down more, knelt to get leverage, and took his penis into my mouth until it was cool in the back of my throat, ice cream soothing the ghost of my tonsils—the dog whimpered, and Walter thrust first right, then left, then back toward the couch. A car took the street fast. I mimicked the motion with my tongue. The refrigerator clacked on in the next room and began to hum, so I did too—Walter's penis like a Jew's harp vibrating.

"I'll come," Walter warned.

"No, you won't."

I pulled his pants down to his knees. The hair on his thighs was wet. I dried it with my breath. The dog barked and my elbows hurt, but Walter had his hand on my neck, rotating his thumb and forefinger on the knob at the top of my spine, tapping my head back to his penis—well, I'd started this, and now I had to finish.

After too long, moments after the record switched off, Walter said "Ah," in the voice of a little boy who has done something wrong. He came jerkily, jarring my head so radically that I lost my balance; one knee slid off the couch, where the Doberman growled, yelped, and bit my ankle.

"Ow!" I said. "Fuck!"

I slapped the dog and regained my balance. The dog whined, backed off. Walter purred, then reached out and grabbed the buckle of my belt, trying to undo it swiftly, one-handed. This irritated me—it reminded me of how seventh-graders light their cigarettes when they've just learned how to smoke. I ducked from his hand and got my cigarettes from the floor.

"Don't smoke," Walter said. "Come back here."

I moved into his reach, lighting the cigarette, as Walter unbuckled the belt and unzipped my pants. The pants didn't fall to my knees, because I'd gained some weight when I quit smoking.

"Don't!" Walter said. "I mean it."

Groaning, shuffling stupidly in the pants, I went into the immaculate kitchen, wet the cigarette under the tap, and threw it in the trash. The dog, who had followed me, nosed the lid off the trash can.

"Stay here, idiot," I advised.

"Don't be mean to my dog," Walter said, pulling my pants to my knees before I was even seated.

"You don't have to, you know," I said. "It's like fifth grade, when you had to give a Valentine's Day card to everyone in the class."

He stroked my waist. "Thanks."

"Any time."

"Remember it's been three years since I came with a woman. I'm very grateful."

"I'm surprised you didn't try coming with a man, then. There are about ten of them pacing at any moment on the corner of Pine and Twentieth who would probably do it much better than I do."

Walter glared, then slackened his face in a way that made it clear he refused to be daunted by my predictable resistance; he responded with a muffled series of kisses from my navel down to my pubic hair, which he touched now with what struck me as excessive reverence and gentility, given the fact of his recent hit-and-run penetration.

Cunnilingus made me nervous because, despite years of reading women's magazines, I still worried that it took me too long to come. Walter set in on me with great aplomb. I closed my eyes and tried to concentrate on pleasure. Walter must have had some training with equally self-conscious women. His tongue didn't dart about too violently, so I didn't have to worry that I wasn't yet as excited as he thought I was. The Doberman was stationed behind him, watching and whimpering, and every so often Walter would lazily ruffle the dog's crew cut. I knew this because I opened my eyes occasionally to get my bearings. Walter had quite a repertoire of things to do with a tongue. He did something for a while that reminded me of dulcimer music, then something like the swift wrist movement that Theo and I had mastered for catching long-legged spiders on water, then something very small and light and delicate that put me in mind of illuminated manuscripts—the big initial letter that starts the chapter and the cramped German Gothic letters marching across the page. I opened my eyes for just long enough to catch a detail on a column of the Palladio poster, and knew that if I focused on the column, that if Walter adjusted the pressure just a notch, I'd come. Since I get quietest right before I come, Walter was surprised when I pushed his head away. He smiled, his face a little puffy, proud of himself. I waited for him to speak. Instead he rubbed his head against the inside of my thigh.

After a while, I said: "I'm cold. I've got to pull up my pants."

He got up, went into the hall, and returned with a fisherman's sweater for me. I rolled up one sleeve so I could smoke. Walter handed me the cigarettes and the saucer, which I balanced on my knee.

"Well?" he asked shyly. "What do you think?"

"I'm too nervous to say," I said. "Let's talk about the weather."

"Okay." He smiled, taking my hand.

"I hate this weather," I said, somewhat weakly, enjoying the warmth of his hand. "Transitional they call it, which inaccurately implies a nice temperate zone between boiling and freezing, not this zigzag back and forth."

"I love it. I feel human again by October. But it is hard to heat the first- and second-floor units in fall. By the time the first floor's comfortable, my bedroom's hell. I'm considering electric baseboards if I annex the second floor—I'm sorry."

He patted my hand as apology, it seemed, for going on too long about logistics. I hadn't been paying full attention because I felt that a new relationship, like the weather, was too unpredictable; then I thought about what it would be like to inhabit the apartment with Walter. As he patted my hand, I caught myself thinking that Walter seemed to be well off financially and scolded myself for thinking of living with a man I wasn't even sure I liked. Walter reached out to turn my head until I was facing him. He looked at me hard. Perhaps because I felt so safe in the sweater, I kissed him. Walter's skin, like his hair, had a reddish cast. After the kiss his face turned tender.

"You're tired," he said.

"This is true."

"Let's go to sleep, then."

"Do you have something I can sleep in? It's so cold. Also, do you mind if I use your toothbrush?"

He brought me an undershirt. I changed in the bathroom and came out with my breath free of nicotine to find Walter putting away the cheeses. He led me to the bedroom. When we got under the covers, he turned me onto my side, facing away from him, and moved me around until he fit into the contours of my back.

"Walter?" I began after a while, but in response his hand went slack—he was already asleep.

Soon I was surprised to be falling asleep myself. I never expect to sleep well with lovers, especially new ones, but Walter slept wonderfully. He wasn't so light a sleeper as to be distraught if I snored or pulled on the sheets, nor so heavy a sleeper not to respond with a stroke when I cuddled up.

It would have been a remarkably restful sleep, were it not so short. The light woke me at seven. Although most of my apartments had faced south, I had never felt a sun that bright, even in summer. It gave off no heat, only light. I knew right away that for years, no matter what happened with Walter, I would associate him with that light: a cool, insistent light, a little too all-pervasive, keeping me awake.

10

Sometimes in the morning, before you've entirely unhooked yourself from sleep, answers will come to you. They don't *come*, exactly. Rather, the answers seep through your body. Some issue that has been tangling you up unwinds: you watch the issue float away on its cord, like an astronaut spinning into space on TV; suddenly it's light, clear, small, whole, without gravity. In Walter

Danner's bedroom, an answer came to me. All at once I understood: *I thought too much about sex.* I needed to find some new
system that better transported me out to the world with its larger
issues.

In Walter's bedroom, open to the weather on three sides, I felt
as if I were on the deck of a ship, looking out to sea. The light
from the window was as refreshing as breeze. The Doberman sat
by the edge of the bed, fixing its most imploring stare at me. I
dressed quickly, brushed teeth and hair, found my shoes, picked
up the dog's leash in the kitchen, and put a hand on Walter's
shoulder.

"I'm going to walk the dog."

"What time is it?"

I looked at the clock on the drafting table. "Seven-thirteen."

"No intercom. Take my keys," Walter said, pressing his head
into the pillow.

"Where are your keys?"

"Jacket pocket."

"Where's your jacket?"

"Closet."

There were at least ten jackets in the closet. I had to concentrate to remember which one Walter had worn the night before.
I was surprised he was so inefficient that he would unlock his
door, put his keys back in his pocket, and hang up the jacket.
There were about thirty keys on the ring. I returned to the
bedroom to ask Walter which key would let me back in. Although
Walter's hair was disheveled and the corners of his eyes were
webbed with sleep, he looked good to me.

On the way out, I couldn't resist the bookshelf. I let the dog
break his eyeballs and tail stump in entreaty as I inspected the
titles, which were mostly standards for undergraduate courses—
a little Lévi-Strauss, a little James, the Samuelson economics, a
book on cell mitosis, *Gravity's Rainbow*. Some biography, some
film scripts, surprisingly little architecture. Out of about four
hundred books, there were maybe fifty I hadn't read, and I
suspected that Walter had read far fewer of them; most of the

books had tight spines, including the Bollingen *I Ching*, which was inscribed from Judy Gold:

1971

For your bathroom, sweetheart. More manageable than the newspaper and more informative too—

As always,

J.

I didn't even know when Walter's birthday was.

I closed the book guiltily and walked the dog.

It was chilly, with a fine light that admonished: *Enjoy; soon the weekend will be over and you'll have to go back to work.* I was fully aware for the first time of how blessed I was to be unemployed. There was a seminar paper that my professor had claimed was imminently publishable. Just because I was unemployed didn't mean that I had to be unproductive. I'd leave Walter's as quickly as possible. If he was still asleep when I returned, I'd walk to Market Street and catch a train—I wasn't afraid of North Liberty in daylight.

But when I got back, Walter was awake and fully dressed. Bacon and coffee were already on; he was sautéing mushrooms, beating eggs. "I think you'll be surprised," he said cheerfully, "by how well I cook. I have to go easy on the spices, though, because I can't taste-test. Will you set the table?"

The plates were a rustic gray ironstone; the napkins were linen. Had Walter kept the kitchen stash from his ex-wife's shower? It didn't fit. The two or three men I knew in real estate had scraps of paper fluttering from every pocket and a sour conviction that others kept them from work, when what held them back was their own disorganization. While I set the table, Walter talked on the phone to his roofer; he hung up and announced breakfast ready. Not only was breakfast ready, but the pots and pans were soaking in fresh suds. He flipped omelets onto plates and delivered the bread—already buttered, ideally crisped—to the table in a cloth-lined wicker basket. Then he slapped his forehead, said he forgot something, and removed my plate before I could taste anything; he brought the plate back, the omelet decorated with a sprig of parsley and an orange wedge.

"You *are* a perfectionist," I said. The mushrooms in the omelet, if I was not deceived, had been touched with brandy.

"It's very important to me how food looks," Walter said, chewing. "That and texture. I like Chinese dishes with cashews and walnuts. Seafood where getting the food to your mouth is a challenge—cracking the shells, dipping things in vats of butter."

"You really can't taste a thing? That's a shame." The way to a woman's heart is through her stomach, I added to myself—I felt blackmailed by the wonder of his domesticity. I could have told Walter as much, but I was tired of being first to introduce the subject of relationships with men, and anyway he would take it wrong. Far too often, my speech undermined my intentions. "One's words must have power"—ah, the *I Ching!*—"and this they can have only when they are based on something real, just as a flame depends on its fuel. Words have influence only when they are pertinent and clearly related to definite circumstances." So I just smiled.

Walter took his napkin from his lap and slapped it on the table with some force, startling his nervous dog. He took my hand intently in both of his and said, "Alex, I need your opinion on something." He fetched the *New York Review*. "I bought this on a whim, and of course I turned right to the personals. This one. The one that starts 'WD.' "

I read the entry:

WD: NOW's your chance. If you read this you'll know what to do. JG

"Judy," I said.

"Just like Judy," he said, "to assume that if I saw the ad, I was fated to see it, and if not, then it was just as well."

"Maybe it's Jane Green, writing to William Doe?"

"I called her in New York. Her husband said she'd left him. It must be true or he certainly wouldn't admit it to me. She isn't at her parents' and my sister hasn't heard from her. She isn't at any of her good friends'."

"Does she run off a lot?"

"Unfortunately, yes."

"So you expect her here any second."

"I don't know."

"Do you want her here?"

"I don't think so." Walter turned toward me gravely. "But what if she buys a one-way ticket to San Francisco and jumps off the Bay Bridge?"

"Are you still in love with her?"

"We may be beyond love now, to the way you love family—the way you can't help but love family."

"Lots of people help loving their families."

"I shouldn't have brought it up except that I feel responsible. Alex, please understand that I want you."

"I can't imagine why; you don't know what my family's like or what I do or what my brother does or what music I listen to."

"I know plenty. I saw your apartment. You like order. What *does* your brother do?"

"He's a psychohistorian. He teaches psychohistory in Boston."

"Huh?"

"Don't ask."

"Have some faith, Alex. Have some patience."

"I have to admit I feel very suspicious."

"Last night wasn't bad, was it?"

"No. And breakfast was fun. Nevertheless, I should get home."

I stood. Walter rose to embrace me, and soon we found ourselves in bed, where—with the help of a condom that Walter retrieved from the back of his sock drawer—we had real sex, affectionate sex. It was so pleasant that it made me want to stay in bed for a long time, feeling secure in that terrible immunity good sex gives you to everything else.

"You're beautiful when you're not talking," Walter said after a while.

"Thanks so much."

"This part of your mouth—here, under your chin—settles nicely. See? You look entirely different. You look softer."

He tried to convince me to spend the afternoon, but I wanted to go. I was half afraid of him and half afraid of myself—that I'd start wanting him.

Walter insisted on bringing the dog for the ride to my place. It tried to stand on the back seat of the car, but it kept nosing the stick shift and losing its balance. At every light, Walter turned to look at me. It made me nervous, so I chattered about the weather—and briefly about the dog.

"You should take him to obedience school. Paper-training him is an exercise in futility unless you live in a high-rise and are enough of a sociopath that you want to eventually move the paper to the balcony so he can learn to piss over the railing. The only reason you're paper-training him is you're too lazy to take him out. If you don't give him any water after six o'clock, he won't do anything during the night. It'd probably only take you a couple of weeks to get him to sit, stay, lie down, and come when called. You want to have him obedience-trained, of course, and not attack-trained. Most of the time will be spent training you. You'll have to spend about a half hour a day with him, on and off the leash, at different times of day and in different environments—for example, you'll want to train him to stay at a shopping mall so he learns to obey despite distractions."

"You know a lot about dogs," Walter said, "for a person who hates them. You have any advice on how I could train you to be less guarded?"

"People are harder," I said dryly.

Walter ran a light, throwing the dog off balance again. "The week is going to be very busy. I'm having problems with the roofing contract. I should have been over there three hours ago. If it snows, I'm up the creek. What are you going to do today?"

"Work on a paper."

He pulled up in front of my building. "I have to confess I'm distracted by work right now, but don't think I'm not thinking of you. I'll call."

He moved toward me as if to kiss me, but he changed his mind and just touched my face instead. I got out of the car and waved foolishly—a flutter of fingers. I said goodbye to Walter and the dog, and watched the car pull away the moment I closed the passenger's door, if not a second before.

The best part of living alone is that you never come home to find glasses with congealed liquids in them making rings on the table, the refrigerator door not properly closed. I turned to a laconic sax tune on the radio, thought about playing my cello, and watched Waverly Street from my kitchen window as coffee brewed, trying to imagine what journal might like a review of the controversial literature about divorce patterns among the Gonja peoples of Northern Ghana. But all I could think about was how the bridge had looked from Walter's bedroom window—strangely British, muted and far-off, as if photographed at dusk, in the rain, with very slow film.

11

I'd begun unemployment like the ant storing for the long winter. There were enough books on my shelves that I still hadn't read to keep me away from bookstores. My kitchen was stocked for a lifetime of home cooking, from the salad spinner and German carving knives to the saffron and hoisin sauce; my bathroom was stocked with imported soaps. I was excited about the $550 a year I would save on cigarettes and I had promised myself to cut down on phone bills.

I got a little over $400 a month from unemployment, which was consigned to about $480 of basic expenses, not counting food. I don't know how much I was spending on food, but I was still eating out, and I could no more stop buying Brie, gourmet coffee, and veal than I could stop bringing wine when I was invited for dinner or treating myself to croissants and the *Times* on Sunday mornings. If you counted accidental expenses, I'd estimate that I was exceeding my "income" by at least $250 a month.

I had $1,200 saved, $1,300 in credit on the cards I'd gotten while still an upstanding citizen, $500 due from a free-lance editing job, and $400 due from the I.R.S., so I was cushioned, but only for the thirty-three weeks of joblessness that the State would pay for.

If I wasn't as worried as I should have been—and I wasn't—it was because I am to the quick a daughter of the middle class. Pat said that only a Jewish American Princess who counted on her parents bailing her out could be so blithe about money. It's true that I'd fumbled into quitting PR and collecting unemployment, but now that I found myself with some time to consider my future, I was determined not to waste it. Obviously my unemployment wasn't motivated by stale 1960s anti-materialism. I had no desire to streamline my life. A monk can't exorcise his dirty thoughts just by wearing a hair shirt; Thoreau, I knew, only embraced poverty as a hobby, commuting to Walden Pond from his nice house in town. I would rather be rich, but I had to discover exactly what it was I could do that would get me there, exactly why I hadn't yet been able to find anything engaging.

How I should go about this process of discovery, however, was a problem whose solution had so far eluded me, and the only tangible change that unemployment had brought was a much-increased craving for *things*. I wanted track lighting, a recording of Samuel Barber's *Excursions*, Pernod, a black Alfa Romeo. Mostly I wanted clothes—a mauve silk blouse, large triangular earrings, a black car coat with a royal-blue collar, elbow-length gray kid gloves.

That many of the items on this list were luxuries, fated for

ALEXANDRA FREED

obsolescence, didn't surprise me. My wardrobe especially—full
of ill-fitting clothes bought on whims or sales, clothes that quickly
went out of style—was a testament to my father's lament that I
had never learned how to delay gratification in the interests of
long-term planning. Indeed my attempts to save money had been
very similar to my attempts at dieting: money squandered in
small quantities, like the calories in tiny pretzels, didn't seem so
much a violation of the rules. My relationships with men, too, despite their bounty, had been more frivolous than sustaining—a diet
of munchies. All that was stable, all that lasted, was the longing.

I tried to console myself that I wasn't alone in my craving for
things. At the labyrinthian department store where my credit
line was open, it was clear that other shoppers were equally
aimless in their consumer behavior. We touched cashmere and
silk, sniffed cologne and leather with the hypnotic fervor of pinball
addicts. During lunch hour, while shoppers somnambulated, the
store treated us to a rendition of "Some Enchanted Evening" or
"The Shadow of Your Smile" on a grand old organ better suited
to Handel. I'd forget what I wanted to buy in soulful thoughts
of the store's overhead. Wanting was the human condition;
unemployed, I was shoved right up against it.

But secretly I was waiting for something dramatic to happen.
What if nothing happened? What if the savings just ran out?
What if, on the other hand, the situation really did get desperate
and I did something commensurately desperate, like marrying
Walter Danner?

Between shopping bouts, I stayed at home and thought far
too much about Walter—or, rather, about his apartment, to which
he seemed more attached than most people are to their pets.
It scared me that Walter could so quickly, after what I still
half-ironically called the rape, seem, as he'd claimed in his self-
aggrandizing letter, a model of stability.

He called as promised, with quirky regularity, once a day for
the week before Thanksgiving. Though we barely knew each
other, he acted like a husband checking in from the office, and I
was as curt as a housewife, busy separating eggs for a soufflé,

practicing a partita on the cello, or searching for a reference, for the ninth time, through a shoe box of index cards. Walter would inquire flatly what I was doing and each time I'd tell him.

"I mean are you happy?" he said on Monday. "Is it enough?"

"What are you, the shop steward of my soul?"

"I think we should just be a couple and get it over with," he said.

"Great idea. If we wait until Wednesday, my brother can witness."

"I'd like to meet Theo. I'm serious."

"He's quite meetable."

"I mean about getting together."

"Maybe we should wait until the hostages are freed."

"Grown-ups," Walter said, "are worse than children. We want the same things. I make the offer in earnest. Talk to you tomorrow?"

I'm always snappy when I feel vulnerable. I was especially snappy with Walter because he recognized the showiness of my gun-moll mannerisms. I'd had more than my share of fires and so was more on guard against pyromaniacs. But what could I do? My instinct was to dote over men. Soon I would be taking the phone off the hook when I went to the basement to move my clothes to the dryer, lest Walter call and think me out. He seemed to be going easy with me, not making plans but calling every day, giving me time to exhaust my fears. I was afraid of how much he seemed to want me.

When he called on Tuesday morning and asked how I was feeling about him, I said, "If I told you I was relenting, you'd hop the next train to Zanzibar disguised as a leper."

"Do you have to make everything so complicated?" he asked.

"Yes," I said. "Me and Hamlet—two late-blooming graduate students."

But as we chatted he seemed to understand my reservations, and that encouraged me.

That evening Pat Graci and I had just come from a movie when a mutt flanked me. Amid the bums and pimps on Chestnut

Street the dog seemed so friendly that I petted it, and it responded so gratefully that I bent over to give it a kiss. Pat grabbed my elbow and pulled me away. The dog's entire back was rotted, pink and ragged as carrion. I hadn't noticed. I was probably the only person in America stupid enough to have touched the creature in months. As I held my infested hands away from me like claws, the dog continued to follow us. Pat stamped her foot. "She doesn't really like you," she told the dog sternly. "She was only pretending. Go away." So the dog crossed the street and kept pace with us, watching me from the distance with a hurt face. Only when we ducked into a restaurant so I could wash my hands did the dog vanish.

Pat said the mutt looked as if it had been in a bad fight, or been clawed while in heat, but later that night, haunted by the incident, I talked about it with Walter—he'd called to say he was too busy to talk long, but wanted to see how I was. He suggested that the dog probably had mange.

"As if crab lice my freshman year weren't bad enough," I said, "now I have to get mange! I'll need a long needle in my stomach. I hate needles!"

"That's rabies," Walter said. "I wouldn't worry about it. There's nothing you can do now anyway. Listen, I really have to run."

"Enjoy Thanksgiving," I said.

"With Margaret? With Jacob? You serious? Maybe I can get both dinners done and drop by to meet your brother."

I called Vivian West, who was absorbed with a brief and had no idea whether or not mange was contagious to humans. The SPCA assured me that it wasn't, but I still couldn't sleep. I sat up in bed, smoking and reading *Vogue*. As my upstairs neighbors began to make love, I couldn't shake the image of the poor dog begging to be petted.

12

Nothing in the world seemed more soothing at that point than the promise of spending some time with Theo, who arrived in Philadelphia at dusk on Wednesday in his ailing purple Fiat (held together almost entirely with magnetic tape), bearing a pound of fresh pasta, a fifth of Irish, and the notes for his China book.

He had got a haircut. He wore a slim silk tie, a white shirt, and a leather jacket he'd had since the eighth grade, too short in the sleeve. He looked like an English rock star, not a professor, and he wasn't doing it on purpose. His paleness, his skinniness, the rings under his eyes gave him the look of a consumptive poet or a dissolute dropout. Women found him very attractive. This surprised my parents, but then they had never stayed up until dawn with him, having a last cigarette and embarking on some topic that turned the last cigarette into a last pack. Dilettantism, the Freed curse, transformed itself into range in Theo. He knows that if you keep a dog awake for twenty-four hours, it will go crazy and die. He knows why Swedish teens are so nihilistic. But that afternoon he looked troubled.

"What is it?" I asked.

"Long drive," he said, offering his cheek. "Also I had a rather unsettling post-breakup confrontation with Pam this morning."

"She wants you back?"

"On the contrary. She wanted me to know that she has replaced me with a poet who writes sonnets to her."

"Good for her! She hurt your feelings at last."

"I'm not jealous. I don't like sonnets."

"Theo, Theo, Theo! Sit down and tell me all about it."

"Do I have to?"

He did. Theo talked mournfully about Pam for a while, and I told him about Walter. Theo hated talking about relationships almost as much as I loved it. "Sounds like another entry in your endless boyfriend series," he snorted, and I pointed out that I had not, after all, had that many more boyfriends than he'd had girlfriends. Then, before he challenged me, I asked him if he remembered his theory about formers and arrangers, about how Jung was a former and Freud an arranger, da Vinci a former and Picasso an arranger, how most arrangers secretly longed to be formers but few formers ever dreamed of being arrangers?

Theo didn't remember. He said he'd undoubtedly been joking. He'd rather discuss the state of psychology in China, the subject he was presently researching. What were the consequences, personal and political, of not believing in repression, denial, transference? He told me about China for a while. I told him that the Chinese didn't need psychology if they'd done without Christianity, since psychology and Christianity are pretty much the same thing. Theo did some more snorting while I reviewed the similarities between id and hell, superego and Bible, psychologist and confessor; Theo asked if Skinnerians were Shakers or Baptists, and while I mulled that over—how far, after all, was the *I Ching* from the Bible in preaching passivity?—he reminded me that I'd never had much of a grasp of political subtleties. "You've always *said* I haven't," I retorted, and then confessed that I'd applied to take the exam for the Foreign Service in December. Theo laughed. I was kidding. No, I wasn't. "You and Shirley Temple," he said.

"Thank God you're not a Marxist yet," I said. "You're still one of us—the glorious dying middle class. We're dying, you know."

"No chance."

"Uh-huh. The middle class is being pulled asunder. Remember how they used to tie one foot to one horse and one foot to another horse and drive people in opposite directions? The middle class is being drawn and quartered. Or Poe's contracting room. The walls, the ceilings, the floors are all closing in on the middle class."

Theo smiled his inimitable smile, a leer softened by the fun in his eyes. He told me that I should have stayed in graduate school to make use of my talent for myopia, and he lectured me on American class structure. Then we made pasta with mushrooms, zucchini, and cream. Over coffee, I broke down and reached for Theo's lovely new pack of Marlboros, letting him joke about my eternal abstinences.

I don't mind when Theo mocks my smoking, because he's as addicted as I am and smokes the same way, holding the cigarette too far down past the knuckles, bumping it against the nose. We have the same eyebrows, the same eyelids. Theo is the only person I know, other than myself, who cries at Pepsi commercials because of how horribly the grinning, hugging interracial friends lie about the state of the Union, our bombs subsidized by soft drinks that are rotting the teeth and stomachs of Third World children. His cynicism badly masks a soppy heart. We learned to smoke dope together. We still enjoy the late news together, remembering our gleeful incredulity when we watched it in our parents' basement after having smoked a joint while we walked the dog. Theo does an imitation of the dog that nobody laughs at but me. We can sit in a restaurant and Theo will say, Over there, you know who that looks like? and I'll answer, Yes, Mrs. L——, a minor friend of Connie's whom we haven't seen in years.

There are differences, of course. While I'm only a secular Jew, Christianity still makes me uneasy. Theo loves the religion in much the same spirit that I love old movies. He's a minor expert on medieval iconography. He lingers at the crucifixes in museums and thinks that the Bible is the greatest story ever told. Theo doesn't worry, as I do, about escaping conformity. If he's reading Foucault or *Anti-Oedipus*, if he's bowling or watching "60 Minutes," he has a good time or doesn't and that's the end of it. This is because Theo is much smarter than I am in every sense. It astonishes me that he's a Freed, so open is he, so able to improvise.

"Bull," Theo said when I paid him this compliment for the millionth time. It was already the next day, Thanksgiving, and we'd just drawn lots to see who would have to touch the giblets. "I'm just less libidinous. You think you're dumb because every time you get an idea you also get some itch—you spill a drink or cough."

"You have some molten flesh yourself," I sneered, pointing with a knife to the fine scars on both of his eyelids—in a fit of sibling rivalry almost a quarter of a century before, I'd applied eyeliner to him with a fountain pen, to make him up as the witch in a play we were putting on for our parents' guests. "Not much of one, it's true, although you've got it over me by having had a homosexual experience."

"I wouldn't call it an experience."

"We're so different that way. I've probably slept with a zillion men but am basically unadventurous; you've only slept with four women, but you've been in an orgy and sampled men."

"Sampled them? I got sucked off hitchhiking once when I was twenty."

"Did you ever tell Pam that?"

"I'm sorry I ever told you. I want a candy apple suddenly. Can I get one around here?"

"Maybe you're pregnant."

"We need brown sugar anyway."

By the time I'd swept up the fallout from the turkey, Theo was back with candy apples, brown sugar, and snapdragons. He suggested Scrabble. We played for the rest of the afternoon and well into the evening, obsessively, as is the Freed wont. He made JAGUAR on a triple-word score and we had a tiff when I tried to play RESQUAT. Then we set the table very seriously and dressed for dinner. My idea: both of us in our Sunday best, the smoke out of our hair. I perched on the edge of the tub and smoked while Theo shaved. "Know what?" I said.

"We forgot to buy wine."

"I was going to say isn't this silly? We should have invited people. We have food for ten."

"I'm willing to do without extended family *or* your weird displaced friends."

"But it blows the whole purpose."

"The whole purpose is not going home so we have time to talk."

"Talk about what? Everything I introduce makes you roll your eyes. Maybe Pat'll drop by with Nessie."

"Maybe that's Pat now," Theo said, rolling his eyes showily as the doorbell rang.

It wasn't. "It's us," Walter told the intercom. "Can we come up for a minute?"

By "us," I assumed he meant himself and the Doberman, but he didn't. He meant himself and—though I hadn't yet seen a picture of her—a woman I immediately recognized as Judy Gold.

I was shocked by her plainness. In her gray skirt and high-collared blouse, she looked almost matronly, especially next to Walter: his head peering over a bag full of wine, he seemed as intense and willing as the delivery boys who screw war widows in films about sexual awakenings.

"Stole four bottles from Jacob," Walter said. "Alex, this is Judy. That must be Theo. Theo, this is Judy."

"Hope we're not disturbing you," Judy said.

I said, "I'm used to Walter's panty raids by now."

"Nicely put," Judy said.

Theo said, "Walter, right?" casually, as if I'd mentioned an architect friend in some passing context—I suppose I had. We'd rushed onto China before I'd told Theo about Judy or the rape. How did Theo get so suave as to pull off that line, take the bag from Walter, bring the bag into the kitchen, and return to hang up coats in the hall closet, while I stood trying not to exchange a duplicitous look with Walter about why he'd brought his ex-wife to my apartment on Thanksgiving without calling?

Judy laughed as if she couldn't help laughing: one grand guffaw followed by an abrupt series of stifled, smaller guffaws. "You're both so—well, *dressed*."

Theo and I looked down at our bodies.

"A bit on the dressed side," I agreed.

"It's charming," Judy said, smiling with her many teeth.

Walter, who wore a shirt so new-looking that I was sure Judy had just brought it for him and unpinned it from the cardboard, gave me the first look of the last minutes that I could read: *I'm sorry about Judy. She showed up and what could I do? I'd prefer to be alone with you. You look good in black. Will you give me a blow job? Just kidding. It's important that I meet Theo. Judy is not a threat to us. Please bear with me.* All of this with an eyebrow, a pressure of the tongue against the lower lip, a slight tightening of the jaw. Either I was a mind reader or Walter had a future in the movies— probably neither, since Judy saw the look too. She looked from Walter to me, back to Walter, inclining toward him a bit, moving her hair behind her ear in a way that could have meant she had seniority, she was resigned to being usurped, she'd already figured out she had no mutiny to fear from me, she didn't care, or it had been a long day. In any case, the signal was meant for Walter and not for me. Though I'd caught it, I couldn't be expected to read it—I hardly knew Walter, much less his ex-wife.

I wasn't jealous yet, but I would be any minute.

Theo crossed his arms, furrowed his brow, and said, "Really? I didn't know! How interesting!"

Another two minutes had passed. A further half minute passed before we got our bearings back to laugh, and the laugh itself took another half minute, or at least mine and Walter's did— Judy's laugh was a photocopy of her last laugh. The way the little laughs quickly spilled from the gut of the big laugh reminded me of a dream a mathematician friend of mine from college used to have, about a big square root giving birth to whimsical baby square roots in a rapidly multiplying Chinese-trick-box Malthusian tempo. It also reminded me of Freud's theory that a laugh is the human equivalent of an animal baring its teeth in self-protection.

"Off to a flying start." Theo grinned, giving me a gruff look that I could read quite easily: *You and your weird friends.* But I could also tell he didn't mind at all.

"Fifth dimension," Walter apologized.

"True," Judy said. "What was that game called where you had to freeze in whatever position you were in?"

" 'Freeze,' " Walter offered, freezing with one hand scratching his head, his mouth open. Judy nudged him, he unfroze, and all of us laughed again until Theo suggested that we continue laughing in the living room. We were still in the hall. We laughed.

Judy said, "What is this, 1969 and blotter acid?"

"It's the turkey fumes," I said. "They feed them nitrous oxide so they'll die happy."

"Really?" Judy said, in an admirable mimic of Theo, right down to his thin man's slouch. "I didn't know. How interesting!"

"Not bad," Theo admitted.

We sat while Theo chose Aretha Franklin. Walter groaned, but Judy said, "I approve. Thanksgiving is a Motown holiday—happy Americans singing in the street with their shoes off, like in a Marx Brothers movie."

Walter looked at me, half proud of Judy, half embarrassed. Before we could get sucked into another black hole of subterranean communication, Judy added, "It smells wonderful in here."

"Have you eaten?" I asked. "There's plenty of food."

"Twice," Walter said.

"Once at Margaret's and once at Jacob's," Judy said.

"First at Jacob's," Walter said. "Jacob served hot-and-sour soup, Peking duck, and eight-treasures rice. Margaret served—catch this—spaghetti and meat sauce."

"The only advantage of eating bad spaghetti at Margaret's," Judy told us, "is that she's so busy talking she doesn't notice if you get up to dump your spaghetti in the garbage. At Jacob's you have to make a witty gourmet comment about each mouthful. How Craig and Judy got out of the dinner shift to go to Vermont this year I'll never know. You won't like the dinner shift, Alex."

"They're not so bad," Walter said. "Actually I thought the duck was pretty good."

"But you couldn't taste it. The pancakes were like doilies. 'You put the sauce on *first*, as *such*' "—this apparently a Jacob Danner imitation. Judy shuddered.

Walter said, "You didn't have to go."

Theo laughed. "Sounds like 'The Newlywed Game.' "

Silence all around, except from Aretha.

"Oh," Theo said. "I see. You two must have dated before."

"They were even married once," I drawled.

Theo is the only male I know who blushes like a country lass from an eighteenth-century novel. It's virtually impossible to dislike him, but especially when he blushes.

"So," I said, "would you like to eat a third time?"

"Is it turkey and stuffing and sweet potatoes and cranberry sauce?" Judy asked.

"You bet your ass," Theo said.

"And hot rolls and salad," I added, "except it's nine-thirty and probably ruined."

"It wouldn't dare be ruined," Theo said.

"I'm on," Judy said. To Walter: "You on, lightweight?"

Judy was a little *zaftig*. Only seconds before, I'd been noticing her breasts, which were unfashionably large. Large eyes, large breasts, and lots of teeth.

The record skipped.

"I think," Theo said—correcting the skip, just now recovering from his mistake, never excelling in small talk in any event—"that dinner is served."

"And wine," Walter said, finding the corkscrew so effortlessly that you'd think he'd been cooking in my kitchen for months. "Who's giving the toast?"

"I am," I said.

The food was on the table within minutes owing to an almost spooky spasm of efficiency from all of us. The food looked good in the candlelight, and so did we.

"To the hostages," I said. "May they get enough exercise and rest so they can look and feel their best. May the Ayatollah die of something unglamorous like the chicken pox; may America regain her rightful place in the world without sticking her foot in her mouth; and may the Shah—"

"I don't like it," Theo said.

"Me either," Walter said.

"And you, Judy?" I asked.

We were still raising our glasses.

Judy put on the face of a graduate seminar student chewing it over, checking it out against the tertiary sources. "To tell you the truth, it's too camp for my taste. We're all adults, you've made this posh dinner, and half of us are almost in black tie, so why not something that pays a little more homage to the wonder of it all?"

"Right," Walter said, "like 'To our host and hostess.' "

"And to our guests," Theo said.

We touched glasses.

I couldn't quite believe how good the food was. Theo and I had been temporarily possessed. The conversation wasn't bad either. It's true that as we started on the third bottle of wine I began to lose track of what was being said, but that was more Walter's fault than the wine's—he was breathtaking in the soft light and his feet were playing with my ankles under the table. Despite the short-term erection problem, Walter had a matchless sexual sense. I knew I could count on him to not touch the wrong legs or to call attention to us; I was grateful for the reaffirmation of his interest in me against the competition; and I knew that as the records dropped onto the turntable one after another, I could count on Theo and Judy to keep the conversation going. They were comparing notes about psychology, about academic-sponsored research, and I was writing rock songs in my head ("The rapist's ex-wife gets along with my brother/Maybe they'll fall in love with one another"). Theo and I smoked. Judy and Walter's visit hadn't left me advance time to worry about how Theo and Walter would get along, so I worried a bit at the table. Did Walter recognize Theo's genius and wit? Had Theo written off Walter as a dumb stud? I couldn't worry much, because the evening was as tidy, as lively, as a Virginia reel. Theo and Judy talked about habit: Freudian versus Skinnerian views of habit, habit as the danger in research, habit as the crux of human life.

"My grant ran out just when it should have," Judy was telling Theo. "I'll need time to write up the results. Besides, after a while I just got bats on the brain. Who finally cares at what range they'll hear the walls? Wouldn't it be more interesting to get them to sing 'O say can you see' every time you showed them a girlie magazine—more interesting and ultimately just as arbitrary—"

"Arbitrary?" I interrupted. "They bash noise into those poor things until their eardrums pop, then turn off the stopwatch and write on the little chart."

"My sister would give more money to animal protection agencies," Theo said, "if she didn't spend so much of it on milk-fed veal."

I thumbed my nose.

"She's right, though," Judy said. "I never got used to killing the critters after they schized out."

"Maybe you'd be better off with rats," Theo suggested. "Or a private practice."

"A psychiatrist doesn't get his hands wet," Judy said. "He files 'em in, they talk about their premature ejaculations"—Walter winced—"then he goes home to read the papers in case there are any new tax bills that might affect him. So what's the alternative to research?"

"Do you note some venom toward psychiatry?" Walter asked me.

"You could always become a bureaucrat," Theo told Judy. "You could spend your days assessing other people's grant proposals, like our father. Talking about habit, he has a ritual like a military burial for everything. He's the world's great quantifier. Everything's ranked; everything has odds."

"Time for Theo to beat up on our cute father," I said.

"Oh, boy," Judy said.

"In the dessert ritual," Theo explained, "he heaps ice cream on peaches and drowns it in Drambuie, then asks you if it's the best dessert you've ever tasted, how it compares to the last dessert he made you, and if you think the dessert would taste better in a different bowl, which leads us right into the china ritual. They have two complete sets of china as an inheritance for me and Alex. The gold set is more expensive but the everyday set has more pieces—"

"Sounds like Jacob," Judy said.

"Not from what I've heard," I said. "When Phil does it, it's all ironic."

"Hah!" Theo said. "The dog ritual is ironic?"

"Not the dog ritual," I conceded.

"This dog," Theo said, "has undergone more tests than the talking apes, than Eliza in *My Fair Lady*. Phil knows what cheeses Sam likes, what brands of chocolate. Sam has been trained to attack people who dance. Certain songs hummed under the breath make him growl. He's the universe's only anhedonic dog. Phil feeds him bones, inadvertently makes him sick, then gets to quiz the vet on the probability of the dog's survival, the odds of the dog recovering by Tuesday."

"You're drunk," I told Theo.

"Then we should do the dishes so as to create an artificial wall between this part of the evening and the next," he retorted.

"What's the next?" Judy asked.

"The next," I announced, "is you and Theo going into the living room, changing the record, and chatting while Walter and I do the dishes."

"I'll do the dishes," Theo said.

"No," I said, "go away so Walter and I can compare house construction techniques of the Mountain People and the Villanovans."

"Gotcha," Judy said.

After Judy and Theo left, Walter leaned me up against the sink and kissed me for a good while. It was the kind of kiss you can only participate in while drunk and a little numb, because otherwise it would hurt too much. The kiss was defined by teeth and tongues as fast and goal-oriented as long car trips. We kissed as if we were swimming laps, as if it were good for our health. I'd have rather not stopped, but there was the little problem of getting some oxygen into the lungs to make the chest go up and down.

"What a kisser." I sighed. "Well?"

Walter held my hands and let me swing backward so I could uncrimp my calves. "Well," he said, "looks like Judy is done with Keith. Remember when I called at Judy's and Keith said she wasn't there, he didn't know where she was? That wasn't Keith. That was Keith's brother. They sound just alike. Keith has checked himself into a mental institution, which, as you can guess, wreaks havoc on his practice. Looks like it's going to be an amicable separation, on account of Keith, though self-avowed crazy, has decided that Judy isn't good for him. So Judy is going to give up her research associate thing to live off her alimony if there's any money left. She says she's going crazy but she seems okay to me. In fact, I think she's relieved. Doesn't she seem okay to you?"

"I'm not a Judy Gold authority, but you know, Walt, I like her."

"Good. Do you want to wash or dry?"

"I want to kiss more."

"We've got a lifetime to kiss. Meanwhile the food's getting barnacled on these dishes."

" 'We've got a lifetime to kiss.' Oh, Walt, that's sweet. Once more, okay, because it's so good to see you?"

This was an even longer kiss than the last kiss, and for its duration I was metaphorically doing dishes. In the slog and suds of the Freed brain, all the tongue and tooth and lip and face was soap and water and silver and china, and all of it was clean, clean, clean—wishful thinking, like getting up, turning off the alarm, getting dressed, and going to work in your dreams, with the covers over your head.

"I've got a better idea," Walter said. "Why don't you slump down against this cabinet and keep me company?"

I slumped obediently and tried very hard to imagine how I'd condense the evening for a report to Pat, how I'd get more of a feel for Judy so I could describe her to Pat, but I kept getting distracted by Walter's knees, which were on eye level, bopping up and down, because Walter was humming to himself as he washed dishes.

"I love you," I said.

He smiled, turning.

"Slipped out," I apologized.

"It'll mean more if you can say it tomorrow, lush."

"Who are you calling a lush? Who you think you are, anyhow?"

"How did you know? I've always had this secret delusion of being Anyhow."

"That's very bad. Furthermore you missed my Godfather imitation. That was my Godfather imitation I just did."

"Run it by us again," Judy said.

"You've appeared!" I said. "You're almost tall from here. Theo's taller. Hello, Theo. You're too thin. Will you eat some pumpkin pie?"

"My sister," Theo told our guests, "is a notoriously cheap drunk."

"Nyah-nyah."

"Finished," Walter said. "Let that one soak. Coffee, anyone?"

"While it's true that I'm drunk," I said, "I'm now going to offer *living proof* of my theory that all drug effects vanish with the right kind of hyperkinetic mind control. Ladies and gentlemen, I'm now going to stand and resume my former role as a hostess."

I stood. There was applause, coffee (thank God for Walter), pie, and more talk. We were all drunk, not just me. I pointed this out, somewhat indignantly.

"Sad thing about the world," Judy said, "is that one is rarely 'just me.' One is usually surrounded by all sorts of other stuff, like people and their needs."

"Does this mean more than I think it does?"

"I.e., more than nothing?"

"Correct."

"Of course not."

Theo pointed out that it was after two. Judy and I shook

hands. She said that she'd see me again, because Theo was going to give her a lift to Boston on Sunday so she could visit friends.

"That's great," Walter said.

"Great?" I said. "Have you ever driven with him? Imbibe Valium before you take off, and buckle your seat belt."

We all kissed goodbye, even Theo and I. Only when the door closed and we exchanged the congratulatory sighs of successful hosts did I get the horrific gnawing in my stomach that heralds a fear I'd done something wrong, said something wrong—I'd been too open or not open enough, been rude, talked too much about myself.

"If you're mad about anything," I told Theo, "say it now or forever hold your peace."

There was a joke then circulating about me, prompted by the possibility of a draft for women. The joke had General Freed on the battlefield, asking the enemy: "Do you still like me? Are you bored yet? Have I done anything wrong?"

"I'm so mad at you," Theo said, "that I'm going to make you help me fold out the couch."

"I don't understand couples," I said. "How were they ever married? How were Pat and Preston married? Will we ever get married?"

"I think we'll throw up dinner first."

In folding out the couch, the drunken siblings spilled the rest of the wine and somehow managed to clean it up, but we didn't empty the ashtrays—a sign of something, among fanatical ashtray-emptiers.

I started to cry.

Theo rolled his eyes. "Okay, okay, we'll empty the ashtrays."

"It's not that. It's just—Theo, I'm just so *tired*."

THREE

13

My mother claims that I was born unhappy. I had kicked out of the womb, had scorned mother's milk, and hadn't smiled since. I had folded my arms and frowned before I learned to crawl; I was congenitally misanthropic.

"Now, Mom," I objected. "No baby rejects the breast. You must have been emitting some powerful anti-kid signals."

"When in doubt," she said, "blame the mother."

If you asked my father, my problem was that I suffered from chronic laziness and hedonism. "Pleasure, pleasure, pleasure. Buy me, give me, show me. Why don't you try thinking? Why don't you *do* something, Madame Bovary?"

"What do you suggest?"

"Is your mother a slave? Clear the table."

Parents are not always the best people with whom to discuss the vicissitudes of the soul in battle.

On a Friday in December, during an unseasonable storm in Bethesda, Maryland, lightning hit a tree in my parents' backyard. The tree, an extraordinary oak that I'd hoped to use as the canopy for my wedding, managed to avoid the bedroom windows and crash through the patio glass, leaving the basement exposed to rain. My parents were stranded on the beltway at the time, two miles from a telephone, in the '71 olive-green Dodge Dart that Phil had driven since Nixon froze his salary. By the time they got the car towed and arrived home, the basement, recently refurnished, was under two inches of water, and their octogenarian Schnauzer had gone into the storm through the patio glass to carouse. My mother's car was in the shop, so my parents put on galoshes and went out with umbrellas in search of the dog. They went to bed dogless and wet, and woke up on Saturday with colds and a whimpering dog who had returned on his own with hepatitis—requiring a fat-free diet, three pills twice a day, and $160 in veterinarian's fees.

If the dog died, Phil Freed might have to be buried with him.

This was the weekend on which I decided to surprise them.

I'd taken the train to D.C. Saturday morning to endure the Foreign Service exam along with seventeen thousand other hopefuls. Only three thousand people would pass the written exam and I knew I'd be one of them. Give me a multiple choice and I'm a shoo-in. Though it's no testament to my intelligence—like a lab rat or a Clever Hans, I'm right only when the answers are computed in advance—I've always enjoyed taking tests. In the huge exam room, I was as tidy and self-contained as a computerized answer slot, but not dehumanized, because my new green shoes (a pre-Christmas present from Walter) had caught the attention of the competitor to my left, a man in thick glasses who ran his fingers through his thick black hair as he concentrated. I had him sized up as a corporate lawyer's son from Great Neck who hadn't taken to medical school and was now appeasing his distraught mother. The man smiled at me as I left, and I liked his teeth, but as soon as I began to imagine making love with him I remembered Walter, felt promiscuous, then a little sullen, because I still hadn't defined our relationship, such as it was.

Walter and I had been seeing each other for over a month, which is not, needless to say, much of a panorama in the eye of God. Still, I was almost ready to stop counting. The time I spent with him was so fine that I wanted to believe not only that we had a future together, but that we would glide into it effortlessly, without establishing a timetable. When we made love and Walter was ready to come but stopped to arrange me better so as to see my face, or to move his hand down my back to the bottom of my spine, I felt that what we shared surpassed speech. Not that we were mute. We had our days to discuss, our private jokes. We would start a walk with the Doberman while I ranted about Rousseau's *Confessions* and would end with Walter expounding on the virtues of an old house: our discrete subjects would seem, almost physically, to meld. Then Walter would take my hand into his pocket because I was shivering, take me to his place and make me camomile tea. In bed, watching a film that crowded Dracula, Frankenstein, a hunchbacked nurse, a werewolf, and a mad scientist into the same thunderstruck Gothic mansion, I'd find myself looking instead at the exquisite way that Walter's lower lip joined his chin, at the thickness of his lashes, at the way his hair was a little redder at the part. He'd catch me looking and smile. He made me feel soft and lithe. He didn't think I was a bitch, or zany. He brought me roses and baby's breath; once he brought me an armful of birds-of-paradise.

Goopy, yes, but so is cynicism. The romance was the romance of daily life. My happiness with him didn't seem to depend on any escalation of intensity. For the first time, serenity wasn't sloppy or lobotomizing, the tic of a Hare Krishna proselytizing at a laundromat. For the first time I wasn't hungry, wasn't devouring someone the way children finish their soft drinks in restaurants, knowing their parents will order them another if they wriggle around enough.

Or so I told myself, but I still thought it would be much smoother and less anxiety-producing to be married.

Both my parents are Grade A domestics. My father's duties include strip-mining the leftover turkey and transforming the salvaged meat into dog food, croquettes, and soup, washing the floors and the dog, transferring the dirty clothes from the upstairs hampers to the laundry room, and caring for the lawn. My mother is responsible for all serious cooking, bookkeeping, shopping, and entertaining. She also deals with repairmen. If a storm knocks over a telephone pole, our phone is the first on the block to be reconnected. I have a vivid memory of Connie and Phil changing the sheets together on Sunday mornings: they'd have contests to see who could get the pillows into the pillowcases faster. The match would often end with my father lunging for my mother's ass and my mother saying "Knock it off, Phil," in a voice that meant she didn't want him to knock it off at all. While I can't imagine my parents racing to bed in midafternoon, I remember how they'd look at each other when they'd washed every glass and emptied every ashtray after a big party: the world had been put in its place, the world was out of their way, and now they were allowed to tend to each other.

As paragons of enlightened domesticity, my parents are a hard act to follow. At least I think so—Theo thinks that they use their daily program to shut out reality and risk. In either case, next to them both Theo and I will always seem frenetic and selfish. Time has frozen in my parents' house. No matter how much I change, I'll always be six years old there, decrying some injustice or tedium. When I hit the foyer, I feel like a kid after six weeks of summer camp, restored to the holy, dust-free stillness of my parents' house. It's so safe there it's eerie, because nowhere else will ever feel that safe again.

"It's also clean here," Phil would say, "with your mother making your bed. You smell like an ashtray."

Now, after two hours of irritating public transportation, I had arrived keyless to find no one home.

I indulged in a second of irrational panic before sitting on the doorstep of the house Theo and I had nicknamed Tara (it has structurally useless columns out front), wishing I'd eaten something before leaving Philadelphia and feeling as foolishly homeless as I had in fifth grade, when I'd run away from home and, for lack of more imaginative options, spent the night at the playground at school. Unaware of the fallen tree and the broken patio out back, I leaned against a column and smoked, dropping my ashes into the soil of a dead potted geranium.

My parents arrived a half hour later in the Dart, carrying groceries, the leashed dog, and the dog's X-rays.

"How nice to see you! I hope nothing's wrong," Connie said, kissing me.

"What's wrong with you? You both look terrible."

My mother offered a condensed version of the Friday fiasco as we entered the house. The repairmen were due momentarily; most of the water had already been mopped. Phil asked me what I was doing in Washington and I told him.

"You think you're going to be a girl spy?" he said. "You'll be

sent to a Third World country with malaria and malnutrition—
no movies, no Chinese restaurants. They'll stick you behind a
desk to plow through memos and supply requisitions. For that
you could work for the government here."

Connie and Phil began to put away groceries, forestalling the
basement tour. Ah, the steaks and mixed nuts, the Pop-Tarts
and snow peas, the eighteen varieties of canned soup!

"So, Dad," I said, "how are you progressing emotionally,
intellectually, and physically on a scale of one to ten?"

That was my father's usual greeting. Unlike Theo, I enjoyed
Phil's catechisms. Phil was as dedicated a test administrator as I
was a test taker. It used to embarrass me, infuriate me, when a
math major would pick me up for a date and my father would
shake his hand and say, "If a Dodge pickup goes from Cleveland
at sixty miles per hour and returns from Detroit at fifty miles per
hour, what's the average speed for the round trip, and a hint is
the answer's not fifty-five?" He quizzed the physics majors on
relativity, the English majors on *Don Quixote*. His knowledge,
like mine, is broader than it is deep. Like me, he prizes himself
on being able to size people up quickly. He can guess someone's
age, occupation, and birthplace in ten seconds from speech and
dress; he can select the right contestant on "To Tell the Truth"
in thirty seconds with the sound off, simply by reading gestures.
Where such accuracy gets him is a different matter. To endear
himself to people, he needs my mother, who is much kinder,
much slower to speech and to anger. My parents have the typical
marital division of labor, with the exception that if the car won't
start, it's Connie who looks under the hood.

"Life," my father answered, "is a series of disappointments.
You can't protect yourself, so you might as well relax."

I smiled. "The great dictator of achievement has been reduced
by a basement flood to 'What, me worry?' "

"You better get a job," Phil warned, "because I'm retiring in
June. Your mother and I are going to ditch this albatross, this
House of Usher. I'm going to get a condo and some easy consult-
ing work so your mother and I can enjoy ourselves."

"Can I believe what I'm hearing?" I asked Connie.

"Your father," Connie said—her back was to me as she replenished the dog's water bowl—"is a dreamer. He was so upset about the dog and the flood that he woke me up at four because he couldn't find the Fantastik and he'd decided in his compulsive way that the kitchen floor had to be washed at once. The basement's under water and he's cleaning the kitchen. Then he made a whitefish salad and went to look for the dog again. I ask you, is this man going to relax?"

Connie, a mind reader, had just presented me with a beer and a corned beef on rye. "It could be worse," I told my father, "or maybe not. If the house had burned to the ground, if you'd been taken hostage or lost your job, then you'd get to start over, and there would be a certain sense of pride in having hit rock bottom and struggled up again."

"You'll never get a Foreign Service job," Phil retorted. "Even if you didn't talk like a madwoman, you would never get a government job after what you did in high school with the Czechoslovakian spies' son."

"You're still convinced there are movies filed at the F.B.I. of two sixteen-year-olds making out?"

"Ruined my security clearance," Phil accused, and I would have bantered with him, but he was spying on Sam, his best and oldest friend ("My favorite son," Phil often said); the dog was asleep on its back in the den, its nervous hind legs twitching. It was also time to finish the basement.

Phil headed down with the mop and my mother told me to accompany her to the john, where she whispered, "Don't think I don't know about Thanksgiving."

"What are you talking about?"

"If you wanted to have the holiday in Philly alone with your brother, you didn't have to lie. You think we can't live without you?"

"I'm sorry," I said.

"I didn't tell your father. It would break his heart."

"I thought you'd be relieved for the time off from family."

"What's this surprise visit stuff? You couldn't have called and said you were coming?"

"Any other complaints?"

"Yes. What are you going to wear with green shoes?"

"Everything. Next?"

The basement looked like a World War I documentary photograph and smelled like wet dog. I admired my parents for taking it so well. Most of the objects in the basement were there precisely because they wouldn't be missed—the childhood board games, the grotesque candy dishes—but the treasures were down there too, and I felt I could mourn over the family albums. Wet were the pictures of my father in traction with a full head of hair, my mother freckled in her first prom dress, pictures irreplaceable not only because my parents were no longer young but because they almost never pose for photographs. Their typical expression for the camera isn't sheepish but stern; for them photography is nothing more than culturally approved narcissism.

My mother stood against a stack of wet boxes and rested her head on her palm in a way that always made me want her to write a book, to celebrate this pose on her dust jacket. Connie is unpretentious in her beauty, and even at fifty-five her simplicity belies deep secrecy; she's the kind of woman you label "sweet" immediately and never know.

I grabbed the loaded Polaroid camera my parents had been using to record the flood damage and quickly got a candid of my mother.

"Knock it off," she said.

"Just one more of you and Dad," I pleaded, and she relented because the picture, developing in my palm, was so flattering, and because even my parents had to admit that it was magical how quickly you could represent the world, if not rebuild it.

The repairmen arrived to replace the patio glass. We worked in the basement, chatting about relatives and politics, then made dinner and ate. I announced that I might be in love. Phil grunted and moved into the den for his after-dinner cigar and the news, and my mother snapped, "Another Irish Catholic?"

"You're too smart for the Jewish-doctor routine," I said.

"I don't care if you marry a Puerto Rican plumber. I'm worried about your father. Why don't you think about someone else for a change?"

"I think about other people constantly."

Connie turned sharply from the sink. "Go talk to your father."

Friends have told me about the curious juncture with parents when they stop treating you as a child and you, in turn, have to coddle them. I had assumed that it would never happen to me, not because I'm too selfish to offer the service but because my parents would be too proud and self-sufficient to accept it. Perhaps I'd been wrong. If so, then there was absolutely nothing stable in my life.

"Let's talk about your future," I proposed, joining my father.

"I'm watching the news."

"How about your past?"

"Later."

"How's work?"

"Same."

"How's Uncle Nate?"

"Connie," my father called, "get this girl out of here."

He didn't mind, of course. This is how we talked. Walter would have to be briefed when family introductions came to pass. Already I was bored. I wanted to be with Walter; whenever I'm at home, I want to be somewhere else—a side effect of the regression. This visit, though, I was inclined to agree with Theo: my parents were getting tired. They were more lively in my head, in my descriptions of them to friends. In my rendition, Phil told childhood stories: the time he stole a barrel of herring for his father and was made to scale every fish before he brought the barrel back; the time my grandmother, a fierce matriarch with a grisly sense of humor, was asked by a grandchild what a vagina looked like and responded by pinning a mink collar to her underpants and flashing mink eyes at the child.

"Dad," I said, during a commercial. "What's the dominant quality of Greeks?"

"They talk very close to your ear and bald quickly."

"What's the problem with American youth?"

"They expect immediate results."

"What's the most underrated profession?"

"Schoolteacher."

"What's the world's most anti-Semitic country?"

"Russia."

"So obvious! I fear you've lost your touch."

"Go talk to your mother."

Maybe they hadn't changed. Maybe I was asking too much. I expected to have epiphanies at my parents' house. I still saw the world as an Outward Bound project. I identified with Benny the ant, one of the protagonists from the bedtime stories Phil had told us as children. Benny was my grandfather the immigrant reincarnated as insect. His eternal wish was to return to and be embraced in the bosom of his family. In cartoon style, Benny's life was a series of great escapes. He got caught in envelopes that went through postage meters, on tissues upon which noses were blown, on crumbs that were sponged into the garbage disposal. Every time the ant neared death, my father would contort his face into Edvard Munch's "The Scream" and exclaim, "Wait! It's me! It's Benny!"

"Don't ever die," I told my parents. "Promise me."

"Connie," my father said, "what's wrong with that girl?"

"You tell me," I said. "You're the wizard of behavior around here. If you come up with a convincing answer, I'll do the dishes for a week."

Phil narrowed his eyes at me. "If you'll be here for a week, I'm leaving."

14

Love, like everything else, is mostly a matter of timing. You can't ask too many questions. Some time passes and then you don't have to ask, because whatever you thought you might have been feeling has been ratified or vetoed by history. You discover you love someone because years later, looking at a picture of the two of you sitting together, you hear yourself say, "I loved that shirt." Love asks you to abandon yourself to the present, but demands that you think about the future. Love, for all its claims to citizenship on the exotic edge, is essentially a middle-class emotion. I don't mean to insult love—I love the middle class. Like the middle class, love can ground you or nail your feet to the floor, depending on your mood.

But the immediate question was whether I was in love with Walter Danner.

Pat said, "With Jeff, the only way anything would happen is if we plowed through the courtship with blinders on, but neither of us is trusting enough to do that. Look at people's motives and you're bound to see smoke; see smoke and you're an idiot not to suspect fire."

"Are you endorsing 'following your instincts'?"

"If they're self-protective. Yours aren't. You're like Preston's cat. Every winter she sits on the radiator and burns her ass."

Stacey said, "Tears and sex are meaningless. Almost anyone can make you cry or come."

Vivian said, "As a general rule of thumb, I'd say if you survived the prelims with him you must feel something, unless you're just a masochist."

The *I Ching* said:

> One sees one's companion as a pig covered with dirt,
> As a wagon full of devils.
> First one draws a bow against him,

Then one lays the bow aside.
He is not a robber; he will woo at the right time.

But the *I Ching* also said about ninety other things that had about as much specific relationship to me as the random reinforcement pellets fed to pigeons.

I'd forgotten to ask Judy Gold what she thought of the *I Ching*.

Judy sent me a postcard with a Boston postmark. "Thanks for a great Thanksgiving. I'm sure we'll see each other again. Good luck with Walt. He's a tough nut to crack, but he's fiercely loyal, and that's worth something these days—J."

I didn't show the postcard to Walter. The subject of his ex-wife had happily receded, and I didn't want to reintroduce it. I did wish, however, that Walter would talk more about the nature of *our* relationship, now that we actually had a relationship to discuss. While he was loyal in his attentions, he wasn't verbal about them, and my efforts to draw him out had been unsuccessful. When I asked him if he liked me, he'd say of course he did; when I asked him how much, he'd say enough to spend all his free time with me. I tried to let it go at that. Men hate to be pushed; furthermore, the more crucial question was what *I* thought of *him*, and I still wasn't sure.

I asked everyone how they knew when they were in love. I asked waitresses, salesgirls, the woman who trims my hair. Some people warned against divorced men and some warned against bachelors. Some mistrusted strong silent types and some mistrusted smooth talkers. Some thought good sex was a priority and some thought good sex was misleading. Everyone had figure-skated in the Love Olympics and no one was interested in coaching me.

I called home, got my father, and asked him at what point he knew he was in love with Connie.

"It was the cute way she walked."

"Dad, I'm serious."

"I'm just a bureaucrat. I just take out the trash around here.

Please don't ask me about love. It makes me tired. Ask your mother."

My mother told me to cool off, but she might not have if Walter had been Jewish, and I was becoming convinced that there was a distinct possibility I'd met my match. I could smile in the unemployment line thinking about the time Walter and I cleaned his apartment in order to have Pat and Jeff for dinner: I vacuumed, dusted, washed floors, did dishes, defrosted the refrigerator, made the bed, and scrubbed the tub while Walter cleaned the telephones. He took both phones apart and cleaned the insides, then spent over an hour trying to figure out how to put them back together. There was the time Walter browsed with me in a boutique where I couldn't afford anything. I bemoaned the condescension of the salesgirls. In the store I caressed an eight-hundred-dollar suit, and Walter said in a stage whisper with haughty salesgirls within earshot: "It's a good color for you, dear, and it's a bargain, but look how shoddily it's constructed. Look at this seam. Not that you have to wear it except on Bill's plane, but I beg you, let me take you to my tailor in Paris. For three or four hundred dollars more, he could make you something truly lovely." The shopgirls there hadn't spoken down to me since. There was Walter's politeness to my friends, his gentility. Every time he nestled his hand between my hair and the collar of my shirt, I wanted to marry him and spend the rest of my life sorting his socks. Though he was overfond of puns, he had a sense of humor. He was proud rather than threatened by my knowing more than he did about politics, anthropology, art.

But then there were his temper tantrums about work. Once I'd heard him argue with a mason over the phone. When he hung up, he picked up a two-by-four and hurled it into the sink, where it broke three dishes. Walter had angry-young-man streaks without irony. When he was angry, he looked so childish, but so disconcertingly middle-aged as well, that I felt like Lucy Ball being cursed at in Spanish. He tended to get preoccupied with work but he wasn't always organized. Often he arrived at my house with his hair uncombed, his expensive shirt buttoned wrong, ranting about having forgotten to bring his folder marked "Things to Do," which had twenty pockets marked plumbing, financial, sub-contracts, and so on, divisions he never used: the papers that weren't on his drafting table were all crammed into the first pocket. There was his childishness about his family, his lack of friends (he hadn't time, he said). Most of all, there was the rift between his aggression and certainty in courtship and his present reticence. I didn't know how to weigh the odds, and though friends told me that I shouldn't feel the need to—that truths would emerge more readily without a den-mother consciousness trying to organize—I couldn't stop asking.

It was almost Christmas. Shoppers were out with their hungry looks and their unwieldy packages. I made banana bread and played Vivaldi on the cello. Soon, I knew, I'd no longer be able to resist applying for more jobs, grants, arcane graduate programs. Leisure was not at all what I needed. The Christians were right: water *does* taste better when you're thirsty. My leisure was enforced. I was no better off than an inmate making pot holders, license plates, and soap elephants.

Walter, on the other hand, had never been busier. There was an opportunity open for him to manage the renovation of a suburban shopping mall.

"I don't think you realize," he said on December 21st, "what it'll mean if this mall comes through. The step from residential work to commercial work is giant. If the mall comes through, things'll be tough for a while, but then we can cruise for the rest of our lives."

The "we" thrilled me, as did Walter's casually delivered invitation that I join him that night for dinner at his mother's.

"You won't enjoy it," he warned. "She's going to interrogate you on your feelings for me."

"What should I tell her?"

"Tell her it's none of her business."

"If you don't want her to know about me, why are you bringing me?"

"So I can play with your thigh under the table and keep myself awake."

"She couldn't be that bad," I scolded, and I was right.

I liked Margaret Danner immediately.

"So you're Alex," she greeted me. "Have you been crying, or have you just not gotten enough sleep?"

"Are my eyes that red?"

"Terribly. Shame on you, Walter, for dragging the woman out in this condition."

"Aw, Mom, so early in the evening?"

"He didn't drag me, Mrs. Danner."

"Margaret. Well, come in."

Margaret Danner walked with a chrome contraption and her right arm didn't appear to work very well, but she had a peppery grace, an air of calm independence. Her hair softened her face in effortless waves and she wore her infirmity with a kind of pride: if you couldn't bear to watch her, if you were that cowed by a reminder of your mortality, then you didn't deserve her. She led us through a bland living room—Walter certainly didn't get his taste in interior design from her—into a kitchen, where she gestured to the set table.

"My mother means business," Walter told me.

"Open the wine," Margaret commanded.

Walter obeyed. Margaret put steak, baked potatoes, and salad on the table; we were bidden to eat.

"I didn't ask you how you like your steak," Margaret told me, "because it only comes one way here, and that's medium. I've got no touch with steak. The fanciest of the French dishes I could cook once, but never a pot roast. It's worse, of course, since I became a cripple."

"Actually," I said, "this is how I like my steak."

"So I've been having a hard time getting my son to tell me what you *do*."

"I told you," Walter told me.

"What did he tell you?"

"That you'd quiz me." I smiled.

"Well? What *do* you do?"

"Not a blessed thing."

"Me either, since the stroke. How old are you?"

"Twenty-nine."

"And may I ask where you were educated?"

"Swarthmore and the University of Pennsylvania."

"I wouldn't think Swarthmore suited to you. It's such an understated Quaker school. You seem more of a forthright personality."

"I did have problems there," I said, "but I thought it was good for me to learn to deal with anal types."

"Certainly necessary to exist in Philadelphia, though Lord knows why any of us bother—that haughty silence so cultivated here has completely destroyed our claim to any national leadership or influence. We produce mindless investment bankers and overeducated lounge lizards like you."

"Mom!" Walter objected.

"But she's right," I said. "And we've got New Jersey over there, completely torn between beleaguered Pineys in the Pine Barrens and lower-middle-class nuclear-plant slaves, to keep us smug in our intelligence."

"Plus New York making it useless for us to develop any originality. But one mustn't blame others for one's failures. Don't tell me you're still laboring under a flower-child delusion that employment is a noose on the spirit?"

"I just don't like working very much."

"The usual complaints about the length of the working day, or something more interesting?"

Before I could invent an entertaining reason, she asked me how I was living.

"Unemployment."

"Have more salad. A friend of mine has a grant to research

unemployment among the disaffected middle class of the baby boom. He's a brilliant young fellow, but I'm afraid that his mind tends to outrace his pen. Can you write, Alex?"

"Adequately."

"What did you fail to finish your Ph.D. in?"

"Anthropology."

"I'll put him in touch with you. If you ask me, you need to stop this crap and get a job. Then you won't have to lose sleep over my son."

"For Christ's sake, Mom."

"That's all right, Walter," I said. "My parents have been saying the same thing."

"As well they should," Margaret said. "I'm going to speak to Zoll about you."

"Zoll," Walter laughed. "You should be flattered. Whenever I bring a woman home, my mother tries to fix her up with another man, but you're the first to be offered Zoll."

"Walter, you're going to embarrass the poor girl."

Walter nodded. "*I'm* going to."

"So, Mrs. Danner, how's your health?" I asked cheerfully.

"That's a cheap trick, but it'll work."

The eyebrows that Walter raised my way clearly meant *Now you've done it.* The eyebrows settled into resignation as Margaret talked about her health for the rest of the dinner. She told great malpractice stories. All the incompetent and evil doctors were identified by smells.

"What does Alex smell like?" Walter asked.

Margaret considered. "Tofu."

"Great. Under the expensive perfume, I still smell like bean curd."

"She could have said paint thinner," Walter said. "You're in good shape with her if you smell like food. Speaking of which, we're going to eat and run."

Margaret reached around the table to put her hand on Walter's hand. He smiled and reclaimed his hand to ruffle her hair, as a father would a teenage son's.

"The Brown units okay?" she asked him. "Any word on the mall?"

"Not yet."

"What do you hear from Jacob about the Delancey closing?"

As Margaret and Walter touched each other reassuringly and discussed the developments in their lives that hadn't been covered earlier over the phone, there was a moment when I felt invisible as a phone tap or a house dick. In a way, it's easier to witness other people's families in insult-pitched battle than in scenes of such ordinary tenderness. For the short period that Margaret covered her accountant and Jacob's latest transgression, I wished I could draw or paint so I could create an updated Biblical series: Madonna and Child in a modern kitchen, too bright from over-heads and loud wallpaper. The Parable of the Loaves and the Fishes set at a patio barbecue. A stupid idea, but it distracted me from fretting about how Walter would get along with *my* parents, how Margaret and Connie would talk.

Walter said, "Come on, Alex. Don't get up, Mom. Sit there."

"Let's do the dishes," I said.

"Nurse duty's over," Margaret said. "You can do them next time." She sized me up quickly and laughed. "God, another Jew."

"Mom!"

"You see, Alex, no Jewish mother could compete with me for guilt or doting. He's a sweetheart, isn't he?"

I was going to say yes, but Walter cut me off: "So I've been trying to tell her." He leaned on his mother's walker to bend and kiss her quickly, but not unaffectionately, on her forehead.

"Have a son," Margaret advised me. "In the matter of children it's best to be a misogynist. Men *stay* children—there you have it. They're very devoted. You don't have to kiss me, not on a first date."

"Thanks for dinner, Mrs. Danner."

"*Margaret.* You're a slow learner? You're welcome."

"I enjoyed it."

"Thanks for coming."

Walter and I walked from the kitchen backward, waving. I tried to suppress the feeling that I was six years old on "The Mickey Mouse Show." "A relative," Walter apologized, in the mirrored elevator.

"But she's wonderful."

"Better than Jacob, anyway. She liked *you*."

"How could you tell?"

"She told you to cut the crap."

"Usually I get along well with lonely women who try to intimidate people."

Walter laughed. "Alex, may I make a request?" He took my hand as we passed the reception desk.

"Sure, because presently I'm enamored of you and of all of your kin. When do I meet Jacob?"

"The later the better." When we hit the cold, Walter held my wrist as if he were taking my pulse and said: "I listened to Neanderthals on Brown all day. I went to the suburbs and listened to Margaret. What I'd like right now is for us to be very, very, very *quiet*."

I nodded.

Margaret may not have intimidated me, but she clearly did a number on Walter, who ran two lights and honked at a car with slow pick-up in front of him at the light he did stop for—by escaping the suburbs, he escaped his mother. I snuggled him. Family reduces us all. Even when he elbowed me over to my side of the car, out of the way of the stick shift, I matched his irritation with warmth. His childishness seemed human, more deep than limiting.

The only noise for twenty minutes was wind on the hood, the tires, my cigarette hitting the side of the ashtray, my smoker's cough. The city, when we reached it, was quiet as well—too cold and late for pedestrians. Walter slowed for a stop sign, turned on the car light, and bent to examine my feet. "These aren't good shoes," he said.

"Do you think they offended your mother?" I laughed.

"Are the soles thick?"

"Thick enough. What is this, Walt?"

"Roll up your pants. I want to check out a building I'm thinking of making a bid on tomorrow. I wanted to see it at night. Are you game for a little adventure?"

"When Theo and I were kids," I said, rolling the pants, "there was an abandoned men's club near the house. The Fumindish Pleasure Club—a hunting lodge, maybe, though Lord knows what they hunted in the suburbs. We used to scare ourselves silly there during the day, and we never got further than peering in the windows."

But the Fumindish Pleasure Club, set as it was off a major highway lined even in my childhood with condos and Burger Chefs, was nothing compared to the desolate block behind the Art Museum where Walter parked, opened my door, and fished two huge flashlights, a crowbar, and an old beach blanket from the trunk. He draped the blanket over me Pocahontas-style.

"Walter, we're going there? Those places are all boarded up. The electricity won't be on."

Nor, I added quickly, were my shoes meant for wading through knee-high weeds probably harboring rodents. We walked to the side entrance of a house where Walter bid me aim both flashlights while he pried off the wood nailed to the door.

By the time he'd succeeded in removing the plywood amidst flying dust and plaster, my goodwill for an adventure had entirely fled. I was whining, in fact. Walter leaned into the flashlight to examine his hand, which had a splinter. He shrugged as we entered the building.

"Oh, Walt!"

One step into the building I saw more spiders than I'd ever seen in my life. The air was tamped square foot by square foot from floor to ceiling with spiderwebs, cobwebs. Spiders fled from the random spots of our flashlights; cobwebs settled on my hair and eyelashes. Behind the fear, which was as thick as the stench (Walter's disability was an asset in this business), I was thinking of the New Zealand caves I'd read about in some existentialist tract: caves exist in New Zealand with walls lined by phosphorescent snails, zillions of tiny snails that eat themselves and in their self-destruction produce a brief neon, a light eternal in the caves because of the endless number of suicidal snails. Unlike the caves, this building wasn't pleasantly, philosophically eerie. It was disgusting. I felt as if I'd been plunged into a vat of salt-water taffy and it was completely dark.

"We'll have some patches of moonlight upstairs," Walter assured me, "where the roof's gone. Watch your step."

"I'm not going anywhere," I said, but Walter pulled me forward by my elbow.

It took a few minutes to adjust to the dark, and as my eyes began to distinguish patterns of light, the stench seemed to get worse—dust, excrement (human and animal), trash, mold and mildew, soot.

"Fire damage," Walter said.

No wall, no ceiling, no floor—beamed by our flashlights in what Walter assured me could make a grand living room—was without black stages of disintegration. Indeterminate objects loomed everywhere. Amidst the debris it was both comforting and harrowing to make out familiar objects—a tennis shoe, an old pot, an old-fashioned, naked porcelain doll with half of its face burned away and one leg dangling by a hinge. Walter crouched to examine the doll, grinning. "Anything and everything of value in these places gets pillaged," he said, almost cheerfully, "so what you're faced with is always garbage—and a sofa bed. There it is." He shined the light on the sofa bed, springs exposed, uphol-stery gone. "There's always a sofa bed. I guess they're too heavy to move."

"Let's go."

"Be careful," he said, taking me into what seemed to be the kitchen. "What's strangest"—he opened a cabinet, shined his flash on an ancient box of baking soda, its design identical to the one in my refrigerator at home, on a can of peas—"is that even though everything's trashed, things are still in the right places. In that silverware drawer yesterday, I found a slimy dead black rat and a silverware tray—one of those yellow plastic numbers with the silverware still sorted in it, knives here, forks there. Upstairs"—he led me back to the hall—"the closets are still full of hangers holding up charred rags, melted fabric. Have you ever seen fire-damaged clothes? They're very strange. Some fabrics just melt thinner and thinner, like bubble gum, until they trail on the floor. When I see them, I feel as if I'm in a dream sequence— like the clothes will melt us into a flashback, into some other kind of time. In the basement here there are rusted hammers and screwdrivers, all the accoutrements of a Sunday carpenter. Look at that, Alex."

He scanned a high wall showing about twelve layers of charred wallpaper styles; you could have traced decorative fashions back to the turn of the century if you could see through the soot. The ceiling in the atrium had some ornate details and a chandelier that had somehow escaped damage.

"I want you to see upstairs," Walter said. "There's such a strange little maiden-aunt bedroom there, with a lace bedspread and a Bible opened on the dresser. I swear nothing in there has been touched, even the jewelry—the looters were afraid of it. Almost everything's charred, but there's the Bible with the little pink satin strip marking the place."

"Touching. Can we go now?"

I was shaking. The vile-smelling building was cold. I was already walking like a Chinese woman with bound feet, terrified of rats and roaches, not even afraid anymore but in acute physical discomfort; I was ready to brush roaches from my ankles as Katharine Hepburn plucked leeches off Humphrey Bogart's back in *The African Queen*. But Walter pulled me forward and gave me a lesson in Section Eight walking techniques as we took the steps.

"A lot of the second floor is gone," he said. "Actually, 'gone' is misleading because it's like quicksand—it's there and intact, just waiting to be stepped on and give way. Where it's fire-damaged, you'll see that the sub-floor is white and chalky. If it's rotted, it's dark, warped. In either case, you've got to locate the joists—they're spaced every sixteen inches or so. You can feel them in your toes. It's weird in the dark—it's like when you were a kid, groping for the bathroom in your sleep. That's it."

By the time we reached the top of the infinite stairway, I had realized how hostile it was for Walter to bring me to this house, and I began to moan. At the same moment, something or some-one else at the far end of the hallway began to moan too—a long wail but low enough, strange enough, to be something else.

"Yo," Walter called, taking on the chummy beer-commercial voice I'd heard him use for his carpenters and plumbers.

At the end of the hall, against a wall, in the weak beam of the flash, a man was sleeping. The noise had been the snore of a stirred smoker—a long fire-damaged exhalation. I froze, then clutched Walter's sleeve, but Walter repeated his "yo" and stepped forward, bidding me with his hand on my stomach to stay put.

"Sorry to wake you," Walter said.

The man grunted, stared into the flash belligerently. I was gripping the crowbar. The man had few teeth, and that was about all I could tell about him in the dark, other than his size. I could tell he was toothless because of the way he slurred his speech when he said, "You get out of here."

"I'm just showing this woman around," Walter said. "Just have to measure a few things. Won't get in your way."

I fled down the steps.

Fleeing was not a good idea. The wood on the staircase gave way and one of my legs slipped through the step into some ooze and chips. Walter caught me from behind, lifted me from under my armpits, literally hauled me down the remaining steps.

"Fuck you," I whimpered.

"I'm really sorry. There weren't any squatters in here last time I looked. Is your leg okay?"

He crouched to examine it, except in the process he managed to sneak a last look at the floor—I knew he was digging his thumb into the charred wood, determining the extent of the damage. I brushed him off and fumbled toward the door. Walter caught up with me and took my arm.

"I guess the squatters *are* scary if you're not used to them. This is the best of the buildings; I didn't think there was anyone here. In the building two down, the guy has a rabid dog. He shits into a pail; the dog shits all over the place."

"Why did you bring me here?"

Walter shined the flashlight into my face. The light got him as well, from underneath, so that his face looked sinister. "It's just so amazing," he said. "I'm sorry you didn't get a better look upstairs. I would have taken you tomorrow but that's closing day for the bids and I needed another look to decide. I think I'll buy the whole block. I thought it would interest you. In the attic there are sheaves of sheet music all over the floor—Bach, Handel, Chopin. Every time I imagine what these houses must have been like, it sends chills. They're the most wonderful examples of entropy I've ever seen. It's very sad in a way—all those relics just lying around."

We were standing just at the door by then. He put his arms around me, kissed my hairline. "I didn't want to upset you," he whispered.

I stepped outside without answering. While Walter pounded the board back over the door with the crowbar and the nails he'd apparently put aside for this purpose, I breathed deeply. I felt as if I'd been buried alive and had just been released from my grave.

As we went through the weeds to the car, he took the blanket from me, shook it out as fearlessly as you would a clean sheet you were about to fold at the laundromat. "I love it," he said. "Soon we'll clear it out and put up new drywall, new paint, new stairs. All the old strata of lives will be stripped away, along with the graffiti and debris. All that'll be left of what you just saw is the brick shell. Sometimes I feel like I'm building over Pompeii. Hiroshima. It feels almost criminal."

"What is criminal is subjecting me to that. What did I do to deserve it?"

"I just wanted to show you what I do, what I think about."

The car turned over—I hadn't expected it to. As I stroked my slightly turned ankle and longed for a hot shower, something was clear: either Walter disliked me or he disliked women in general. Maybe both. Maybe he was a latent homosexual after all. The night before he'd begun to make love to me before I'd attended to birth control. I'd suggested that if he didn't want a baby, he should run, not walk, to the nearest exit, but he'd persisted. "You're going to pay for the abortion," I'd warned, then surprised myself by coming noisily. Walter had tried to pull out, had turned on a light to show me the glistening trail of semen on my leg. We'd looked at that for a while, as if it were exceedingly beautiful. Now for two weeks I'd have to obsess about being pregnant. Between rape and the Section Eight housing, forcible entry was the dominant metaphor.

"I'm sorry," Walter said. "I always forget how other people react to the mess. I love you."

That last stopped me almost as forcefully as the stench in the building had.

"Thank God you don't hate me. You would have left me there with the toothless drunk."

The Doberman, he pointed out when we got to his house, hadn't yet eaten. I sat while he fed the dog, wondering how such a violent man could have such a strong nesting instinct. Walter lived in space as totally as I inhabited my interior landscape. More and more, he and I were relating as man of action versus woman of words, and maybe he was beginning to resent it. He didn't want to play Tarzan to my Jane, feared that in my praise of his domesticity there was the condescension one would give to an expert mechanic or an efficient housewife. He was right. More than once he had complained that I didn't trust his intelligence, and I couldn't argue. Why, then, had he taken me to the abandoned house? It only confirmed whatever suspicions I'd had of his desire to conquer danger.

"Walter," I said, "there are things we have to discuss."

"Right away?" He hugged me, burrowed his face in my neck, and asked me if I'd walk with him and the dog.

For once I wasn't going to give a man the satisfaction of

claiming he was pushed. I recalled the way Walter had said he loved me—his earnestness, his simplicity—and thought, I'll wait.

"Look," he said when we left his building. "Look what happened, Alex."

Snow.

It was sticking. The sky had that mystical day-for-night look it gets when it snows in polluted cities.

We watched the snow fall.

I was only partly thinking about how good the snow looked. I was thinking that I ought to brace myself for things with Walter not working out, and, on the other hand, that it wouldn't be a bad life, to inhabit the classy, warm apartment with Walter and the Doberman. The Doberman was checking out the snow with very much the dignified curiosity that Walter used for buildings. I'd begun to like the dog, begun to miss it when Walter slept at my place and left it to guard his apartment on Brown Street. I wondered when that had happened.

15

It was good to be at least partly in love with Walter, because I was even less in love with everyone else.

Vivian West and I sat in my neighborhood bar arguing about holocaust movies. I found it sickening to call the lascivious catharsis of the concentration-camp soap operas "bearing witness." The films dangerously distorted the war, made Jews and Nazis into cops and robbers or cowboys and Indians, made the survivors stronger, smarter, more stoical and large-hearted than their gassed relatives, when survival was more often than not totally arbitrary. Vivian said that in order to get an awareness of prejudice out to a mass audience, some distortion and oversimplification is inevitable. We bantered over the noise of the jukebox, and were half enjoying ourselves until we got to "Roots." I hated "Roots" as much as I hated "Holocaust," for the same reasons. Audiences liked to watch people thrown into ovens, into vats of boiling oil. Vivian told me that I was unconscionably apolitical. I pointed out that I voted Democrat and boycotted pro-Arab big business just as she did; besides, she earned forty thousand a year, drove an Audi, and didn't have a single blouse with polyester content, so she should please spare me the ghetto-life routine, or I'd start in on how I got felt up by a gang of boys in the back of homeroom on the last day of seventh grade.

Needless to say, I went too far. Two hungry-looking black males entered and sat at the table to our right. I automatically took my open purse off the floor by their table and shifted it to my other side. Vivian glared. I spent another hour defending myself against charges of racism and political ignorance.

"Fran, a friend of mine in New York, just had her purse snatched," I said. "She ran after the mugger, caught him, and had him indicted. The guy was eighteen, Puerto Rican, a high-school dropout whose family kicked him out and changed the lock. When he called home from the police station, he found that they'd gotten an unlisted number. But when Fran told her Marxist brother that the mugger had been indicted, her brother said, 'That's too bad.' I'd like to see how he'd react if someone mugged the woman he lives with."

"You'll fit right into the coming Fascist regime," Vivian said. "I'll send you one of those stickers of Mickey Mouse giving the finger to Iran."

"Good work, Viv. Who around here was sitting next to you at the Shah torture protests five years ago? Remember how we met?"

"Sorry," Vivian said.

"Me too," I said, but Vivian and I didn't really speak much for a month, during which I argued with Stacey Easterlin.

Stacey had solicited my approval in condemning her boyfriend, who, she claimed, was simply jealous of her success as a photographer. I agreed that once or twice he had behaved badly, but Stacey's "success," so far as I could determine, had very little to do with it. In fact, Stacey had been strutting her success too much for my taste, and for everyone else's. Several shows in Philadelphia and several thousand free-lance dollars hardly made her a star. Even if everyone in America had heard of her, it didn't give her the right to dismiss her boyfriend's opinion about a movie or a restaurant décor because he "had no sophistication about the visual image." This "sophistication" appeared to consist of wearing pedal-pushers to a pink bar that looked like a waiting room for the shuttle to Saturn and listening to music from the reactionary fifties. Since I couldn't tell Stacey I thought her taste was not all that original, I suggested that what her boyfriend thought about a movie didn't have to be so crucial. She told me that, unlike me, she was a feminist, that she wouldn't play games or compromise her personality for a man. When I mentioned that my history with men wasn't characterized by blissful compliance, she said that, like her boyfriend, I was just jealous, that I had no direction in my life and was taking it out on her.

There's nothing like a gorgeous, rich woman dismissing you as a lousy feminist. Stacey was a closet flirt, the most successful kind of flirt; she could monopolize most of the male attention at a party and later insist that it wasn't calculated, refusing to admit that her careful indifference to men was her most successful bait. We had become friends mainly because I was one of the few women she didn't threaten into resentment, and because I was one of the few "intellectuals" who didn't make her feel defensive. But we'd been circling each other in wider and wider arcs. I thought, Fuck this. I also thought that her argument, self-serving as it was, also contained a molecule of truth. I did envy Stacey— Stacey and Vivian—the purity and optimism of their drive. I envied them the belief that the world made sense.

These were mendable breaches. When I fought with Pat, I began to worry.

Pat Graci had been a solid B student who'd never got picked

last for volleyball teams, who'd been exhorted in yearbook autographs to stay as sweet as she was. She had always been sweet, but she hadn't always been happy, mostly out of a fear that it was her lot to be loved the way daisies are loved—for their very commonness—then to be deserted when the occasion required a more exotic bloom. Men who began by praising her service wound up complaining that the menu was bland and predictable. This had happened often enough so that Pat found herself agreeing with them, mistrusting her own capacity for inspiring or having strong emotions. But three years of self-confidence lessons had begun to restore her. Now she often seemed as effortlessly happy as she casually, superbly parallel-parked.

What worried me was that her happiness was too predicated on her economic gains, and therefore ephemeral.

Pat and I were on our way from a hardware store in the '39 Packard that she had got from her neighbor as part of the deal on the house. She had a fixed mortgage and about a half year of repair work ahead of her if she worked alone. She also had the Packard: dark green, mohair interior, white sidewalls, spare wheel mounts, and enough dials and gadgetry on the wooden dash for a Buck Rogers set. It was fun to take the car to the grocery store; in it you felt a tidy transcendental glee. Pat's glee was tripled by the knowledge that she'd managed to get a house full of antiques and a car worth $24,000 for $25,000 down—most of that money being Monopoly money won in silver—and have the old man who owned these things feel duly recompensed. I understood her excitement, but I was tired of real estate. Between Pat and Walter, all I heard was plaster, roofing, drywall, wiring, lumber, joists, wainscoting, mortgage. Pat and Walter had spent two hours at dinner one night comparing brands of tile glue. It wasn't just that I was bored. The obsession with place, with ownership of place, seemed stridently superficial. Not that I didn't suffer from obsession and even from some ownership lust myself; I just realized it as such. Real estate made Pat's and Walter's eyes shine.

After an hour in the hardware store together, I asked, "What is this real estate crap? You and Walter. What difference does it make to your psyche if the door and the floor aren't exactly flush?"

"Because the door won't close otherwise?" she said, puzzled.

"I understand why you'd want to make some money, but why are you so *into* it?"

Pat laughed. "Probably because I don't know what I'm doing. Two months ago, all I knew about lumber was that it came from trees."

"The good old days."

"Yeah, when other people worried about the leaks and termites."

"I'm scared for you, Pat. You hate your job. You're seeing Jeff but that isn't going anywhere. You're lonely a lot. You're working yourself to death and you're not happy."

"I'm hardly suicidal. Actually, I think I'm happier than I've ever been."

"You're just distracted with the house. You're not changing anything."

"Believe me, if I could snap my fingers and be ecstatically married or ecstatically employed, I'd snap my skin off."

"You could be more happily employed, at least."

"Yes, and I'm looking."

"Not as hard as you could look if you didn't fool so much with the damn house."

"Maybe, but, Alex, why should it bother you? I realize I've turned into a bit of a house bore, but I'm not as bad as Sue— she's divorced too, and if you try to introduce her to a man, her first question is 'Can he hang Sheetrock?' You certainly don't have to keep working with me over there if you hate it so much."

"My point is you're so smart and you spend your time picking out door handles. Who cares?"

"Are you in a position to pick at my use of time?"

"*Argumentum ad hominem.*"

"You want me to get unemployment and play the cello all day?"

"Hitting below the belt."

"Hitting home. I've got a kid. You don't have to play any violins for me, but the responsibility takes it out of you. I don't understand why you're making a scene about the house."

"Because I care. You're going to wind up like Walter, in Philadelphia your whole life, talking about plumbers."

"Is that how you think of him?"

"Sometimes. My least favorite thing about him is his real estate."

Pat parked the car in front of my building, turned off the motor, and faced me with an expression she most often used with Nessie, to let her know that she'd been pushed far enough. "I don't want to fight dirty—I didn't know we were going to fight at all—but your attitude about the house is very patronizing. You sound like Stacey."

"God forbid."

"I get the feeling sometimes you can't accept me—or yourself—until we have Pulitzers. You make fun of Vivian because she takes the law so seriously and you laugh at Stacey's photography. Then you start in on me and on Walter. It so happens that Walter is excellent at what he does. Granted, he's no Venturi, but he's earning a fine living as a damn fine renovator."

"What we're disagreeing about," I said, "is the whole notion of what constitutes movement in a life. You can't make cosmetic changes on a cancer; you have to fight it from inside."

"Walter doesn't have cancer, and neither do I. The person who's unhappy, love, is you."

"At least I'm honest about it. At least I'm trying. Walter has been an emotional wreck for three years and what does he think about? New lines of Formica. It's basically busywork but he acts like he's Tarzan, conquering his environment. I'm getting quite fond of him—it's just the real estate that sickens me."

"Alex, you don't know anything *about* real estate. Real estate is complicated, but not in the ways you know. Buildings aren't books. They aren't a reflection of self. They're there, all the brick and wood and amount of weight that this and that can take. You should listen to Walter sometime. It's fascinating. It isn't child's play."

"Gee," I said.

"Gee's right. Stop shooting off about things you don't understand."

From mild Pat, these were fierce words. "I'm sorry," I said.

"You should be."

"I am. You're always right. My mother always told me I'd die by the tongue. Is the wound fatal?"

"Not at all."

"You know I've never learned to keep my mouth shut, but why do people assume that the smartest people are mum, the most heartfelt sentiments unspoken? It's superstitious. It's the childish sixties' notion that reality is a kind of secret spell, that you know something's real if you don't share it and can still believe in it. So we got stoned and had fascinating ideas that we were just too stoned to express. It took us a while to admit that there are no ideas without expression, that our brilliance was merely buzz on the synapses. I'm not condoning cruel honesty. I'm just saying that with people you care deeply about, it's useful to try to talk things through. I'm also saying I'm sick of this strong-silent-type visual-person trend. Everyone's tired of talk; everyone wants Marlboro men again, quiet but soulful. I think it's bull. I don't want you to get sucked in. You're too smart for that. I criticize you out of my respect for you."

"Right," Pat said, starting the engine.

"You're still mad at me."

Pat smiled. I must have looked mournful, because she hugged me, then added wryly: "Why don't you write a book?"

"I'm on hand and knee, begging your forgiveness."

"Granted, but I'm serious. You could write about the Freed theory of movement in a life, and the death of the middle class."

"How long do you estimate I'll be incurring your wrath?"

Pat looked at her watch. "Until nine, more or less."

"I'll call you then. Really, I'm sorry."

We kissed goodbye.

Walter had a meeting that night about his mall; I wouldn't see him until later. In lieu of Walter in the flesh, I had the bad snapshot of him that I'd recently stolen from his photo album and was already very attached to: Walter looking over his shoulder, caught inspecting a house he'd renovated. Though his hair had been longer then, his clothing less meticulous, his skin a little too boyishly pink, his expression—a dialectic of woolliness and almost savage precision—was the one I'd come to recognize. I liked the picture so much that I could overlook the fact that it had been taken by Judy Gold, that his tender surprise was aimed at her. That snapshot, along with the one of my parents I'd taken in the fall, leaned against my clock radio on the dresser, because Walter and I were not yet established enough as a couple to justify a good picture of him, expensively framed. Ironically, I knew that when we got that established, I wouldn't be interested in documenting our progress. An unfortunate thing about my shoe boxes full of pictures: I generally had none of the people who mattered to me most. I had not one picture, for instance, of Theo as an adult. Like my parents, Theo is not hot on posing. I used to have a picture of him at his desk, so peculiarly lit that he looked like Rembrandt's Nightwatchman with flashlights up his sleeve. Pam had begged me for that snapshot, promised to make me a copy, which she hadn't, of course; now I regretted it. Never again would Theo look so spooky, although he'd been acting strangely of late, and certainly owed me a letter.

16

Dear Alex,

I have two pieces of news, one great, one strange, or at least strange enough that I didn't want to tell you on the phone.

Do you realize it has been over two months since Thanksgiving? My typing chair has been broken since around then. For the last half hour I've been sitting in it shakily, trying to figure out why we haven't been in closer touch. Part of it, I know, is that Walter has kept you occupied (doesn't he ever sleep at your place?). I'm glad that things with him have been going well.

Most of our lack of contact, at least on my end, has been due to how busy I've been. Aside from teaching and research, I've had Chinese class, which meets for two hours five days a week at 8 a.m. and which is permuting my perceptions of language and life so completely that yesterday at a Baskin-Robbins I got completely tongue-tied over Jamoca Almond Fudge: I was sure the girl wouldn't understand my dialect; I was trying to visualize the character for said flavor (a bird? a plane?); I eventually just cleared my throat and pointed.

What's weirdest is that by June—if I'm lucky—I'll only be able to say hello how are you and ask for the check. If I can find a context, I'll be able to drop *maou tsaou* (a scholar not succeeding and giving himself over to liquor), *heaou* (a well-informed female mind), and *pa* (a short man standing as high as he can).

You've always been good at languages. I'm not, especially at one whose rules make symbolic logic look like ABC. But I've just received an immense head-pat: my grant came through; $13,000, plus the department is giving me a sabbatical at full pay for the fall semester—quite astonishing given that I've only been there a year, have only published a couple of diddly-shit papers.

Alex, they *like* me—either that or someone on high has chosen to smile on me enough to drug the department chairman and the entire staff at the Endowment.

At first I jumped up and down, squealed, wished I had cigars to pass out. But within hours I was scared. I don't know a thing about China. Certainly having completed a dissertation on Veblen doesn't prepare me. For a moment yesterday I couldn't even remember what a psychohistorian is supposed to do. It'd be easier—and probably only slightly less ambitious—to wait ten years until my Chinese is passable and translate *The Lives of the Saints*. But I'm calming down and beginning the long campaign of study to spend fall in China speaking to psychologists.

Do you think they use acupuncture there for schizophrenia?

Now the strange news. It doesn't seem strange from this end anymore, but you should make sure that you're sitting.

Judy Gold has moved in with me. When her divorce is final, we're going to get married.

Some explanation, I think, is in order.

I didn't expect to fall in love with her. But we drove to Boston, got dinner, and spent the evening together. We've spent every evening together since and a good part of most days; the day before yesterday I proposed, and she said yes.

That simple—but why, you may well ask, did I spend three years with Pam without her having been able to squeeze so much as an "I love you" out of me, and propose to Judy in less than three months? The only explanation I can think of is that, unlike Pam, Judy never pushed me. She wants to be exactly who she is. She doesn't want to be taller or thinner or richer or more articulate. She doesn't test herself, and therefore I'm less on the spot, more free to act.

Are you over the shock?

Her life, as you've heard, has been in some state of flux—for the first time in her life she's carless, unemployed. But somehow she doesn't become less solid from the instability. I feel the same way about you. No matter how many times you call me to announce you're falling apart, I never believe it. Actually, you and Judy are a lot alike. You both speak quickly, get accused of being overly judgmental but are in fact usually right, more inse-cure about your perceptions than you let on—it's that insecurity that keeps you watching, keeps you open, yet you never let it shake the foundations.

You're very different in some ways, though. You're a peculiar mixture of cynicism and romanticism, doom-saying and hope—qualities that are usually found together, just as insecurity and conceit are found together. But in you the contrast is acute. One second you've got the corner of your lip up, speaking disparagingly of a man's inadequacies; the next second you're moon-eyed because he sent you flowers, or in tears because he didn't. Judy wouldn't do either. There's a rare consistency to her behavior. (In a way I feel she's the first *adult* I've met in years—she's got Connie's generosity without Connie's air of martyrdom.) On the one hand, she's very organized, very rational, totally hooked in with how much money you need to draw from the bank and what our government's policy is toward human rights in South America. Then there are moments when her face goes blank and she's off to some other planet, so distant even she doesn't know what she's thinking about. Then even her plainness turns exotic, extraterrestrial. There's such an endless *privacy* to her; she's both straightforward and a galaxy of secrets.

Writing this praise, I'm aware that you'd damn it as more than faintly sexist. You're right that it smacks of the old Womb as Veil of Mystery. My only defense is that I've hardly placed her on a pedestal. I know how noisy her sinuses get when she's within a mile of a cat. Her mystery isn't soft or yin or in any conventional way *feminine*. It isn't, in fact, sexual at all. This for me is a new experience.

Obviously this wasn't planned. You know I don't as a rule make snap decisions. Don't think I haven't questioned the speed of the whole process. But all I can say is it feels right, and I don't feel drugged. I don't think it'll wear off. I feel calm and I feel clearheaded.

Giddy, it's true—about her, about the grant—but clearheaded.

One time (I think it was about Victor, though it doesn't much matter since it's always the same newsreel of Nazis marching with your boyfriends), you tried to ask me whether people are ever "right for each other," or whether they simply hook up at the right time in their lives, when they have similar ambitions for a relationship. Now I can answer you: both. There's a point when commitment becomes almost a biological imperative. But there are also some people who are easier to be committed to than others. All of the questions I'm used to asking don't apply.

Not that Judy and I don't talk. For the first couple of weeks—when we weren't in bed or eating, or both—we were like a seminar in Civilization and Its Discontents. Judy was trained as a behaviorist and was married to a psychoanalyst, so her ideas on the interaction of nature and nurture are fairly complex. Do you change the self or the world from the inside out, or the outside in? Can/should you change the world at all, or merely resign yourself to the world as it is? Remember how Dad used to proclaim "Selection, Not Training" on the subject of your boyfriends? He was right for a change. Eighty years with Pam and it still wouldn't have been natural. I'm not saying Judy and I won't have some work. We'll just have less work, and the work will be more fun.

We've talked about Connie and Phil's marriage, the Golds' marriage, in this regard. Both good marriages, neither of which can serve as a model for any of us. I can't wait to hear the two of you brainstorm on this. Both of you have gnashed your teeth over the paradox that you want old-fashioned families but haven't the stomach for the compromises family entails. This whole question, of course, doesn't exist in China, but not simply because Chinese culture is so patriarchal—it's exciting to look at the way Chinese psychologists talk about family. Try talking to them about doing-your-own-thing and they look at you as if you're crazy. Try substituting the Tao for the way analysts discuss Pattern, and you've really got something (I hope!).

The present plan is we marry in June, settle here (I think we'll try to buy a house), and in August we leave for China. Judy will work with me on the book and she can wrap up her own research there as well as anywhere.

I realize a lot could backfire between now and June—or, rather, never go off. I don't think so, but I'm aware of the dangers, the most immediate of which is how we survive the family reactions. Judy and I will do the D.C. circuit of family sometime in March. I hope you can join us at home. We'll make parental proclamations soon, but I wanted you to be, as they say, the first to know.

We're working on strategies to break the news to the Freeds that Judy is six years older than me and going on her third marriage—suggestions welcome.

Judy hasn't said anything to Walter yet. Don't tell Walter if you can help it. Let Judy tell him. I don't know exactly what you and Walter are up to, but I hope you don't let this affect it much—incestuous, I know, but such is life.

A minute ago the doorbell rang. The mailman with your birthday present, which is, as usual, exactly one day early and wonderful. The sweater fits perfectly; the ties are snazzy and much needed; as for the dolphin-shaped water pistol, I don't know how I've lived to be twenty-seven without one.

Do me a favor: don't lose Pat as a friend over a house. That's stupid. I've always liked Pat. Give her a break. Not everyone is going to have exactly your priorities, thank God—have some tolerance.

Needless to say, I'm anxious to hear from you, see you. Truth is I'm worried about you. I hate to sound like Connie and Phil, but when are you going to *do* something? I'm not at all sure I get the point of paralysis, no matter how gravely undertaken. Enough of nothing is enough—

Always,

T.

17

So Judy had Theo signing with his initial already.

That was my first reaction.

My second reaction was a shudder at the fear that wunderkind Theo, who excelled at everything worldly without sacrificing his cheerful spiritual haze, would soon buy a house and speak of nothing but property taxes.

Why not just kill him at once, rather than subject him to the slow death of paint-sample chips?

I had spent a cozy night at Walter's. On February 15th, Walter swung me and the dog, who was my charge for the afternoon, past my apartment so I could pick up my mail; then I walked to the unemployment office. I leashed the Doberman to a hydrant in the slush and read the other mail first while I waited in line for my check—two letters from college friends who were never friends themselves, one in Maine, one in San Francisco, both announcing weddings on the same Saturday in June. I read the letter from Theo walking home, with the Doberman several steps ahead, in seeing-eye fashion.

Reading on the move always makes me feel thirteen, on the cusp of adolescence. I got my adult library card in winter three months before I first menstruated, and tackled *Middlemarch*, *The Possessed*, and *Tropic of Cancer* at about the same time I was interrogating my friends to find out how one French-kissed. I had discovered that if you concentrated hard enough on what you read as you walked slowly in winter, you could anesthetize yourself to the cold, and to the world. The suburbs seemed at once less threatening and more exotic. The traffic, the kids shoveling driveways, the mothers with bundled babies became milky and distant, like the changes happening inside my breasts. Of course I didn't understand what I read. I knew all the words, and I could usually recite the plots, but the meaning, like sex or adult life, was beyond me, as out of my range as a perfect cartwheel or a facility with algebra.

That's how I felt when I read Theo's letter. It was like a movie I'd missed the first twenty minutes of. Once I caught on to the plot, I was angry. I should have been told earlier. Once told, I should have been spared the apologetic prologue, the condescending earnestness of the explanation—the affianced think their capers make the *Kama Sutra* seem pedestrian while you've been languishing your life away in the missionary position. I resented Theo saying that I "did nothing" (even now, I cooked, played the cello, talked to friends), that I'd never felt love. Not that Theo hadn't derided my boyfriends for years, but the tone of his mockery had always tacitly acknowledged that if my love I.Q. was low, his was lower. Now he spoke as if he and Judy were adults, and everyone else in the world—I particularly— was a wayward child.

But what hurt was the certainty that if I expressed concern, if I questioned motives, I'd be accused of the predictable vulgar display of jealousy. "You want to be the birthday girl," Pat had said at Stacey's opening; indeed, as a child, I had to be given gifts on Theo's birthdays, so uncontrollably would I rain on his parade. (I recalled a Barbie doll I got during one Theo birthday party, and for a moment the doll's mountainous breasts and tense neck, its manic good cheer, reminded me of Judy Gold.) It's true that I was jealous, to the extent that I wanted a marriage myself and wasn't necessarily dying to share my brother, but why was jealousy assumed *a priori* to cloud my judgment? While I realized that Theo was anticipating my objections at such length because they were his own as well, not because he wanted to make me feel inferior or excluded, I also felt that he didn't really want to hear what I thought. All he wanted was my congratulations, and I was too protective—of him more than of myself—to give them. By the time I reread the letter on the slow walk, made slower by the Doberman's desire to check out every tree, I'd decided that what Theo felt was at least in his mind real, or at least as real as it could be after less than three months—and anything I could say would be read as denying him his happiness.

Before I could reflect on the ramifications of this news for Walter and me, I'd reached my building, where I literally tripped over my upstairs neighbor, a large-boned blonde who was sitting on the steps. "Sorry," I said.

"Me too," she said, and began to cry.

"Don't worry. I won't sue."

She continued to cry. Her hands were between her knees as she shivered on the wet steps; her long bangs were wet with tears. Her entire face was swollen. She'd cried hard enough so that she couldn't breathe through her nose. She wasn't wearing a coat.

"I should have figured you weren't getting a tan out here," I said. "What's wrong?"

She didn't look at me as she answered: "Sorry for the scene. I'm a little shaky. I'm waiting for the police. I've been robbed."

"How awful!"

"I was just picking up suits at the dry cleaner's and doing grocery shopping. I don't care about the things. But they dumped everything on the floor. I have to move in all over again, or move out. And they took a plant. Can you believe that? A huge potted plant. I suppose it makes it look more natural, walking out with a plant in daylight."

"I'm sorry. Don't you think you should get a coat?"

"I can wait inside," she agreed. She stood and patted the Doberman as I opened the door to the building. On the second-floor landing we both paused to study my door. "It hadn't even occurred to me," she said.

"Me either. Shall we?"

The door was closed, but unlocked. We followed the Doberman into my apartment, which was orderly as usual, but by the time the dog had completed a quick round of sniffing and settled into his habitual resting place in front of the stereo, I'd noticed the dust-free rectangles where the turntable and receiver had been. The books on top of the bookshelf had slipped without the speakers holding them up. The connecting wires were still draped over the books. In the kitchen my Cuisinart was gone, my good knives; in the bedroom there was an absence of television, typewriter.

"Camera?" my neighbor said.

"Nikon, and gone," I said, checking my desk drawer. My jewelry box was open, and empty, on my dresser. I opened my lingerie drawer and found the yellow sock in which I kept my only valuable jewelry, a pearl choker and the gold bracelet I got for my sweet sixteen, before gold went up. Both pieces were there. So was my sable coat from Walter's Aunt Hattie and my cello, in the corner by the bed.

"Cellos are worth more than Cuisinarts," I said.

"Hardly feels like the same burglar," my neighbor said. "You should see my place."

"I guess he worked from the top down and didn't have time for a thorough job here. Well, the police can kill two birds. Would you like some coffee?"

While I was brewing it, she called the police to say that she was on the second-floor front, which had also been robbed, and would they please hurry. I gave her some coffee.

"Thanks. Actually," she said, wiping at the rivulets of mascara on her cheeks, "I wasn't crying about this. My husband is out of town. His mother died last year. His father is dying now. He loves his family. His younger sister has been at home since she graduated from college, nursing her parents. She's so sweet and she's had no life. We finally convinced her to get her own place so at least she could date. One week there—she'd just unpacked, gotten used to sleeping in her own place—and a man breaks into her apartment, rapes her, and—well, she's dead. She was murdered. Twenty-eight."

"God, I'm so sorry."

"They caught him. We were supposed to feel lucky. Now he gets due process. Not that I'd want it otherwise, but"—she smiled, trying not to cry, staring at the dust around the turntable's spot behind the Doberman—"it turns your world inside out. My husband is the gentlest man on earth. Now he's ready to join a vigilante group, beat people's hands off with chains. I keep thinking about *The Exorcist*, when the little girl is convulsing on the bed and the psychiatrists are watching her on their videoscreen—they're talking about the superhuman strength of schizophrenics. Get someone angry enough and he can bend telephone poles, jump from the World Trade Center and land on his feet. I'm watching Rob get madder and madder and I know he has it in him. So do I. I could chop someone up if I was pushed far enough."

"But you can't feel guilty. It's not your fault."

"I know."

As she began to cry again, I moved closer to her on the couch, put my arm around her, and took her hand, which was very soft. I was startled to find myself thinking, She doesn't seem like the kind of woman who would make so much noise screwing. The Doberman watched us indifferently, then went to the bedroom. Though I didn't even know her first name, I thought I might cry myself, but I felt false to do so: other people's misfortunes, like the misfortunes in books or newspapers, are too easy.

"You're very kind," my neighbor said. "I'm supposed to go to Buffalo tonight. The funeral's tomorrow. This all hit yesterday. I'm in hospital administration. Hospital workers all over the country do a booming black-market business in stolen dentures. Yesterday we had twenty pairs of teeth stolen. At lunchtime a mob of furious geriatrics descends on my office and I've got a husband phoning me who's so distraught he doesn't want me to come home from work—he can't deal with my pain about the death. What do I do? I finish work. I eat dinner. I let him go to Buffalo alone so I can finish up stuff at work. I wake up this morning and put on makeup, take out trash, pick up laundry. The captain going down with the ship—you want to hang in there. You know the saddest part is that if it wasn't for the robbery, it might have worked."

I hugged her. The doorbell rang.

"Thanks," she said. "Believe it or not, under ordinary circumstances I'm fairly reserved."

The policeman whom I buzzed up had the husky, gruff, good-natured saunter of television policemen. I offered him coffee. He raised the mug to me in a toast, having determined that I was the more stoical of the present victims, and took the clipped pad from under his arm. "Tidy job," he said, looking around.

"You should see what the bastard did upstairs," my neighbor said.

"Bastard? Last ring we busted in this area was a gang of young mothers. Went out with their strollers and those metal carts you haul groceries and laundry in. Under the sheets and detergent were televisions, silverware. Some of them were working mothers, too. A legal secretary, a C.P.A. Look at this, will you? This is a parody of a door. Let me have a bobby pin."

I fetched him one. He showed us the lightness of the door, the leeway between door and frame, the frailty of the lock. "I'd talk to your landlord," he said, "for future reference. Hey!"

The Doberman had come out from the bedroom to bark at the policeman, and was trying to nose through the open door.

"A little late," I said.

"I take it this dog wasn't here for your burglar," the policeman said. "On second thought . . ." The Doberman had approached him shyly, and was licking his hand. "Why, pooch."

"He's just a puppy," I apologized.

"Dobermans," the policeman said. "Most of them go mad. Turn against their masters. They've got some kind of pressure on the brain, right here." He tapped his forehead, then asked the usual questions: where I'd been, when I'd made the discovery, what was missing. He made the usual disclaimers about the likelihood of finding the culprit, then discussed my insurance. He turned to my neighbor and made an ironic formal bow. "Next?"

"Ellen Mayer," she said, offering me her hand with the same formality.

"Alex Freed. Can I help you upstairs?"

"You've helped quite enough. I'm not going to clean today. I'll wait for Rob. I've got a six-o'clock flight."

"Do you need a ride to the airport?"

"No, no, thanks, my sister—my own, not my sister-in-law"— her voice caught, remembering—"is taking me. Thanks for asking."

"If you need anything, please just call or knock."

"Or pick the lock," the policeman offered.

Ellen Mayer thanked me again and left with the policeman. I went to switch on the radio, and actually stood with my hand in the air where the receiver should have been for a while before I figured out what was going on. Only then did I feel the rush, the shock, of the robbery. I switched on the clock radio, which made all singers sound as if they had socks over their faces. In the kitchen I poured the last of the coffee and saw the letter from Theo, out of its envelope, on the table where I'd dropped it. I didn't want to think about that, so I returned to the bedroom and rested, calming myself. Overhead I could hear Ellen Mayer's step, the policeman's heavier one, shifting, walking. Except for sympathy with Ellen, I didn't feel sad. I didn't have a right to. If anything, I should feel a wry giddiness about the robbery: despite myself, I was finally going to travel light. My only worry was that itch you get backstage in the head when you think there's something you've forgotten to do.

When the doorbell rang, I remembered what it was.

I'd forgotten Vanessa Graci's first ballet recital.

"Forgive me," I told the intercom.

"The fledgling has to date not apprehended the lack," Pat said, in the silly language we used to talk over Nessie's head. "Since protestations refer to other misdemeanors, one thinks it preferable not to call attention to aforementioned wound."

"Gotcha."

Nessie was crying as they took the stairs. I was prepared for Pat's mouth tightened in resigned disappointment, but she looked mostly bemused. Nessie was costumed as a bee—black leotard, yellow tights, black-and-yellow striped wings. "What happened?" I asked.

"She fell. She thinks her career is shot. I've been trying to convince her that few failures in the first decade are permanent."

"I was bad," Nessie snapped. "I stunk."

"I'm sure you weren't all that bad," I soothed, taking Nessie into my lap. "May I tell you a little story?"

"No."

"When I was not much older than you, I was in a talent show at summer camp, singing 'Stranger in Paradise.' This was back when I had a voice. In front of everyone, Ness, I forgot the lyrics. Took me three tries to remember. Know what?"

"What," Nessie sighed.

"I won. Imperfection is likable, especially in a child. I didn't get the prize, however, because in order to claim it you had to climb onto the stage and be mockingly kissed by the male counselor whom all the girl counselors had a crush on. I refused. What a to-do. Lost a case of Pepsi. None of the girls in my bunk would speak to me for a week."

"This is supposed to comfort her?" Pat said.

"The point," I told Nessie, who was struggling off my lap to search for cookies and to play with the Doberman, "is perspective. One usually survives everything but death. Speaking of which—"

"You're the only person I know," Pat said, "who can sedate a child with boredom. Eat the cookies over the sink; you know Alex doesn't like crumbs. Don't turn on the television! I'm illegally parked. You can watch at home."

"She certainly can't watch here, because the television's gone. I've been robbed. Ergo my absence."

"Oh, Alex, how terrible."

"That's not all. My brother's going to marry Judy Gold."

"Of Walter fame?"

"I'll read you Theo's shocking treatise on the way, unless you have pressing news."

"As a matter of fact, I do."

"Further felonies from Jeff?"

"Correct."

"Tears, guilt, and indecision?"

"More than you can shake a stick at—Ness! Dogs don't eat cookies."

"My upstairs neighbor was robbed too, plus her sister-in-law was raped and killed in Buffalo."

"Great. When it rains it pours. That's horrible."

Nessie, a remarkably polite child, had waited for us to pause before she cried again. Pat led Nessie down the stairs and I led the Doberman. Outside, a police tow truck was hitching up the Packard.

"Please, please, please," Pat said, her hands pressed together. "I know this never works, but please have mercy."

"Sorry, sister."

Nessie, Pat, the Doberman, and I lined up and looked at the policeman dolefully. He grunted, put away the chain, and began to write a ticket. "I'm a sucker," he said. "Hurt my heart to touch this beauty anyway. Where'd you find it? How does it run?"

Pat spent ten minutes detailing the work she'd done to the Packard with her bare hands. The policeman was so impressed that he ripped up the ticket. Pat and the policeman shook hands.

Pat and I smiled at each other, then drove in silence. The plan had been to spend the afternoon working on the new house, then go to the old house for dinner. That was, I hoped, still the plan. Quite despite myself, I'd begun to enjoy working with Pat on the house. It was relaxing. I smoked less there, and the exercise was tightening my thighs.

18

It has been said that there are two kinds of people in the world, those who divide the world into two kinds of people and those who don't. I belong to the former category, insofar as I divide people into mind and body. I'm decidedly on the mind side of the fence. This doesn't mean that I'm smart. Just because I think more doesn't mean that I think better—I'm like a person turning an apartment upside down in search of a key that has been in the door all along. Because people take me for an abstract-thinking city girl, they're often surprised at how moved I become by some crickets and a slow dusk, but my pastoral streak makes sense. My married friends envy me my "adorable" cramped apartment, my "peaceful" isolation. We all want what we don't have. That's the primal axiom: lessened supply increases demand.

My environment was suddenly becoming dominated by body people. Everyone worshipped the material world. Walter and Pat were in real estate; Stacey took photographs. My friend Greg was marrying a dentist in a small town in Maine; my friend Jessica was marrying a sculptor. The only mind people I knew were psychologists. The mind people and the body people were facing off as cleanly as Rorschach blots. All marriages were marriages of mind and body; the question was when opposites would interlock to form a complete picture and when they'd merely splinter each other. Judy and Walter, Margaret and Jacob, Pat and Preston clearly belonged to the failures—square pegs in round holes. On the other hand, if you coupled people who were *too* much alike, they either killed each other or bored each other to death. Balance of mind and body was everything in a relationship, and Walter and I must have had some of that balance, for we were getting along enormously well.

On the day I was robbed, Walter balanced his checkbook. He'd been threatening to since I met him, but because of the huge sums of cash flowing daily, the task was monumental. For the first time in years, Walter's business was solidly in the black and guaranteed not only to stay solvent but to expand. That knowledge made his voice deeper, his stride smoother. While his shopping-mall deal fell through, another deal he'd been simmering proved possible, just as daring, and even more profitable. He bought a condemned nursing home in Atlantic City for less than a quarter of a million. He would put up condominiums—thirty units, which he could sell for $100,000 to $140,000 a unit. In record time, he got backers for the front money, collected amiable partners for the construction money, and began to contract for the work.

"What are you going to do with the old people?" I asked. "Cremate them?"

"If you saw the place, you'd thank me for getting them out. It makes the Section Eight housing you saw look like Versailles."

"And what are you going to do with the poor Puerto Ricans you're displacing up there?"

"Let the government take care of them."

"The government won't take care of any of us for long."

"Why don't you do some volunteer work," Walter grinned, "while you have time on your hands?"

Our routine of bleeding-heart liberal versus heartless businessman was playful now that growing respect for each other had made our lovemaking richer, our conversation more animated. I'd begun to be interested in his real estate speculations, and he, in turn, was intrigued by the kinds of speeches on politics and art that Theo, Pat, and Vivian derided. I was beginning to think it possible I'd never want to sleep with another man.

"I've heard all this before," Pat said. "You spewed the same hearts and flowers about Victor. You'd never laughed as much with anyone as Victor, never trusted anyone as much."

"For a week or so. Walter and I have kept this up for almost five months."

"Four. You were with Victor longer than that."

"Not happily, and anyway not quite."

"Pretty close, not counting the Edgar episode. You're depending on Walter too much. It won't be much fun when your unemployment runs out and you beg him to support you—watch how fast he runs from *that*."

"By then I'll be in the Foreign Service."

"Alex, aren't you tired of this silliness?"

"Why should I be?" I bristled, but I was getting there. Though the parental focus on Theo's marriage (they didn't like Judy's age or marriage track record) and Walter's focus on the condo took some of the heat off me, I hadn't forgotten that the only real changes in my life since I'd quit work were Walter and a growing friendship with Ellen Mayer, who cried a little less every day— every day, she and her husband stepped a little out of mourning. That progress was more than I could lay claim to. Sneaking back to friendship with Stacey and Vivian didn't count—friendship rarely pays the rent. I was very happy, therefore, to find out that I had passed the written exam for the Foreign Service and been invited for an interview. That news came on the same day that I was told the anthropology article I'd finished in the fall had been accepted for publication. For about twenty seconds I considered finishing my Ph.D.

Like everyone else, Ellen thought my Foreign Service idea was silly. I didn't understand. The Foreign Service was a slightly longer shot than an M.B.A. from Wharton, but it was in the same spirit. Thousands of people tried every year. It hurt my feelings when people were surprised that I'd passed the exam. I began to crave the respect accorded to people with successes. Stacey had one show and now everyone deferred to her on matters of art. Vivian was Our Lady of the Litigations, and Pat had begun to join Walter as the Housing Authority. The only thing that people asked me is if X is someone they should have read. Phil Freed was right: one was expected to specialize, and in something other than Self.

By the beginning of March, when spring wasn't present but palpable, Pat and I had completed the living room, half the dining room, and the foyer of her new house. Those antiques which hadn't been sold to fund the renovation had been stripped and laid on the sanded floors. At the end of each day, Pat and I would have tea in the living room, with a view of the gleaming Packard out the window and a smug certainty that we were getting somewhere. I began to understand the thrill of real estate. Property was the bottom line, the only bedrock. If a house burned down, you could still take a clump of soil in your fist and mourn like Scarlett O'Hara.

Because nothing else in my life was progressing, because I was about to turn thirty and would have to quit smoking again, because everyone I knew was in a happy struggle with love or about to be married, I fought with Walter.

On the first day warm enough for just a jacket, Pat dropped me off at his place. It was late afternoon, early for Walter to be back from Brown Street or Atlantic City, so I didn't ring; I just used the key he'd given me. The Doberman—now full-grown, still unnamed—had a time-lag mechanism: he waited until you were inside to bark once; then he became as bored as a cat. I turned on the radio, poured cider, and patted the dog before I heard a noise from the bedroom. Walter was at the window, his back to me, on the phone.

"Yeah," he said. "Right. We'll discuss further. Sure. Right. See you. Okay."

By the time I approached, he'd hung up.

"Not your roofer," I said, kissing him.

"Atlantic City," he said. "How are you?"

I have a sure nose for infidelity. We made love, cooked chicken breasts in tarragon-almond cream sauce with rice pilaf and zucchini, and I tried to think about the woman other than me that Margaret Danner had met after Judy, about the woman who had whispered to him at Stacey's opening, about Stacey herself.

"Well, who is it?" I blurted, over dessert.

"Who's who?"

"The other woman you're seeing."

Walter smiled. "I've made you jealous?"

"Who is it? Fess up."

"Can we do this later? I've got to finish the Brown bookkeeping tonight. I'm very behind."

"How serious are we? Why haven't you asked me to move in with you?"

"What?" Walter said sharply.

"You heard me."

"What about your lease?"

"Fuck it."

"You know you wouldn't do it, so why are you asking? If I thought you would, I'd have asked. It isn't time."

"Why not?"

"It just isn't."

"Shit."

Walter studied me as I began to cry. "What's the word for this?" he asked. "Starts with a 'd.' Judy used to say I was good at it."

"Judy! You're seeing Judy. All those purported trips to Atlantic City! But Theo hasn't said Judy's been away, except to visit Keith in New York. Have you been flying to Boston?"

"Displacement. It's the rest of your life that's fucked up, Alex, not me."

"Or lack thereof. You're probably right."

"You knew it from the beginning. What's moving in here going to do for you? I don't want you to do it because you don't know what else to do. Stop crying, will you?"

"Say you love me and all."

"I love you and all."

"Say it with more heart."

"I love you and all with more heart."

"Has anyone ever told you that you have a very childish sense of humor?"

"You have, several times."

"So this was just a little practice after all until you confirmed that you could get erections and come. Now you're going to marry a nice assistant professor of tax law, with her own mortgage and car, who doesn't smoke or cry."

"Am I expected to take this seriously?"

"You were only interested as long as I stood off."

Walter got up to do the dishes, his face expressionless.

"Oh, Walt, I'm sorry. I'll do them."

"Just sit there and cool off."

"I'm sorry."

"Don't apologize."

"Are you really not seeing someone else?"

"Alex, I know you're keyed up, but I have a lot of work. If you're going to keep this up all night, I wish you'd do it at home."

"Let's make love."

"We just finished making love."

"Okay, drive me home."

We didn't say a word in the car. I was thinking about how little I wanted to worry about Walter's faithfulness. "Our first fight," I noted when we arrived.

"Probably not our last."

"I love you, you know."

"Love you too."

ALEXANDRA FREED

"But not enough to include the personal pronoun—uh-oh. Here we go. Can I take the dog for company?"

"If you want."

"See you tomorrow?"

"Tomorrow's the shore. I won't get back until eight or so. I'll call."

"Don't. Just come right by and I'll cook dinner."

"Cool *off*, will you?" Walter pleaded, with his head drawn back on his neck as it always was when he was cross.

The only advantage of being robbed of all valuables is that it eliminates the need for a moment of anxiety when you open your door after a night's absence. I got the dog his water and went straight for the phone, but no one was home. No mail and everyone was out—Pat, Theo, my parents, Frank, Fran, Ken, Greg, Stacey, Vivian, Ellen. A conspiracy.

I dialed every five minutes until I got my mother.

"Relationships are like house plants," she said. "Stick them in the sun, water them, and they generally grow. You can't speed their growth, unless you buy the crap that they respond to Bach and babytalk. Prod them, overwater them, and you kill them. You've got to know when to leave them alone, when to let them go."

"You and your metaphors."

"So I've got a limited repertoire, but I can talk myself out of the blues and you've never learned to—you and your father. He's worried sick about retirement. He'll snap out of it, though, and there's nothing I can do but be patient."

"Patience isn't my forte. Maybe I ought to kill myself on my thirtieth birthday as planned."

"It'd be very rude to kill yourself before your brother's wedding. What do you hear from him?"

"Nothing since last time you asked."

"I called there the other day and he said he was busy, he'd call right back, and never did. Tried to get him again and no one was home. What's going on?"

"Theo's fine. You worry about him too much."

"I worry about you too, my dear. And your father."

I cried myself to sleep.

For the rest of the week, mainly because there was too much to do, Walter and I didn't discuss our fight and were sweet to each other. On top of his bookkeeping, he had decided that it was imperative to knock out the wall between his living room and kitchen at once, to install an island doubling as counter and storage space. The crew worked overtime all week; the floors were rewaxed, the walls repainted, the couch sent away to be reupholstered in a brighter blue. The kitchen island was so pretty that if you stood at the counter, under the skylight, dipping veal in egg and flour, you felt as if you were on the deck of a luxury cruiser. The cabinets had been dabbed with little lights that you could dim or brighten, so when you sat at the table, the island seemed the harbor of a good new country beckoning to you. Even dirty dishes on the counter looked interesting. By the door was Walter's new taupe umbrella stand, in which our twin black umbrellas leaned together easily. On the wall over the spot where the couch would go, Walter had hung Stacey Easterlin's Halloween photographs, framed at last; from my place at the table I stared at myself, an image brimming with all of the original calm desire I'd felt toward Walter.

The couch was delivered in time for my birthday on March 15th. I was sad because it was going to take at least two weeks to get Walter completely recovered from our argument, two months to get him less busy so he had more time for me, and at least two years to get him to propose, to recover after I quit smoking. I'd wait. I had friends. By 1985, I still might not be too old to have children.

Everyone I knew in Philadelphia was at my surprise birthday party, as well as several of Walter's real estate connections. That he had bothered to track down all my cohorts soothed me into thinking that he couldn't be indifferent to me after all, as did the fact that out-of-town friends who hadn't sent cards knew they could reach me at his place. Greg called to announce that he and his dentist fiancée had sold the porn murder mystery they'd written when they were stoned on their Christmas vacation; Jessica called to see if her official wedding invitation had arrived and to wax rhapsodic about the gentle hands of *her* fiancé; Theo and Judy called to say that my gift would be delivered in Washington, where we'd convene in two weeks. I hadn't answered either Greg's or Jessica's invitation yet. I was holding out—for a vacation with Walt, for a job from which I couldn't tear myself away.

All the couples at my party seemed so calm. This was an illusion, of course—the effects of liquor and marijuana. Pat and Jeff were fighting; Vivian and Rich were madly in love and at each other's throats every minute; after half a year, Stacey still called her boyfriend "the mathematician" with a sneer; Stacey and Pat spent the party avoiding Preston and his present date; only Ellen and Rob Mayer were actually married, but they'd known each other since the eighth grade, so they could hardly serve as a model for any of us. It was amazing, given all this instability, that people could drink, dance, talk; that they could smile and nod as I opened my gifts—two bottles of wine, a bottle of Scotch, a book of crossword puzzles, two hardbacks I'd been intrigued by, a skirt Pat had seen me salivate over in a shopwindow, and, from Walter, a sleek blue ten-speed bicycle. The bicycle, and the nicotine withdrawal, made me cry. Nonetheless I rose to my usual party performance, sauntering like my father and expounding on why Jews make lousy alcoholics, why the tenor saxophone is the closest equivalent to the sound of a woman's pleasure. I wanted a cigarette so badly that I told Walter as he passed to replenish drinks and dips—Walter loved to play house, and this was as much a redecoration party as a birthday celebration—that if he didn't stick his tongue deep into my mouth and keep it there for at least three minutes, I'd collapse. He did, in the bedroom closet. I put my hand down his pants. The doorbell rang.

"Margaret," Walter said. "I guess Zoll dropped her off."

"Walter, I want you so much."

"You've got me, but you better not be too drunk to talk to

my mother. She doesn't know anyone else here, and she hates parties."

"Then why did she come?"

"I invited her."

"Stay here. Let someone else buzz her up. Let her talk to Ellen about hospitals."

"Come on, sweetheart."

"Is all forgiven?"

"Nothing to forgive. Whatever happens, I'll always love you."

"Is something about to happen?"

"Oh, Alex, please."

"Tell me."

"I love you."

"Through thick and thin?"

"Even through these stupid cross-examinations."

From the moment Margaret Danner entered, she looked stricken, isolated, uncomfortable. I felt bad for her but also a bit resentful that for the rest of the evening I'd be responsible for talking to her about real estate, joblessness, her health, my brother and Judy. "Their marriage will never happen," Margaret proclaimed.

"That seems to be the general consensus, but they seem very confident it will happen."

"They're too different."

"My brother claims it's nice that he's green and she isn't. He still gets a kick out of grocery shopping with her, down the aisles with one of each of their hands on the cart; she's pleased that he'll go—not only go, but enjoy it."

"So many of you girls look for male wives now. Can't you do your own grocery shopping?"

"It's true"—I laughed—"that I haven't met a man in years who isn't a better cook than me."

"This vogue of homey men is misleading. Underneath the candlelit suppers, the men are the same. Sadder yet, so are the women—much as you go on about 'nice' men who don't threaten you, you still crave the danger, the disapproval. Oh. I brought you a present." She handed me a wrapped gift from her side of the couch.

"You didn't have to."

"Of course I didn't. Unwrap it."

"You're right in a way," I said, unwrapping. "But it's like learning to write or to play an instrument—critical understanding always outdistances ability. I think we know intellectually what kind of relationship makes sense, but we're not able to embrace it yet emotionally. Oh, Margaret, that's beautiful."

She'd given me a dress—white, with unusual details.

"I'm glad you like it."

"How did you know I would?"

"Wild guess."

We embraced with some emotion—mine the recognition that a gift from Walter's mother had to indicate some approval of us as a couple.

"How are things with you and my son?" she asked.

"Good, though I'm not sure exactly what'll happen."

I was debating whether or not to tell her more when she said, "Do you want me to tell you?"

She put her hand on my knee, then drew the hand away, embarrassed. "Nothing."

"Nothing forget you said anything, or nothing nothing will happen?"

"Nothing will happen."

"Is there something I ought to know?"

Across the room, Walter was laughing, his hand on Stacey's back.

"Nothing you couldn't figure out yourself. For you, Walter's a job. He's a challenging job with flexible hours and some variety, and the description of your duties is loose, but he's a job nonetheless. He's not a vocation. You need a vocation."

"Granted. That aside, Walter's wonderful."

"If you met his father or his sister, you'd understand."

"Understand what?"

"His limitations. Let me just say it. Walter's incapable of giving love. His father is too, and so is his sister. While Walter has risen a good deal above them, emotionally he has a very narrow range."

I looked at her harshly. "I don't think that's true. Why are you saying this, anyway? Are you trying to scare me off?"

"Why would I do that?"

"Maybe you prefer to keep your son single."

She shook her head. "Forget I said anything. I'm a bitter woman, as my son has no doubt told you, and I'm dying. Makes you want to be blunt, dispense with formalities."

"Why are you picking on me?"

Margaret put her face in her hands. She looked old, sad, and very tired.

"Christ," I said. "Don't. Don't cry. I won't know what to do. I can't deal with you crying without a cigarette."

"I quit smoking March 11, 1963, and you know I still miss it?"

"Don't tell me that. Say something pleasant."

Walter approached with the lit cake and placed it on the coffee table in front of the couch where Margaret and I sat. Several friends gave me knowing smiles—Alex with her future mother-in-law. But as the twenty-odd spectators began to sing happy birthday, I could easily see myself as a single middle-aged woman, lonely and bitter.

"She looks distressed," Ellen said.

"She's just not smoking," Vivian said.

"And she's thirty," Pat said.

Stacey took a picture. As the flash fired, Margaret yelped and put her hands over her face. It was an automatic gesture that only took a second, but when I got the picture from Stacey several months later, Margaret would be shielding her face like a criminal leaving a courthouse.

Walter squinted at me, then glared at his mother. He handed the cake knife to Pat, turned up the stereo, took me by the hand, helped me around Margaret and off the couch, put his arms around me, and began to slow-dance me into the bedroom. I closed my eyes. There wasn't any noise from the living room for a moment; then people laughed and began to talk again. He kissed me.

"Your mother was telling me," I said into his neck, "that nothing will ever happen between us."

"I figured."

"That isn't true, is it?"

"Something's happening right now. We're having a birthday party and I'm kissing you."

"Come on. Be honest."

"I am."

"Why is she doing this?"

"Quiet."

Maybe you never knew what you'd get. You could wind up being a sculptor when your real aptitude was for math; you could wind up being an efficiency expert in Detroit when you always wanted to live in Florence, speak fluent Italian, and make, by hand, intricate glassware. Maybe you never got what you wanted, or had to train yourself to want what you got. Walter was a nice man. That was all I knew and all I was going to know for a while. If I could just be in Walter's arms and not want anything else, I'd be all right.

"Quiet," Walter whispered.

"I didn't say anything."

"You know what I mean. Come on, sweetheart. Try. Quiet your brain."

FOUR

19

Borrowing Walter's car to go to my Foreign Service interview in Alexandria, Virginia, was probably not a brilliant strategy. Even if I were fully at ease with a stick shift and the turnpike, adding four hours of driving to the six hours of testing I was to undergo probably added injury to insult. I had hoped to think in the car. At 6 a.m., however, I rarely think very well. Mostly I did mental math. If 12,000 people took the exam, 3,000 people passed, 2,000 people were invited for interviews, and 6 people were interviewed daily, what were the chances that I'd bump into the black-haired man who had smiled at me on December 8th? If 300 people were appointed, what were the odds that the black-haired man would be assigned to Ethiopia and me to Sudan so we could entertain the possibility of a commuting relationship?

A solitary car trip, like after-dinner coffee, is a trial for the ex-smoker. It was day seventeen and phase two: after two weeks, all of the physical withdrawal has faded, as well as the pride in abstaining, and you wonder if you've proved your point enough to start again.

The car trip was as challenging as the interview itself. For six hours I was interrogated aloud and on paper. What were my drawbacks for the job? Would I mind critiquing several issues of foreign policy? If I were a consulate and an older U.S. citizen claimed to have lost her passport and money, what would I do? Ten years of fanatical newspaper reading served me well. After the essay test, two people interviewed six of us. The interviewers gave us copies of their biographies and asked if we had any questions. I was the only candidate who wasn't fresh out of college. This gave me an edge with the interviewers: we'd been to the same moratoriums; we felt the same disdain toward the kids who had plowed through school and jobs with no self-doubt. None of this sympathy was expressed, but it was perceptible. My respect for the interviewers' ability to represent the interests of a country they didn't fully like meant more than the cloying respect of our juniors.

When asked to explain my sudden interest in government, I said: "For a while I believed that if you had inner resources you could survive the nuclear holocaust or a year blindfolded in prison. All such notions of mystical expansiveness were propagated in direct proportion to the shrinking economy. Despite our pleas for calm individuality, we still loved to see Goldfinger, in an expensive futuristic watch, feeling up a buxom blonde with more makeup than Nefertiti. The sixties eschewed the Protestant work ethic without replacing it with anything better."

One of my interrogators, a genial black woman around my age who had warmed to me, agreed. "There were no models for how to use leisure time except for the rich—Jackie O. having her breakfast caviar flown in."

"You haven't answered the question," the other interviewer scolded—we'd already determined that he'd known my high-school boyfriend at Harvard.

"I'm practicing diplomacy," I said.

"Not funny," he said, smiling.

"Seriously? It took me a while to recover from the recognition that the whole globe is run like a tenure committee—that politicians are backbiting, sly, and soulless; that in challenging them you lose your soul as well."

I was the last candidate to leave the room. As I left, the woman interviewer managed to communicate, with a professional nod and a wave of my folder, that she'd see what she could do, that she was a little doubtful about the good-old-girlism implicit in rooting for me despite my inappropriate background, but that she'd see what she could do anyway.

In the afternoon I was given a room with a desk and a bundle of materials that needed to be evaluated, put in order, dispensed with. I wrote twenty memos and letters in three hours—a drug smuggler being held, a problem with an Embassy cafeteria staff, the Secretary of the Interior's request for a tour at a politically sensitive time.

I enjoyed the combination of excitement and detachment you get on a ride at Disney World or while playing volleyball on a company picnic. I missed working. Even in public relations in provincial Philadelphia, there were moments—usually around three on a Friday afternoon—when all activity stopped and we'd discuss whether advertisers created evil new needs or merely answered existing needs. Maybe even waitressing was good enough. Theo had put himself through school as a garçon and hadn't minded. The elaborate serving code was as mysterious to him for a while, as impenetrable, as the history of thought.

For two weeks I'd rehearsed—talked to myself in the mirror, read newspapers for diplomatic statements on critical issues, called friends who had undergone the interview. The knowledge that my chances of actually getting an appointment with my spotty employment record and my unexotic foreign languages spurred me on. There's comfort in the quixotic. If it's impossible, it's more understandable to fail. Thinking about the Foreign Service had also provided a satisfying relief from absorption with Theo and Judy, whose imminent marriage demanded more and more airtime.

It was Tuesday, April 1st—April Fool's Day and Passover, too early for cherry blossoms.

My parents hadn't said much yet about how they liked Judy. They didn't have to. Whatever suspicions I had of Judy Gold were bound to be mild next to my parents'. I expected to mediate between them and Theo, to practice on a personal scale what I might soon be doing for the State Department.

When I arrived, Theo and Judy were out, and my diplomatic duties, I knew, could start at once.

From the way Phil tilted in his chair, the way his head was cocked, the thin way his lips were stretched, I could tell he was distressed. Connie was miserable. Her eyes were blank behind her glasses. She sat the way people sat for the old cameras, her only movement an occasional twitch as she bit the inside of her lip.

"Well?" I said.

"We're trying to look on the bright side," Connie said. "She certainly can't be marrying for money."

"Or looks," Phil said.

" 'Those who never change their opinions,' " I laughed, " 'ought to be secure of judging properly at first.' "

"What?"

"*Pride and Prejudice.* I prepared the quote for your inevitable disapprobation."

"Do you understand how your brother could have fallen for her?" Connie asked.

"Her parents are small-minded and insincere," my father said, "and so is she. We feel very sorry for your brother."

"You've got to talk to him," my mother said. "He listens to you. Can't you convince him to continue living with her for a while until he comes to his senses?"

"We can't put pressure on him," Phil said.

"But maybe we can scare *her* off," my mother said.

I laughed.

"Laugh," Connie said. "I tried to be open-minded. If it were just the age difference, but Judy has been married twice, isn't even divorced yet, and moved in with your brother the moment she met him. Her parents are understandably tired of her marriages, besides which they're cold shits. I realize the ceremony is primarily for our benefit. So why have no introductions been arranged before now? Why did you and Theo stay home over Thanksgiving? Your brother is thumbing his nose at us like a teenager."

"You're hurt that you weren't more included in the decision," I said. "I can understand that. I was too."

"Bullshit," my father said. "We're sad for him, pure and simple."

"Have you discussed any of this with Theo?" I asked.

"How can we? You know what he'd say," Connie said.

"He'd ask—rightly, I think—to be told what on earth she *did*."

Before they could answer, Sam barked to announce the arrival of a car. My parents snapped out of their fatigued postures, my father to trim a cigar, my mother to empty the dishwasher. I went to the door, still giddy from the interview and, I confess, satisfied at having so accurately predicted my parents' mood.

Outside, my brother and Judy Gold were kissing, each with a bag of groceries on a hip.

I cleared my throat and the three of us made a football huddle of greeting before braving the kitchen, where my parents nodded to Judy, greeted Theo more energetically, and accepted the bags of gourmet cheeses, dips, and wine, intended to help us enjoy each other before Theo and Judy left for the Starks' for dinner ("Why Theo has to meet his fiancée's ex-husband's sister is beyond me," Connie would later declare).

"Come, sit," Theo instructed my parents. Judy gave me a look of sincere gratitude for showing up as ally. With her white teeth, impeccable dress, and new hairstyle effectively undercutting the roundness of her face, she looked quite fit, not oblivious to the tension but not crushed by it, as did Theo, who asked, "How was the interview?"

"Fun. I got to use your line about how entropy is life's biggest rule."

"In what conceivable context?"

"The hostage crisis. Remember the number we used to do about people bowling? How if they happen to scratch their noses before a strike they attribute their success to the scratch, just like laboratory pigeons?"

"Don't even mention labs," Judy said. My parents grimaced at her as if she'd just farted.

"How's China?" I asked.

"*Sib*," Judy said.

Theo grinned, lit a cigarette, and shifted it to his other hand so he could put his arm around Judy. "That means 'Water dried us so as to make it difficult to sail a boat,' " he explained. "I teach

Judy all the useful words. The difference in the Eastern and Western treatment of the mentally ill becomes a perfect metaphor for our separate gestalts. There's little despair there, you know. No snideness, no underhanded flirting, no drunken confessions—no neurosis, in short."

As Theo talked, everyone competed to see who could listen to him more attentively. My mother and Judy posed as adoring wives, my father quizzed him on history, Theo unwittingly slipped into his teacher's posture, and our gathering developed the adrenaline undertow of a graduate seminar.

"That's some stone," I said after more than a half hour of this. Judy held up her engagement ring for me to see and Theo took her hand proudly.

"She melted down the stones from the other two marriages," Phil said.

My mouth dropped open, but Judy smiled.

"Actually," Judy said, a smile proclaiming her intention to ignore the comment before I could protest, "I never had an engagement ring before. This is a new experience."

"Not one engagement ring?" my mother said sweetly. I glared at her empty chair—she had left the room.

"We should give Alex her birthday present," Judy said.

"Right!" Theo sprung up, leaving my father to give Judy hostile glances, and returned with a large box, which I unwrapped after the usual birthday fanfare.

"A microscope?" I gasped.

Judy smiled. "Just what you always wanted?"

Theo pulled a piece of hair from my head with staged aggression and got it in focus for me under the lens. "Do you like it?"

"Can't say it isn't a surprise. Is that a healthy hair?"

"This gift," Theo said, "has a two-fold purpose. One is to allow you to diagnose your own yeast infections. You didn't hear that, Dad. The more important reason is to get you interested in the physical universe. If you're good, Alex, we'll get you a telescope for your next birthday. There's a lot going on out there."

"So I've heard. Stars and cells and such. Well, thanks. You're clearly insane, but you're very nice."

"We thought you could get it back to Philly since you have Walter's car," Theo said.

"How's Walter?" Judy asked.

My mother entered, assessing the table with its pepper Brie and rice crackers next to the microscope as if it were the set for a bad absurdist drama, and announced, "It's six. Don't you have an engagement?"

"We should go," Judy said promptly.

"I'll walk you to the car," I said.

My parents didn't even see us to the door. By every estimate among the most hospitable people in America, they didn't even say goodbye. When the front door closed behind me, I shook my brother's shoulder and said, "We've got to talk."

"There's nothing to discuss," Theo said. "They're just going to do that for a while, and I'm going to be a charitable son and not hate them for being so narrow-minded. Aren't you proud of Judy?"

"I'm a trooper," Judy said. "First the Golds, now this. I'm ready to join Keith on the ward. Thank God we leave tomorrow."

In the house my mother cried, my father paced. I'd seen my mother cry like this only three times before: when her grandmother died, during the Six-Day War, and when my father's high blood pressure was diagnosed. We begged off Passover dinner at Uncle Nate and Aunt Barb's on account of illness, ate leftover take-home Chinese, and spent two hours discussing my parents' aversion to Judy.

"Why do you do it?" Connie asked. "You and your brother. You go out with such cold, self-absorbed people."

"Maybe we don't think they're cold and self-absorbed."

Walter called. I stretched the telephone cord into the laundry room and explained the situation to him.

"Don't worry about it," he said. "Just hurry home with my car."

"But I'm enlisted as go-between."

"Fuck 'em. Ask me how I am."

"Don't tell me you're upset too."

"Happy. I may be able to pull off historical certification in Atlantic City after all. Then the construction can be depreciated in five years. My investors love me. I'm going to be able to hold the costs to thirty-five dollars a foot, even though all the sub-contractors are in Mafia-controlled unions. I keep waiting to be shot. Today it was so gray and rainy at the shore I felt like I was in a forties movie."

"I'm in TV soap. Do you miss me?"

We talked a while longer, said we missed each other, said we loved each other. Connie brightened as I hung up. "Maybe we can fix them up again," she said.

"Thanks."

"I mean Judy and Walter."

"That's a sickening remark. Just because you're losing your baby boy doesn't mean you should begrudge me a happy relationship."

Phil groaned.

"You haven't met Walter," I objected. "He's sweet."

"Sweet is the word your asinine brother used about that bitch."

"*Mother!*"

"That's how I feel about it."

"You want to know how I feel?"

"No," Phil said.

"I'm disappointed in you both. Especially you, Mom. You're being irrational. You're also being sexist. You're assuming Judy has done something to him."

"How can you understand anything when you don't think about anything but yourself?"

"I resent that."

"Your brother is about to ruin his life and we have to discuss your resentments."

"The hell with you," I said.

My father made a gesture to slap me and I dodged.

"Phil," Connie said.

"Get out of my sight!" my father said.

"Apologize," I said, choking back tears.

"You started it," my mother said.

Phil gave me a look so rich in sadness and defeat, so dispirited, that I just threw up my hands and left my mother to do the crying. When she came out of the bathroom, she asked me to accompany her to the grocery store. My father was already in the den, watching TV. He waved to us weakly as we left.

My mother and I didn't speak in the car, and in the grocery store we talked exclusively about food. Argued about food, in fact. I wanted fresh peas; Connie wanted frozen ones. I thought three pounds of sirloin was more than sufficient; my Jewish mother thought we needed four. Anyway, I thought veal would be easier and more special. I'd be happy to cook it. Connie, whose hand-me-down shoes in childhood had deformed her feet, thought that veal was too expensive. I chased her like a child, trying to shove veal into the basket. I tried to talk her out of chicken coating that was 90 percent sugar and she berated me for drinking so much coffee.

"The symbolism's so blatant," I said at the register, "that it cancels us out even as comics."

"You don't care about anything, do you?" Connie said.

"Oh, come on, Mom."

"You who claim to so love and admire your brother."

"For God's sake!" I almost whined.

"I'm sorry," Connie sighed.

"You ought to be."

When we returned, my father was already in bed, red-eyed, staring at the TV. My mother joined him, announcing that they were exhausted. I was tired myself, but I wanted to wait for Theo, so I brought the microscope into the den and watched a rerun of "Columbo," resisting a hunt for one of my brother's cigarette butts in the trash and taking advantage of the commercials to inspect various items under the microscope—a cuticle, one of my hairs versus one of the Schnauzer's. I'd never thought about whether hairs were all alike or as different as snowflakes.

Judy and Theo arrived around one, slightly drunk and looking much happier.

"Not everyone hates me," Judy said.

"We need to talk," I said.

Theo and Judy looked at each other. "I don't think we missed much," Judy told him.

Theo sat down and let Judy stretch out on the couch with her head in his lap. "Well," he said, "what did they say?"

"They want you to continue cohabiting for a while and stall the actual ceremony."

Judy put her hands over her ears.

"Remember when parents liked the idea of marriage?" Theo asked, offering me a cigarette.

"You didn't notice I quit?"

"How far will you get this time?"

"Eternity."

Theo opened his eyes the way he does when he's about to say something he thinks you'll dismiss, but as he began to speak Judy made a muffled whine and my brother smiled. "She's already asleep," he proclaimed. "She falls asleep faster than anyone. It's a talent." He lifted strands of Judy's hair and let them fall onto her shoulders. "It has different colors," he confided. "Reds and blondes."

"I wonder if the different pigmentations would show up under the microscope."

Judy shifted and Theo held the smoke he'd begun to exhale until she was comfortable. I gave him an ashtray. "May I?" I said.

"Shoot."

"You've perennially taken a dim view of public displays of affection. Connie says you aren't acting like yourself and the change corroborates her view."

"Well, I'm in love. Anyway how would *she* know if I'm acting like myself?"

"She wouldn't, because you score a consistent ninety-ninth percentile on the Private Person Scale. You can understand why she's so puzzled and threatened by your openness to someone you've just met. I know we must sound like Desdemona's father claiming she'd have to have been drugged to have fallen for Othello, but you know, Theo, you'd make it a lot easier if you included us more."

"You sound more like Phil by the minute."

"It won't do to accuse me of being like Dad every time you don't agree with me."

"You want an exegesis? It's this simple. I love her."

"Theo, in graduate school you'd come up with an ornate, quirky argument, then try to tamp it into a simple form, try to present it to your professors as if you were a good boy just following orders. You'd try to be accommodating and they'd consistently read you as pompous. It took you a long time to handle that two-edged sword with which you can bow down to your superiors, to the history and etiquette of your field, without sacrificing your originality—"

"I definitely need another cigarette to see where you're going to dribble *this* ball."

"I'd suggest that you haven't yet learned that balance in your love life. You're acting the part too well. It's not convincing."

"Neither is this older-sister routine. Judy's convinced. I am."

"Come on. I know you. When you love people, you hold your head back to get distance. Remember after we were in Disney World and I realized that the repulsive Tikki-Bird show was sponsored by the Florida Orange Growers' Association, that we'd just patronized Anita Bryant and thus anti-homosexual legislation? I was so indignant. 'Since when have you been such a fan of homosexuals?' you asked, and I said, 'I'm not, but—' and you said, 'I know, I know, they're better than the Tikki Birds?' That's Theodore. You're not—"

"One, you have no idea 'how I am' with Judy. How can you? I hardly know myself."

"That's the point."

"You're trying to typecast me. You're demanding consistency. Two, Judy's wonderful. Let's take that into account. It's not beside the point."

"Granted."

"You say that, but you don't believe it. Three, you're jealous."

"Of course I am." I grinned. Well, I'd certainly anticipated this.

"There you go."

"Naturally we're jealous. That's the first premise."

"Then I rest my case. Ashtray, please."

In reaching to put out his cigarette, Theo roused Judy, who murmured, jumped upright, recognized us, and smiled apologetically as you smile at people who've probably watched you snore on a train with your mouth open, your head jerking around.

Theo and Judy kissed. For a moment they looked like low-budget porn. Theo's cigarette, I noticed, hadn't been properly extinguished. I dragged on it until I was inhaling filter.

"I saw that," Theo said.

"Did you two work everything out?" Judy yawned.

"No," I said, "and now it's a choice between an entire cigarette of my own or bed. The latter, I think." I stood, hating myself.

"Do you know your parents have given us separate bedrooms?"

"Doesn't surprise me, and you know what? You know exactly what kind of tiny sweetnesses would put them at ease, Theo, and it wouldn't cost you a thing to be nice to them."

Theo jutted up his chin contentiously. "You can't actually"— the *actually*, I noticed, was a Judy Gold word, used with her tinny precision—"believe that there's something one does to 'put them at ease'? That they even want to be at ease?"

"Don't bother to change the light bulb, I'll just sit here in the dark," Judy said, the back of her hand to her forehead.

"*Actually*," I said, "I do believe that."

Theo caught the challenge. He smiled, glinted a bit. "What I can't figure out is if they've set you up to mediate or if you've simply inherited verbatim their streak of melancholy paranoia."

I considered, still dizzy from the cigarette. "You know what else? Who's exactly like them isn't me, dear; it's you. Generally, I like them, so I don't mind, but sooner or later you're going to have to confront that."

Judy did an imitation of a man doubling over after being hit in the groin. "I think you won that set, Alex."

Theo glowered. Judy scratched him in cat fashion behind his ear. "Careful," she said, "or you're not going to have Alex to kick around anymore."

I left them to kiss.

The door to my parents' bedroom was always open to give the dog freedom of movement. My father was snoring. My mother raised herself on her elbows. I tiptoed in. By the hall light she looked very pale. The distinctive smell of their bedroom—cigar smoke, air freshener, cologne—hit me as I bent to kiss my mother.

"What did he say?" she asked, her nose stuffed from crying.

"Nothing we can do. Sleep."

"What a role reversal," she sighed. "I'm sorry I'm acting this way."

"I'm sorry Theo is."

The Foreign Service interview, which had been background music in my head all evening, took over as I closed my eyes. The Foreign Service was much more exciting and important than all the histrionics about relationships. The relationship I had, as I revved into sleep, struck me as sane and delicious.

By the next morning, my parents had changed their tactics.

I woke up to find Theo, Judy, Connie, and Phil around the kitchen table, showered and dressed, all of them smiling and talking, so captivated by each other that no one wanted to inflict the interruption of clearing the breakfast dishes. My mother kissed the top of my head and offered coffee. I drank it, waiting for this dream of warmth to steam away along with my sleepiness and urge for a cigarette fix—it didn't. China was once more the topic.

"Psychology there is basically industrial," Theo was saying. "The sane man is the good worker. You think about Rilke's objection to psychoanalysis—that if he lost his devils, he'd lose his angels as well—and wonder if the Chinese are lucky or missing out."

My father said that the Chinese didn't have enough housing for individual psychology and grabbed center stage with his best black comedy about childhood with an extended family, speaking to Judy with so much courtliness that I was sure Theo would see through it—he didn't. He seemed to believe that Judy's good qualities had finally won them over. He wore his most winning sheepish smile; he smoked in his most endearing fashion, holding the smoke in and letting it out slowly, so the smoke didn't conflict with the rhythm of what he was hearing. Connie smiled at Theo, Theo smiled at Connie, Judy smiled at everyone, and everyone smiled at Phil as he told stories about his eccentric brother Nate.

"You're all unbelievable," I snorted.

Everyone paused to look at me.

"Is that you?" Theo offered mock-brightly. "Good morning!"

I ate my bagel and listened.

When the conversation moved into the den, I offered to help my mother with the dishes.

"Killing her with kindness," I whispered at the sink, "or trying to gross her out with the in-laws?"

"Trying hard to make the best of things," my mother responded.

The pitch of martyrdom was so thick in her resignation that I didn't imagine she and my father could keep it up for long. Subsequent phone calls would prove me right. For all our flaws, the Freed clan is honest. We may not think enough before we speak and we may tend to believe too strongly what we say, as if opinion is elevated to fact by the act of speech, but at least we're not secretive or devious.

That afternoon, however, my parents were so convincing about their growing affection and admiration for Judy that they must have almost convinced themselves. For a little while they all looked like one small happy family—Judy the blushing bride, Theo the kind and brilliant husband, Phil and Connie the proud parents of young professionals.

I was dizzy from talk. I missed Walter, his rich and resonant silence. I missed Walter more than I'd ever missed anything in my life, with the possible exception of cigarettes (I snuck one while walking the dog).

On the walk I surprised myself by remembering Samantha Litwin.

Samantha Litwin was my best friend in seventh grade. Her parents, who owned a restaurant in Georgetown, were very rich and much older than the rest of our parents, because Sam was adopted. She knew she was adopted. This gave her an exotic edge with us and much leverage over her adoptive parents. She was quite spoiled. For her birthday one year, she had a slumber party; we were supposed to go bowling in the morning, but it snowed so hard that her mother called it off. Samantha made a terrific scene, berating her mother in front of us all. My parents would never have tolerated such behavior from me. I'd have been thrown down the steps, spanked, locked in my room, denied phone privileges, or, more likely, threatened with all of this. A year later, when Sam and I ceased to be friends (she was already getting felt up on the back of the school bus and reading *Candy*), I marveled that her parents still had to live with her tantrums and sullenness. For years I thought, Samantha Litwin still has her parents. Samantha may well have changed, but in my mind she's forever thirteen, scowling and crying.

In my mind Judy was a Sam Litwin. I didn't imagine I would know her for long. Though I couldn't justify myself, I agreed with my parents: Judy Gold didn't belong in our family. The difference between my parents' disgust with her and what they'd correctly identified as my indifference to the engagement was that I didn't believe Judy *would* be in our family, and therefore I couldn't worry.

20

I should have worried. I was too happy.

The tree that brushed my kitchen window had leaves. My lungs were squeaky clean. Each day my mailbox had good news from a friend, a magazine with a provocative article, a bill that was lower than I'd expected. My spring wardrobe emerged from the garment bags unwrinkled, the vegetable stands began to sell blueberries, and though I was still frozen five or six times an hour by nicotine cravings as fierce as labor contractions, the pangs were beginning to thaw. There was some new buffer between me and dissatisfaction—primitive, like weather stripping, but I felt less draft.

The same rain had fallen for two weeks. Periodically I got the same calls from Connie bemoaning Theo's fate and from Theo bemoaning my parents. My theft insurance check still hadn't arrived. Stacey arranged for another show; Phil Freed interviewed for consulting jobs; Pat got an interview for a job as the public-relations director for an environmental coalition in Boston; Ellen Mayer got pregnant and bought a house; Vivian won three pivotal cases. Walter put miles on his car commuting to Atlantic City, finished his units on Brown, and made progress on the Section Eight housing I'd seen in December. So what if all I had to show for myself was a new growth on my tiger plant? My progress was arithmetic while everyone else's was geometric; it was progress nonetheless.

For a while that April, my happiness was easy and sufficient. Perhaps I'd been perceiving my life as more underdeveloped than it really was. I thought of myself as a person nothing important ever happened to, but my friends thought of me as resilient. When I broke up with a man, I always met another one. Though I was vocal about my depressions, they never overwhelmed me. For years I'd been demanding acceleration as others told me to slow down. Between those two imperatives was the balance: leisurely momentum, self-satisfaction without complacency.

There's a question on the Minnesota Multiphasic Personality Inventory that has haunted me for years. It is the only test with a built-in lie-detector scale designed to determine if the subject is merely trying to psych out the right answers. True or false: *I must admit that at times I have worried about things more than they warranted.* On the one hand, sure I had. I couldn't count the episodes of insomnia over unfaithful men I didn't like, over finals in pass-fail electives. On the other hand, anxiety is so much a staple of the Western diet that I was loath to say "true" to a statement so tortured—of course I worried about things more than they warranted. Didn't everyone? Why should I have trouble admitting it? I was a neurotic all right, but not so neurotic as to worry not only about the trivial situation at hand but about the worry itself. I wasn't a meta-neurotic, or was I? Was that why I deliberated so long over one true-or-false question on a silly test, why I was unemployed?

The gyres of anxiety, I decided, were the Western equivalents of Zen paradoxes. "Today I did not think about you," the Zen master would say. "But to think that I did not think about you is still to think about you." Best to forget about it.

My good mood seemed to happen slightly away from the self, like weather or politics, perhaps because I'd been so quiet about it. With the mood in the Freed family ranging from my parents' grief (by turns frantic and resigned) to Theo's steady exultation, there was little room for—or interest in—my calm, but I cherished it, felt it in my bones as I felt the promise of spring.

As the light rain that had been falling for so long turned into a torrent, I had the secure feeling that everyone gets when it pours and you're safely inside. I hemmed a pair of white pants I wouldn't be able to wear until it was warmer, until I'd taken off the five pounds I always put on when I quit smoking. As the rain slowed down, as my needle went in and out of the cotton, attractive men outside walked by with umbrellas, with groceries, their pantslegs soaked, smiling to themselves.

Everyone was happy, or almost everyone.

It was Tuesday, April 15th, the fifteenth anniversary of Walter's car accident and the loss of his smell and taste. The day before, Pat had taken her daughter and her Packard to the job interview in Boston, promising to look in on Theo and Judy; Walter had gone to Atlantic City, promising to return early enough on Tuesday so that we could enjoy a fancy meal out. Earlier that morning, I'd helped Ellen and Rob Mayer move the rest of their belongings into a van and met my new neighbor, a friend of theirs, a gay pulmonary resident who was now upstairs dragging furniture across the floor as I hemmed the pants.

The doorbell rang.

"Hello, honey," I said to the intercom. "You're early. I'm not dressed yet."

"It's me," a woman's voice said. "Judy."

I buzzed her up. She was very wet. At my door she shook out her umbrella. "I was in the neighborhood." She smiled.

"Where's Theo?"

She looked at her watch. "Teaching. Didn't he tell you I might drop by?"

"No. I'm surprised."

"Me too. May I come in?"

She took off her raincoat and hung it on the doorknob, so it trailed the floor like the limp and melting Witch of the West in *The Wizard of Oz*. She wore jeans and a bright T-shirt; she appeared to have lost some weight, to have somehow acquired a tan. She looked much healthier than she had the last time we'd seen each other. I showed her to the table and poured her some coffee.

"How do you keep this place so neat?" she said appreciatively.

"I put things away," I said, staring at her.

"It's makeup," she said. "I look tan, don't I? I had some kind of attack yesterday. Spent three hundred bucks on clothes that won't fit me any second, then went to a makeup consultant who got me to part with another sixty for the illusion of cheekbones.

I feel as if I have a mask on. Also fingernails," she said, displaying ten gleaming rose ones. "Do you ever get this way?"

"About twice a year—exactly as often, in fact, as I crave having children." Judy laughed, encouraging me to continue. "Trouble is maintenance. The problem with children as well: what if the diapers and crying jags outweigh the flashes of communion with the flesh of your flesh? I don't know if I'm prepared for that."

"No one is," Judy said. "It's like sex. I was ready to moan and sigh long before I could deal with dripping diaphragm jelly. Your friend Pat seems to make a great mother."

"You met her?"

"Last night. And Vanessa—it was strange. I was just getting back with the clothes and the face and the nails. Pat has such a— I don't know, a *shine* to her. Between her and the kid with the coal-black eyes, it made me feel very inadequate."

Over that I could feel sisterly.

"You don't smoke," I told Judy as she lit a cigarette.

"You didn't know I was a fellow addict? I give in under pressure."

The cigarette kept flipping too close to her eyes, which were watering from smoke and mascara. She inhaled too vigorously; every time she tried to flick the ash, the cigarette went out, and not one ash targeted the ashtray. Just as I was torn between grabbing one of her cigarettes and celebrating my release (cheating aside) from a dirty habit, I was torn between sympathy and disdain for Judy Gold: she was brethren, smart and unemployed, fighting nicotine and insecurity; she was also dangerously close to the two men I valued most, and had a nasty penchant for melodramatic entrances.

"When did you leave Boston?" I asked.

My cigarette cravings cushioned the full shock as Judy announced: "I don't think Theo and me getting married right away is such a good idea, for a host of reasons involving Keith and, on a larger and more complicated scale, my future as a human being."

"Have you told Theo?"

"Yes, but you two are so close I thought you could explain it to him better."

I nodded. My concentration was low. It was hard to resist dialing my mother posthaste to share the terrible news. It was also hard to resist Judy's cigarettes.

The phone rang. "Don't answer it," Judy said. "It's probably Theo. I lied. He doesn't know I'm here."

"We'll tell him," I said, rising.

"I need to talk to you first. Alex, please. I'm pregnant."

"Are you sure?"

"Positive."

"Does Theo know?"

"No."

"Give me a cigarette."

"Are you sure?"

The phone had already rung five or six times. I lit the cigarette and tried to keep from enjoying it too much. I only let myself inhale every other ring. Whoever was calling really wanted to speak with me. I'm constitutionally unable to ignore phones, but didn't answer this as penance for the cigarette. It wasn't Walter. Reliable Walter (thank God he'd bored Judy!) would arrive as planned very shortly. I wanted Judy gone. I felt bad for Theo; I had my fingers crossed for Pat in Boston; but I'd had a wonderful day and I intended to have a wonderful night with my boyfriend.

After that, I planned to call Margaret and ask her what she thought Judy was doing. Judy clearly didn't know. My parents thought Judy was mad, and though I couldn't persuasively disagree, I also knew that Judy, like me, would always seem most wild in her self-reports. Life was more real for her in the narration than in the living. With this, too, I could sympathize. I was prepared to serve Theo's interests by mistrusting Judy, by reading between her lines. But there was still a part of me that was inclined to believe her. It was almost as if between Margaret, Judy, and me, we could understand all men, all relationships, once and for all. In some sense, Judy couldn't have ordered a more respectful audience.

"Would you hate me," she asked, "if I left your brother, or would you think I was doing him a favor?"

"My parents would sure say the latter."

"Mine too," Judy said. "And you?"

"I confess I never took you and Theo too seriously as a couple. The other night I saw a sappy movie in which Ronald Reagan gets his legs unnecessarily cut off because the sadistic small-town surgeon thinks Ron is after his daughter—"

"*King's Row.*"

"I was thinking, on the one hand, Now there's something real, to wake up and discover you have no legs—I've made more of a fuss about a cold; and, on the other hand, I thought, The important things that have happened to me, like a rape and a robbery and unemployment and my own brother getting married, don't affect me."

"You've been raped?" Judy asked cheerfully.

I shrugged. The cigarette was making me loquacious.

"Women never open up to me," Judy complained. "Here I am engaged to your brother and even you aren't interested in me. I'd trade all eight of my marriage proposals for one good female friend."

"I'd trade one or two of my less exalted female friends for one quasi-decent marriage."

"Theo tells me you're very good to your friends. He told me how you canceled a vacation once to sit in the hospital with a suicidal friend—do you hate me, Alex?"

The question—it was generally my question—was disarming. "Not yet." I lit another cigarette and thought about my friend Jessica in San Francisco trying to kill herself over some dumb schmuck.

"Do you hear something?" Judy asked.

I listened. "Sounds like it's from the bedroom."

Judy laughed. "It's the fifteenth, isn't it?"

"Yes," I said, puzzled.

"Walter in a rock-throwing mood," she explained. "Not a good sign. I'll stay and say hello to him, okay?"

I went to the bedroom.

Walter stood outside in the rain with the Doberman, flinging pebbles at my window. I opened the window and made a small show of hurling my hair as a ladder. He began to serenade me— a medley of "Maria" and "On the Street Where You Live."

"I told you," Judy called, over the singing.

"Stop screaming," I called down. "Come round front."

I went downstairs to meet Walter in the foyer. He fell into my arms so hard that he almost knocked me over. "Rambunctious, aren't we?" I said.

He pretended to bite my neck. The Doberman nipped at my heel.

"Ow. Judy's here."

"Yeah?"

"Aren't you surprised?"

"Let's get rid of her. We've got a six-o'clock seating."

Needless to say, his indifference pleased me.

"What ho," Judy greeted us. She'd moved to the couch, back-lit by the late sun that had recently begun to penetrate the drizzle.

"Jude," Walter responded, not even looking at her. "How did it go?"

"How did what go?" I asked.

"He means the trip," Judy said, her lips pursed to indicate that she didn't want to open up the previous topics with him.

Before I could pursue this further, Walter darted into the kitchen and emerged with a box of dried apricots and an almost-empty bag of taco chips. "Oh, my God," he said. "Look at this." He was studying the apricot box. "I can't believe it."

"You look good," Judy told him.

He lay down on the floor, leaned on one elbow, and held the apricot box close to his face as a jeweler would a diamond. His left arm was tan from hanging out the car window, the hairs a burnished auburn; the rest of him was freckled and rosy. The contour of his thigh against the pantsleg of his raised knee filled me with the delicious proprietary longing that a hundred and sixty-seven days of acquaintance had enhanced rather than diminished. The fact that I'm not ordinarily attracted to redheads had made me think more than once that my thirst for Walter augured love. I thought with pride about how well he'd age.

"See this picture of the apricot?" he said. "It's *moving*. Shifting around like testicles." He removed an apricot from the box, elbowed the Doberman, and smiled the forehead-furrowed, bemused smile he usually reserved for my coming too quietly after too long.

"Did I ever tell you about the time that Preston drove the turntable arm through his foot?" he asked. "He'd gotten a new turntable and was tripping, having a good time destroying the old turntable, stomping on it like grapes. The arm drove right through his shoe into his foot. He couldn't yank it out. He was trying to pull it out like a sword. When we found him, he was sitting right there looking at the foot and crying tears of laughter. He had to have about eighty stitches. For a couple of days, he just stayed in bed—he had the top bunk—in a bloodstained T-shirt, staring at the shoe with the turntable arm still wedged in it. He'd strung the shoe from the ceiling and pretended it was strung from the dash of a car, that the dorm room was a car and he was going to Mexico. The room was so small because it was an M.G. The room didn't seem to be moving because, he said, there was acid sewn into his foot and he was only driving as fast as the speed limit so he wouldn't get busted."

"Do you know I've heard that story eight million times?" Judy said.

"How his genes didn't ruin Nessie I'll never know," I said. "Last time I tripped, it took me two hours to eat a Big Mac. The layers of bread, tomato, meat, lettuce, and mayonnaise were fascinating. Then my head turned into a hall of mirrors through which every voice echoed and spun until whatever was said came out as '*You* looking at *you* looking at *you*.' My only auditory hallucination. When I came out of it, all of my friends were loading their U-Hauls to leave for the summer. I called my mother and asked her who I was. She said if I remembered my home phone number I must still know."

Walter said nothing.

"Just trying to make conversation," I said.

"Let's put the apricot under your microscope," Walter said.

Walter had been cruel to me before, but he'd never been rude. If this was how he was siphoning off the tension of Judy's presence, I didn't like it. It would have been more rewarding if he'd acted like my husband, home from a long day's work, greeting a friend of mine with controlled but visible impatience.

Judy leaned forward to look solemnly into Walter's eyes. "Walter, are you tripping?"

"Jesus," I said when he nodded.

"You can say that again," Judy said.

"*Tripping?*"

"I forgot to offer you some. A roofer in A.C. was handing it out." He removed a piece of paper from the part of his wallet where he kept business cards and offered it to us.

"Last time *I* tripped," Judy said, "I hitchhiked and wound up on the back of a motorcycle. Everything was water. The guy's back, my legs vibrating, the pavement, the stores we passed, the Capitol Dome. The whole world turned into amniotic fluid."

"That must have been pleasant," Walter said.

"It was a nice change of pace until the guy stopped at a gas station—I had no idea where we were by this point—and asked me if I'd ever been on a waterbed. Here I was in water and the guy had no teeth. He was young to be toothless, too."

I lit a cigarette and inhaled with a vengeance.

"Don't you think it's pathetic," Judy asked, "how original we thought our antics were? We needed help to act like the kids in 'Dennis the Menace' or 'Leave It to Beaver'—"

"If you're coming to dinner with us," Walter interrupted her, "I'll change the reservation, but we've got to get moving."

"That's all right," Judy said. "I don't want to intrude."

"Yes, you do," Walter said.

"Is it all right, Alex?" Judy asked meekly.

After giving her long enough pause to retract the request—she didn't—I said fine without enthusiasm, glaring at Walter. He smiled warmly.

"I hate to trouble you even further," Judy said, "but do you have something I could borrow to wear that might fit me? I only have what I came in."

"Don't take the peach dress. I'm wearing it," I offered, with smoke.

Only the greatest control had kept me from instigating the inevitable argument I was going to have with Walter. His present indifference to Judy, her rather staged treatment of us as a couple, didn't shake my growing certainty that Walter and Judy were up to some complicity, the extent of which I wouldn't gather from Walter in his present state. When Judy ensconced herself in my bedroom, I tried to smile as Walter kissed my knee.

The kiss traveled up my knee into my crotch. "Did you just start your period?" he asked.

"No scare even this month."

Walter burrowed the inside seam of my pants. "I can smell the blood," he said.

"You couldn't even if your nose worked. I'm recently showered."

"Should I call the restaurant?" Judy asked through the closed bedroom door.

"Le Bec Fin," Walter called.

"Phone's by the bed," I added, already exhausted from silent suffering. "Hey, Danner, what's going on?"

"I can smell the soap," he whispered, with a scared and incredulous expression intensified by the dilation of his pupils. "I swear—Safeguard. I smell the baby powder."

"You know what I use. Walter—"

"Kiss me."

His tongue was as tentative as it would have been exploring the abyss of a lost filling. I drew back, puzzled, but Walter pressed forward, upsetting the coffee table in the process—the bag of chips overturned on the floor and was sniffed by the

Doberman. Walter stood and planted a firm foot in the chips. I sighed and went for the broom. The dog growled when I pushed his nose aside with the dustpan.

Walter grabbed my arm in a way he hadn't done since our visit to the fire-damaged house, and whispered: "I can smell the cigarettes, Alex."

"You didn't even say anything when you saw me smoking. What's the matter with you?"

"I can taste lunch on the back of your teeth through the toothpaste. You had a BLT."

"That's right." I blinked.

He burrowed in my shirt. "Deodorant. The shirt stinks of tobacco and the last time you wore it you made spaghetti sauce with Italian sausage."

I considered. "Walter, that's true—at Vivian's last Tuesday."

He laughed, took my hand, led me and the Doberman into the kitchen. He held a kitchen towel over his eyes. "Tie it back," he commanded. "Start with the spices."

He was blindfolded now, his hands behind his back, and with his eyes covered his grin was preposterous. I brought one bottle from the cabinet to his nose with the flourish of a chef testing soup—a useless gesture, since he couldn't see it. "Lemon pepper?" he asked.

"Right."

He correctly identified basil, garlic powder, curry, bay leaf, thyme, celery salt, paprika. After each right response, he laughed and shook his head. "How is this possible?" he asked.

"It isn't. Must have to do with the acid."

He groped for the refrigerator. "Taste! Jesus, Alex."

I gave him a spoonful of yogurt.

"Yogurt," he said.

I gave him leftover Chinese food from a cardboard box.

"Lamb," he said.

He identified corned beef, peanut butter, apple sauce, mint chocolate chip ice cream, a scallion, a carrot. He identified a piece

of leftover meat loaf and announced that my Brie was ammo-
niated. His hands were no longer behind his back. We were
locked into a bear hug, and on every correct answer Walter kissed
me. "That's it," I said. "Stop feeding me so well and I'll be better
stocked."

"I'm cured!"

"Don't jump any guns. Maybe you're just recognizing the
textures and the LSD's providing a heightened memory of the
smell and taste."

"I've been in a sensory deprivation tank for the last fifteen
years. Alex, your perfume's wonderful. Start on the dried goods,
the canned goods. Granola, dishwashing liquid—I don't care."

"What's going on?" Judy asked.

"You tell me," I said. "I've got to be missing something."

By now, almost all of my food and spices were on the counter,
in the dish rack, on the stove. Judy was wearing the dress that
Margaret had given me for my birthday. It was white, sexy by
virtue of its coy propriety, with a Cinderella waistline and a
flouncy, full skirt such as Dorothy might have worn in Kansas—
a dress I hadn't had the courage or the coloring to wear yet. On
Judy it seemed long, a little tight in the breast and sleeve, but
rather than looking ill-fitting the effect was of a political under-
mining of the whole notion of dressing up. The irony was doubled
by her shoes (mine had undoubtedly been too large): navy espadrilles. I found myself thinking of my friend Fran in New York
whose nearly completed dissertation, dissertation notes, and
belongings had been destroyed in a fire, along with her cat, her
plants, and her books. Fran had been finally pulling a life together
after a traumatic divorce when the fire happened. The only thing
that escaped the flames was her wedding dress, an antique white
satin gown she'd taken to a tailor earlier in the week to be converted
into a short formal. Fran claimed that she would recall the pungent
smell of fire every time she saw a white dress for the rest of her
life.

"Okay?" Judy asked, twirling for inspection.

I nodded, almost smelling fire damage myself.

"My sense of smell and taste are back," Walter said. "I just passed spices and refrigerator."

"Have you felt it coming back lately?"

"No. Will you help test me on dry goods while Alex dresses? Hurry, Alex!"

I hurried, mostly so as not to leave them alone. With some perfunctory makeup restoration, my eyes revealed little of my present anger. While my mother would never be stuck for an evening with a tripping boyfriend and his intruding ex-wife, Connie's dignity and reserve, I thought, might serve me well, so I counted to ten backward—a trick of hers—until I could re-enter the kitchen with composure. Walter was out of the blind-fold, putting things away.

"When Keith was a resident at Rockland," Judy said, turning to include me, "there was a paranoid schiz who'd been through a million shock treatments and every drug known to man. One of the aides was a young thing with ass-length black hair who even-tually got fired for slipping acid into the patients' orange juice, then having heart-to-hearts with them. With this old man it seemed to work. For ten years he'd only rocked and drooled. Suddenly he was writing poetry. When the girl got booted, he slipped right back."

"Maybe that was just the effect of attention from a young thing with long black hair," I said.

"Exactly. There's no control group. Like quizzing *Cosmo* readers on multiple orgasm, or Harvard grads on their income."

"Hop to," Walter said.

We were mostly quiet as he drove to his place so he could deposit the Doberman and change, but in the car Walter's happi-ness began to involve me, a contact high. We entered Le Bec Fin with our arms linked. Walter gripped one hand of each of us across the table as we sat. "There are ninety of us," he said.

"Mirrors," I assured him. "Behave yourself."

"I think he has managed quite well," Judy said.

For over three hours, our attention was on the five-course

meal, the wine, the French-speaking waiters, the indecipherable menu, and the other customers, one of whom—a woman in Felliniesque makeup and a blouse with a collar elaborate enough for a Tudor queen—wore a star sapphire so large and brilliant that every time she raised her glass, Walter started back as if he'd stopped on a dime before a total eclipse. Walter was a Geiger counter of the palate. He lifted reverently each spoonful of his soupe de moule, each forkful of my pâté and Judy's raw oysters. We did a skit of doctor, nurses, and scalpel with the exchanged morsels of food. Before we knew it, we had more wine and entrées.

"That's one of those dirty smelly things you see in the park," I scolded when I saw Walter's pigeon, its scrawny legs in rigor mortis dressed in fluted pink booties; but Walter assured me that smelly was beautiful and praised the brown sauce.

"As simple a thing as this," he said, his mouth full of Judy's veal, "with the subtlest nip of lemon through clarified butter, is what I missed most. I can't get enough."

The renowned dessert tray took twenty minutes to explain. By the time we'd sampled six kinds of torte and glacé and mousse, settled the check, whipped past Walter's to get the Doberman, and returned to my neighborhood for a quick walk, Judy had missed the last train back to Boston and Walter's trip was fading. I asked Judy where she planned to sleep; she said a car expanded her options, but she hadn't yet considered her game plan. I realized I didn't even know how long she had been in town. In the car we had missed almost every light and I had felt painstakingly aware of the time. Though the wine bridged the canyon between Walter's LSD trip and the threat of an olfactory relapse, the rift was still palpable. Moreover, after we had sat so long among the mirrors and crystal, the street had the disconcerting clarity it does when you emerge from a movie matinée.

Judy said, "It's spooky out here. I don't feel so good. Let's go in."

"Let's," I said. "I feel like the snake in *The Little Prince* that ate the elephant."

"Could you guys nurse your stomachs on the steps for a while," Walter asked, "so I can be outside? There's the smell after the rain. Please?"

Judy and I sat and watched Walter playing catch with the Doberman. After a while, the movement of Walter's arm releasing the stick and the whisk of the dog going after it began to hypnotize me. The fatigue you get after wine and a heavy meal was increased by the pendulum of Walter's toss, the dog's journey and return. The seductive regularity provided a contrast to the commotion in my stomach, which I tried to ignore along with a deepening awareness of the strangeness of Judy's presence. I shouldn't be out like an old lady with family on the steps of a Baltimore row house. I should be calling Theo and my parents. A phone rang upstairs—not mine, but it jarred me. Had it jarred me a bit more, I might have been able to prevent what happened.

The Doberman's death arrested the languor of the evening so abruptly that I thought *I* was tripping, for I had a violent flashback: for a moment I wasn't on my steps in April, but on Pat's steps on Halloween; Walter, in red scarf, had just walked in front of Stacey Easterlin's camera.

A car with only one headlight took the corner quickly as Walter threw the stick. Judy stood up and ran, calling to the dog; she had almost reached it when the car hit. All of this and what followed didn't seem fast so much as badly edited—a choppy documentary in which you couldn't tell what happened when, and how you got from one place to the next. The dog made a sound I've only heard before in burglar alarms. Judy screamed. You couldn't hear the scream over the dog's but you could see her open mouth; she was standing by a streetlamp, flapping her arms. The white dress was splattered with blood. For a moment I *was* in a documentary: this was 1963 and Judy, in her bloody dress, was Jackie Kennedy. The driver of the car knelt by the dog, blocking my view, bending over that horrific noise. She was a tall woman in dark clothes, glasses, and white tennis shoes, which I noticed because they were so near to the unbearable vortex of the dog. In the dark, the shoes seemed to be dismembered. Walter was frozen where he'd been when he'd thrown the stick, as if the slightest movement would finish off the dog. Though I couldn't see him clearly, I knew that he was crying. The driver— I'd moved close enough now to see that she was about our age, a young woman in jeans—pushed the car until it moved a little, revealing the dog's back, all exposed organ, even more raw than the back of the dog that had followed me on Chestnut Street in November. The howling ceased. Now you could hear Walter crying, Judy screaming. I threw up in the vicinity of my shoes. The tall woman had her hand on my shoulder. Part of my brain had revolted with my stomach, but she was talking persistently very close to my ear, and finally I got it: *Phone.*

I led her up to my apartment, pointed to the phone, and went into the bathroom to wash out my mouth.

In the living room, the driver talked, paced, her hand gripping the back of her neck. From my window you couldn't see the dog, only the people who'd started to collect, standing at a safe distance to gawk. I could hear a baby crying and a radio from the house across the way. Walter and Judy sat on the opposite curb. The woman joined me at the window. "I'm so sorry," she said.

"Not your fault."

Outside, Walter cried, shook, pulled his hair—a silent movie. In her bloody dress, Judy had one hand on Walter's knee, one hand around his shoulder. She rocked him, her face on the crown of his head. A siren became audible. The phone rang.

"I'd better move the car," the driver said. "I'll meet you downstairs."

Walter and Judy were still rocking outside. The steps they occupied were so symmetrically framed in my window, the streetlight so supernaturally confined to the crown of Walter's head and to Judy's face, that the two seemed like a portrait of themselves—or, rather, a portrait of the emotion they exemplified: "Grief" or something else unabashedly symbolic, even Madonna with dead son. Their rocking seemed less a sign of their three-dimensionality than the optical illusion you get when you stare at something for too long, with too much intensity. Either the phone rang for a very long time or my vision of them stretched time. When I picked up the receiver, still facing the window, I already felt past pain, in a shock that protected me against full recognition of the ensuing losses.

"Yes," I said.

"Is Walter Danner there?"

"Who's this?"

"Judy Stark. May I speak to my brother?"

"He can't come to the phone. May he call you back?"

"Put him on."

"His dog just got run over. He's outside with the animal squad."

"Give my brother this message, then. Tell him that Margaret is dead. Tell him that she died around four this afternoon with her address book opened to his name. Tell him that since she was unable to locate him she called Zoll. Tell him that Craig and Jacob and I are at her place making funeral arrangements and have been going through a list of Walter's girlfriends' numbers past and present in her address book trying to find him. Tell him that if he has a minute he might want to give us a ring. Have you got all that?"

"I'll tell him."

"If it isn't too much trouble."

"Listen," I said. "I know you're upset, but Walter's dog just got run over. Please give him a minute to assimilate all this."

She hung up.

Bitch.

Why hadn't Theo or Walter told me?

Outside, the driver was helping the animal squad. I sat below Walter and Judy on the steps and put my hand on Walter's foot, the most accessible part of his body.

"Your sister just called, Walter. I'm so sorry. Your mother's dead."

Judy sobbed at once. Walter loosened her embrace and drew back to look at her. "What did you say?"

"Judy, Craig, and Jacob are at Margaret's," I said quietly. "You should go there, Walter."

"Stop crying," Walter told Judy. She cried more softly. "Judy, what time did you leave her?"

"Three, two-thirty."

"And what time did she die?"

"Your sister said four," I said.

Judy and I looked at each other. The call. The one we hadn't answered.

"The smells," Walter said.

"Come on," Judy said, hugging him. He pushed her away and looked from her to me.

"The smells," he whispered. "It wasn't the acid. It was Margaret. It's Margaret's smell and taste. They flew from her body to mine. It's a transmigration."

"Give me your keys," Judy commanded.

He complied. She helped him up. "And the dog," he said. "The dog's smell too. I inherited them both. Everything circles back. Oh, God!"

The Cortina was parked yards away. Judy opened the passenger door and helped Walter in. She walked around to the driver's side, got in the car, closed the door, and drove a foot or two; Walter leaned toward her and she slammed on the brakes, covering her face with both hands. He insisted on some point with rhythmic karate chops to the steering wheel, strobed in the weak light. Judy threw the car into reverse and backed it up so fast that I had to jump onto the curb. She opened the door, got out, and walked stiffly to where I was standing. Walter had slid into the driver's seat and taken off before Judy reached me. Tears were streaming from her eyes in such a torrent that they didn't look real. Between her crying and mine, the street swam so much that I expected her voice to swim as well; I was surprised by its steadiness.

"I was the last person to see her alive," Judy said.

Her head was slightly turned from me. "Alex," she gasped, "I really, really, really, really need to talk to you"—her lips drawn tight, with the closed smile of people trying not to offend you with their breath.

21

By her own account, Judy Gold suffered from a facsimile of the borderline psychotic state called "the as-if syndrome." Judy aimed to please at the risk of losing her identity. If she was dating a Hell's Angel, she developed a sudden interest in tattoos and helmets. A month later, she could meet a musicologist and find that her strongest desire was to listen to Mahler in a jacket with elbow patches. She scuba-dived with oceanographers, read the *Wall Street Journal* with stockbrokers, had séances with occultists. This is an exaggeration, of course, but "suggestible" is an understatement.

All children have secret lives, other dimensions that they enter through the trapdoors and one-way mirrors and crawl-spaces of imagination. However colorful, the fantasies are shed for the three-piece suit of adulthood. Judy refused to make the compromise—for good reason, because, from the start, the daily life offered her was far too mean and dull.

Judy's parents met while her father was still a product-market analyst, her mother a secretary at the company office. Albert Gold designed some of the original tests to gauge consumer reaction to packaging color. Shirley Gold typed his statistical tables. Her typing was very fast, as precise as her housekeeping and her hair, which thirty-six years later she still wears in the same stiff halo. No one has ever accused Al and Shirl of being warm. Their idol is Sherlock Holmes. With detachment, you discover that even the master criminal is a consumer, as much in thrall to his needs as Pavlov's dogs.

An oldest child, Judy saw her parents' coldness more readily than her brother and sister, who have continued to wear the family mantle of cynicism. Michael Gold, thirty, is a gynecologist whose waiting room in Los Angeles is decorated with the stuffed heads of moose and bear he has shot; he tells lurid jokes on the examining table and likes to diagnose everything—including pregnancy—as syphilis. Sarah Gold, twenty-eight, is a litigation lawyer for a New York pharmaceutical company, the kind of lawyer who finds defending thalidomide or the Dalkon Shield "challenging."

Judy wasn't close to her brother and sister. She had more sympathy for her parents, who at least had poor childhoods as immigrants' children to justify their suspicion and their love of money. They did love something, and in their ascent on the economic ladder they'd shown some imagination. Al's last contribution to marketing had been the pilot studies on theme restaurants—restaurants dressed up as speakeasies, saloons, bank vaults, Noah's Arks. He'd made some money, invested it, quadrupled his investment, and gone into the restaurant supply business, where he made an easy living with little pressure, so he could enjoy his house, his pool, his hot tub, favorite tables at the best restaurants in town, and sophisticated movie equipment to document his frequent vacations.

By the time she was twenty, Judy could criticize her family eloquently. Her early approach was Freudian with a feminist twist. Though she indeed suffered an Electra complex and sibling rivalry at the birth of her male sibling, the penis envy that her (male) therapist was quick to point out was really an accurate perception of the cultural oppression of women. Intellect was unassimilable with femininity and the only way to catch a man was through effective harnessing of approach-avoidance (translate playing hard to get). Men, like dogs, wanted what was on the table for company and not what you put in their dishes; you

had to play by their rules, be as cute and backbiting as Virna
Lisi in *How to Murder Your Wife*.

The only trouble with Judy as a feminist was that she liked
men too much. She liked them deep-voiced and broad-chested;
she liked them ordering for her in restaurants and wrapping her
legs around their backs; she liked to see them transfixed in the
repair of household appliances. She didn't want to be a lesbian.
Women didn't generally like her anyway, because she seduced
men too effortlessly. Though Judy's teeth were too big, her hips
too broad for the current fashion, she had always been blessed
with admirers.

Her secret was woman's oldest secret: compliance with a coat
of resistance. She didn't *try* to be this way. On the contrary, she
was so successful because she tried not to be. Her true nature
was so much that of a pushover—windless air—that she compen-
sated with a veneer of toughness. In fact, she provided so little
resistance that she often felt she was invisible. Men could see
what they wanted to see in her. When she tried to resist such
treatment, it only added spice. Even her wildest balls somehow
stayed in court.

Behaviorism was a workable compromise between her parents'
pragmatism and her own imagination, deeply ingrained as antidote to pragmatism.

Judy had almost come to terms with being a born follower by
the time she finished graduate school, and was fending off her
third marriage proposal when she met Walter.

Walter had many selling points. He got her out of the last
engagement. He was in a different field. The timing was perfect.
And he didn't jump all over her. In fact, he didn't even suggest
sex until their third date. He was a feminist. He liked his mother,
and Judy liked her too. Margaret Danner had the verve, the
conviction, the sheer individuality that the Golds lacked. Jacob
Danner was a scheming egomaniac, but that type was nothing
new. Since Judy was already close to Walter's sister, she liked
three-fourths of the Danners. To ask for more seemed childishly
idealistic.

Then, of course, there was Walter in bed. Judy surely didn't need to sell me on *that* product.

Like most people in love or desiring to be in love, Judy and Walter assumed that their difficulties would disappear like the wrinkles in a garment hung up in the shower. Judy and Walter came home from work, poured drinks, and—curled up on a mauve couch that matched their paintings, their tablecloth, and the flowers on their giant cyclamen—compared notes on their respective days. After four years of marriage, of work, family, Walter, and Philadelphia, Judy felt that her life was as predictable as a color-by-number painting.

Much has been made of our generation's phobia about commitment, and perhaps it's true that the premium on self-sufficiency is just an alibi for egotism; there is certainly a clash between the refusal to feel deep pain in love and the insistence on finding deep pleasure in it. But Judy wasn't thinking clearly. She got to New York and fell in love and did the same thing all over again—new job, new city, new man.

Since the new man, Keith Morgenstern, was so different from Walter, it didn't seem possible that things would turn out the same. Walter was a brooder with a tender heart; Keith was coarse and tender by turns and, at heart, a brooder. A manic-depressive, to be precise. Though he was a Freudian, he insisted that he had a chemical imbalance. He would sink into weeks of paralysis after haggling with a dry cleaner over a bill, then become elated for no reason, drumming his hands on the edge of the table and talking in a loud voice; it made him not sleep to work straight for a week, and the next week refuse to get out of bed. Like most women who fear they're dumb and heartless, Judy was drawn to men who sometimes acted dumb and heartless, whom she could invest with endless depth. About Walter she had decided that anyone who had such a calm surface must have a turbulent heart, a theory confirmed by his outbursts. About Keith she had insisted that anyone whose moods seesawed so violently must be calm and firm in some place; she only had to get to it. At the convention where they met, Judy had even pursued Keith a bit, but once she got him he ignored her as he ignored everyone else. Keeping his attention became a perpetual project.

He slept with a patient. Judy didn't like it, nor did she like it when he committed himself to a fancy mental hospital and claimed that the infidelity was not his fault; he was sick. Judy didn't think so. But Judy had lost faith in the whole notion of "falling." Hurl yourself on the ground, batter your head against the pavement, and you still have the same choice: you stay there until you get run over by pedestrians, befouled by squatting dogs; or you get up and get back to business.

Sickness was no longer interesting. It troubled Judy how little sympathy she had for Keith. She had more sympathy for Walter, unable to get an erection, than she had for Keith, shot full of lithium, shuffling in an institutional robe.

She affected people all right, but it wasn't *her*. Assuming four years to be her limit, she could have ten marriages under her belt if she lived to be sixty-five. Judy was considering all of this with astonishment—astonishment that at thirty-three, after two marriages and eight years of training in psychology, she hadn't admitted it to herself before—when she met my brother.

If Walter was Cary Grant and Keith was Humphrey Bogart, then Theo was Jimmy Stewart. Theo was smart but not tortured. He was skinny, boyish, unpretentious, and straightforward. He refused to wear socks. He wouldn't eat the whites of eggs, though he would eat brains and squid; he didn't look in the mirror when he combed his hair, so his part was never straight. He was positively wonderstruck by the amenities of daily life—clean sheets, clean floors, a cold beer after a stroll. He was an excellent cook; an excellent, if quirky, lover, spending unaccountable amounts of attention on one part of the body at a time, a knee now, an ear next. It was love again, no doubt about it, and that was the problem.

Judy felt the old itch sneaking up on her—fatigue with the domestic. It was the notion of living in China that had fooled her. She'd imagined for a while that since they would begin their marriage there, she and Theo could bypass the usual playing house, could focus on something outside of themselves; for a month or so, she'd even had fantasies about how exciting it would be to work with him on his book.

Judy had been trying to figure out how to discuss this with Theo (in her experience, calling off or delaying engagements only made men want to marry you faster) when she met my parents. She knew that it must have hurt them to be so hostile to her. They seemed like loving people—they had to be, to produce Theo—and they wouldn't have done it unless they felt that their son was in danger. Judy hated to catch herself vying with Connie Freed for Theo's trust—she'd done that with Margaret Danner. But what troubled her even more was Theo's reaction. Theo loved her more because of his parents' disapproval. He was like a teenager who embraces the friends his parents are most likely to deem a bad influence.

The last thing Judy wanted was to "work some things out," but she had things to work out, and so did Theo; meanwhile, they'd started a baby.

Her diaphragm hadn't fit right since she had lost weight.

Seventeen years of steady intercourse and she'd never got pregnant.

So much for self-improvement.

Judy said she had often thought that it was crass of God to link up intercourse and pregnancy. It would have been kinder and more efficient for Him to program a ritual solely for the purpose of conception. It didn't seem fair that only God could *choose* to procreate, whereas humans' children snuck up on them. There was birth control, of course, and abortion, but Judy didn't want an abortion.

She was thirty-three years old, had always wanted a child, and didn't have that much longer for the project. After the doctor in Cambridge had confirmed the pregnancy, she had walked past blank undergraduates with their identical parkas in primary colors, their eyes bright from youth and wealth and the confidence that they'd read the right books, seen the right movies. She had felt not terror but pride. She didn't feel blank. It was hard to feel blank when your blood was being pumped into the production of fingers and toes.

The danger, she realized, was just that sense of righteousness. With her as-if syndrome, Judy was a born hostess, public servant, mother. She could be a terrible mother, using her child as a mirror, a vessel for her own disappointments: she could be a mother of stranglers, or, worse yet, of ordinary broken-record neurotics. On the other hand, Judy could be a magnificent mother. What was so wonderful, so exotic, so *real*, was not knowing, knowing only that whatever happened you were committed for life. There was no wriggling out. You can't divorce a child. You can have him adopted or disinherit him, but the best and truest part of yourself will always rest with the child, and the child will have you in it, with it, in a way a husband never can.

Melodramatic, yes, but Judy wanted the child, and she was going to have it.

Theodore Freed wasn't ready to be a father. He wasn't even ready to be a husband. Fatherhood was clearly not the most timely project for a twenty-seven-year-old with an untenured professorship and an unwritten book.

Besides, Judy would rather raise the child alone.

Single motherhood was hip. There was something unfortunate in jumping on yet another bandwagon, especially since in her fantasies of solitary responsibility there was some residue of romantic chic—the broad pilgrim in bonnet, driving her covered wagon across the hostile expanse. Granted her motivations were too self-serving: she suspected that anyone who pursued her when she was burdened with child would really want her. What could cure you of narcissism faster than the needs of a child?

Eight hundred times she'd told people that she was on the brink of disintegration and they hadn't believed her. But this time they'd tell her she was crazy and she'd know they were wrong.

22

What kept me listening, apart from difficulty in clearing my sinuses to interrupt, was a paralysis born of shock. Judy talked; I smoked. So swept along was she by the tide of her own fortune that she didn't pause when I went to the bathroom, to the bedroom for a change of clothes, or to the phone to dial Walter (no answer). Within an hour, my path from teapot to bathroom to phone to garbage with filthy ashtray was stale, predictable. The blood on the white dress Judy still wore had been absorbed into the weave of the rough cotton and darkened until it looked like a dress in the fashion of punk designed to look blood-splattered. Judy cried some, but most of the time she looked thoughtful, even serene; though crying made me radish-colored and splotchy with swollen-lidded eyes, it made her luminous. She had kicked off her shoes. With her knees drawn up, the dress clasped above her ankles, her rose toenails visible through the mesh of the nylons she'd borrowed from me along with the dress, she was a study in fashionable ease.

That night I understood how she could be appealing to a man, but Theo was lucky to be rid of her. I couldn't cry for Theo. Nor could I cry for myself—I wasn't yet aware that I had anything to cry about, apart from being saddled with Judy when I'd rather be comforting Walter, who would have to return to an apartment with a set of mauve dog bowls (actually ordered from a Bauhaus dog supply company) but no dog, no mother; whose descent into the flat planes of non-hallucination would make his grief unbearable.

Judy waited for my reaction.

"If Pat's any indication," I finally said, "I wouldn't count on men not assailing you just because you have a child. Men like older women with children. They get all of the advantages of family with none of the responsibility—slam-bang-thank-you-ma'am plus home cooking."

"That's fine," Judy retorted. "I don't want a husband. I like sex and food. I don't need anyone to make sacrifices for me."

"Except the kid."

"You're going to sing the sad song of no dad to play baseball in the front yard?"

"The main point of two parents is that it doubles the chances—albeit slim—of kindness."

"Or halves it."

"You don't have children to practice being selfless and responsible on," I said sourly. "There are no A's for effort."

"If you wait for assurance that you'll be a perfect parent, you'll never have kids."

"Your being a *perfect* parent," I remarked, "is not really an issue here."

"You act as if having a kid is gritty and selfish, having an abortion an act of great sacrifice."

"Actually, I can't say I can fully concentrate right now on the subject of your fitness for motherhood."

"Now I'll get accused of narcissism," Judy said mournfully.

"It's true that a woman you claimed was like a mother to you just died, which hasn't stopped you from speaking with great concentration solely about yourself."

Judy sucked in air through her teeth. "I expected more from you than this kind of sexism. Adolf only did it because Eva made him, right?"

I sighed.

"What's Theo's responsibility for all this?" she continued. "Keith's? Walter's? I didn't do it alone."

Judy got a fresh pack of cigarettes and a fresh tissue from her purse, blew her nose, tapped the cigarettes on the edge of my coffee table emphatically. Watching her made me profoundly tired. More than anything I wanted to stand behind Walter, reach around him and stroke his chest, my fingers in the reddish hair there expressing all solicitude. I felt no solicitude for Judy, especially once she accused me of sexism. All I wanted was for her to leave. My lack of response, however, meant to end the conversation, only incensed her.

"It's ridiculous for you to play righteous wife," she said. "This isn't a forties film where I'm the villainess who claws your eyes out. You think Walter and Theo are solidly behind you, haven't talked about you to me behind your back same as we're talking behind theirs? Give me a chance. The first time you met Walter, he raped you and went on and on about himself and you sat there and listened—you gave *him* the benefit of the doubt. I'm just asking for the same courtesy—oh, God. I'm sorry."

I had risen to get her coat. As I held it out for her, absolutely sickened with this last taunt, she began to sob again.

"I'm sorry," she said, "but we're so much *alike*," and I couldn't make out the rest, because she was blubbering too hard and because I was trying to dress her, to get her out.

I'd got her to stand up and was literally removing her wet hands from her face and trying to stuff her arms into the sleeves of her raincoat. It may have been the only moment for weeks when I wasn't crying or about to cry; all my energy was concentrated on getting Judy Gold out of my apartment. Now her coat was on, but her shoes weren't, and she wouldn't cooperate. I squatted in front of her, trying to lift up her foot by the ankle and slide it into one of her espadrilles (the wrong one at first), but since her hands had returned to her face to sieve tears, her balance wasn't good. So intent was I on dressing her that I almost didn't notice how she was wailing in syncopation with the ringing telephone.

"Judy!" I shouted, over crying and phone. "Stop! Just stop!"
She didn't stop.

I grabbed her hair. Since it was short, I was pulling the roots, quite close to her scalp. With her head bent at an obscene angle she followed me, wailing, to her umbrella and out the door. She pounded on the door for a minute, but then I heard her slam out the main entrance.

By the time I answered the phone, it had rung at least twenty times.

"I didn't think you were home," Theo said. "I just got mesmerized by the sound of the ring and forgot to hang up."

"Are you okay, Theo?"

"She took my car."

"What?"

"She took my car. She left a short Dear John letter and half her belongings and made off with my car. Why didn't she rent one?"

"Margaret's dead, Theo."

"I know. Judy Stark called here looking for Judy. I tried to get you and couldn't."

"So's Walter's dog. Both this afternoon."

"The timing couldn't be better. With Margaret and now the dog, it'd be like punching a face with glasses to criticize her. I should've seen it coming. Alex, will you do me a favor? Deal with Connie. I'm not ready to witness her delight."

"Do *me* a favor. Tell me what's happening."

To the best of his knowledge, Theo thought that Judy was calling off the engagement to rejoin Walter Danner.

"Who's the proud father?" I asked.

"What are you talking about?"

"She told me she was pregnant."

"So she told me she was seeing Walter but didn't tell you, and told you she was pregnant but didn't tell me? Connie is going to have a field day with I-told-you-so's. Alex?"

I'd begun to cry.

"Alex, are you okay?"

"Not really."

"Me either. The car's too perverse a symbolism for my castration. That wasn't thoughtless; it was malicious."

"Can I call you back?"

"When?"

"When I can talk."

"We can't hope for any old-fashioned retributions—the long-

suffering orphan getting her prince, the rich siren gambling herself
into prostitution. The old villains were always conscious of their
treachery, whereas now the insanity plea changes our whole notion
of responsibility. We excuse the damage these people do as the
inevitable result of their psychic distress. Judy hurt me, yet I'm
supposed to pity her. It almost makes me wish that everyone still
believed in God, so they'd worry about the afterlife with at least
the fear and loathing they now devote to traffic cops."

"I've got to go. I've got to blow my nose."

"Can't you talk for a while? It's helping."

Crying and chain-smoking had given me a hollow knot in my
chest; I felt cracked, out of tune, an unplayed cello parching in a
closet.

"No," I said. "I'll call you soon."

I hung up and dialed Walter, who didn't answer and would
continue not to answer, or to not be home—for all I knew, he'd
driven his car over a cliff.

Theo's car, it turned out, was parked two blocks away, in
front of the drugstore where I went the next afternoon to buy
cigarettes and the newspaper. The front end of the Fiat was so
badly rusted that it wasn't really purple anymore; it was brown
with a violet tinge, like the shell of a dead beetle. The car already
had a ticket on its windshield by the time its keys were slipped
under my door in an envelope bearing the Danner Associates
logo, the car's location written on one of Walter's duplicate billing forms, underlined in Walter's manic underlining. I still hadn't
heard from him, but it was a sign of my stupidity, my optimism,
or both that even when the car keys arrived I didn't think our
split was definite. I expected a call from him, an apology, a
reconciliation. By then, though I'd smoked a hundred cigarettes,
I was still counting them: any minute I'd quit again, Walter
would call, I'd stop crying and get some sleep. But Walter didn't
call and my sleep was about as soothing as a wet bathing suit.

I wanted a month-long coma—or at least a two-day coma—
so that when I woke up Pat would be back from Boston, bringing
news of her job and of Theo. Maybe in two days my parents

would recover enough from their relief to feign concern over their children's losses. For two days I cried. I was hurt and angry and confused and I wanted to cry for Walter, to scream at him, but for two days and three nights I called Walter's and got no answer. I got Theo, Pat, my parents, but I couldn't get Walter.

"Every minute since February," my mother said, "I've closed my eyes and prayed, Please, let it be over now. I have a confession. I offered to calligraph the envelopes and send out the wedding invitations for Shirley Gold but I never did. No one except us and the Golds know a wedding was even intended. It has weighed on me and weighed on me all week. I didn't even tell your father. Oh, Alex, I'm so happy for you both!"

Theo, from Boston, said perhaps it was just as well Judy had taken his car. It made him walk the two miles to his office, the mile to the shops. Last night he'd walked forever, in rain, to meet Pat Graci for a drink. Breathing deeply was clearing him out, calming him down.

Pat got the job. She would be back in Philadelphia late Thursday night to prepare for her move to Boston. After nine years, she had to change everything in two crazy weeks.

Margaret was buried on Thursday morning. I didn't attend the funeral, but read about it in the paper. *Margaret Danner, 58, realtor.* I sent a card. The last condolence card I'd bought was for my friend Greg in Maine, while he deliberated proposing to his dentist. It was a repulsively sweet rendition of swans in a lake surrounded by flowers: "Our sympathies are with you in this difficult time." Inside, I'd drawn a cartoon of a man vomiting swans and flowers, his hands clutching his stomach. But Walter's card was serious, sent with a note saying I was here if he needed me.

Apparently he didn't.

At thirty I'd never been to a funeral. It was one of the rites of passage I'd missed, along with abortion and the chicken pox. Relatives and friends of my parents had died, but never ones I was close to. I knew of death as I knew of everything except the heartbreaks of failed relationships and failed careers: through the paper, through fiction, through friends. Funerals, plane crashes, mastectomies, murders—they always happened to someone else. Most of my relationships had been formed at the crossroads of deaths, suicides, divorces. But though I convinced other people of my sympathy I rarely convinced myself. I cried for Margaret, but as I cried I feared my sadness was plagiarized. I actually envied Walter his mourning.

Poor Mother, praying since February. She said the person she felt sorriest for was Margaret, to have a son like that.

Another story from the LSD era: once it took me eighty years to get down a flight of steps. No matter how many steps I finished, there were more steps underneath. By the time I finished my descent I'd need a wheelchair. What I had come to, I later realized, was a hallucinatory model of Zeno's paradox, the only thing that has ever impressed me in math class. The teacher had walked halfway across the room. He walked halfway across what was left, then halfway again. Soon he was pressed up against the wall with the tips of his shoes. Only the size of his feet and the fact of infinity, he'd told us, prevented him from completing the journey. Space and time were infinitely divisible. There was my seventh-grade teacher, with his back to us, saying gleefully that he could walk forever—a quarter of an inch, an eighth, a sixteenth! If space and time were like that—if life was an asymptotic curve in which zero was your destination and the closer you got to zero the farther away zero got—then how would any of us ever grow up? How would I menstruate? How would I even finish my homework and make my bed, much less finish my doctorate and marry?

"The wise man knows how little he knows," Phil had comforted me when I'd hinted at my terror. "If you arrive too easily, there's no point to the journey. You personally will grow up, marry, and die, but human life is never 'done.' You kill off the dinosaurs to make room for man. Planets change as fast as neighborhoods; funeral parlors and maternity wards both do steady business. You try to keep the peace between extremes of bliss and misery. Without unhappiness there's no momentum."

I found this only dimly comforting.

I would break up with Walter, start seeing someone else, break up with him too, quit one job, and another, and so on until I was too old to do anything but hire gigolos and pee into a tube.

More dates! More strangers! To get used to solitude again only to have to tell all those dating stories again—do you dream of drowning or falling, are you chipper or groggy in the mornings, do you tend to blow up when angry or clam up?

I couldn't even think about it.

My dominant sensation was guilt. In my dreams the bloody Doberman blended into my father's Schnauzer, into the poodle that had got run over near my parents' house when I was a child, into the mangy mutt on Chestnut Street, and I was somehow responsible for each death. Walter and Judy blended into other unfaithful lovers, other female competitors, my parents. The setting was New York, Boston, Atlantic City, Walter's apartment—people stole my sable coat, and I saw Walter and Judy making love in hit-and-run snatches. In my sleep I reran the footage of the conglomerate dog death, as cold and distant from it as a coroner. I slowed the film, backed it up, ran it in reverse, zoomed in for close-ups, searched for the conclusive piece of evidence that would solve the mystery.

In movies about emotional awakenings, the heroines are always mute, passive creatures whose kaleidoscopic consciousnesses can be tuned to the simple truth, as riveting as a car accident, by a supportive psychiatrist who recognizes the poor woman's hidden talents and vast ability to love. The psychiatrist peers over the top of her glasses maternally if a woman; if a man, he chain-smokes, puts his feet on the coffee table, leans forward humanly. All television psychiatrists like to be called by their first names and to place their hands gently on their patients' backs. All emotionally troubled heroines on television have cold mothers, henpecked or domineering fathers, indifferent siblings, and artistic abilities. They sketch and write poetry. When they unveil their secrets ("I just want to be held"), they're immediately rewarded with men as sensitive as their psychiatrists, with friendly co-workers and warm teachers. Never mind that the world is rarely this obliging. The promise that cleaning your room will coax out the misplaced treasure is a staple of art, if not of reality. But what kind of *deus ex machina* would make a drama of Alexandra Freed? My problems were about as climactic as wallpaper. My unemployment would run out on June 6th, my lease on June 15th; though my family and friends were somewhat supportive, I was low of spirit and of bank account. Worse than that, I wasn't curled in a corner in the fetal position. I'd lost a man I cared about, but I could smoke, play the cello, run up my phone bill, joke to Pat in Boston ("It took a while before you could say 'I told you so' but better late than never"). Because the Freeds prize strength, I'd tried to disguise my pain, so the stiff upper lip had turned into a sneer; because the Freeds pay attention to weakness and need, I'd decided that even negative attention was better than no attention, and I milked my sadness for all the attention I could get; because I'd never fully confronted my anger at my family and my low self-esteem, I could only fluctuate between snideness and self-pity. I could say this calmly. I could even say calmly that the calmness itself was the problem. So what was left to discover? I was like a person with gonorrhea who's allergic to tetracycline.

There was left only the possibility that I had to use losing Walter as the catalyst for doing the whole self-discovery routine again in a different spirit. I needed to go back to the drawing board with the old designs discarded and act as if I'd forgotten how to hold a pencil.

So on Thursday morning I made the old promises. Don't call Walter. Don't go out and screw someone else to fill in the vacancy. Don't call friends for a fix of pity. Ask not what your friends can do for you but what you can do for yourself. Stale adages, but my last resort, a sentiment confirmed by a postcard from Theo.

It was one of Theo's bloody crucifix postcards, this one from the Prado featuring a particularly anorectic Christ, except that under the crown of thorns was not Christ's agonized upturned face, but a photo-booth picture of Theo and me, cut and glued to Christ's neck so that it looked as if he were two-headed. We'd taken the photo two years ago in Ocean City, on a vacation with his old girlfriend Pam—a glorious vacation during one of my brief respites from boyfriends or from mourning boyfriends, on which I didn't feel like a third wheel and I satisfied my libido with sun and seafood. Pam, Theo, and I had posed in the booth, but Pam wasn't present on Christ's neck. She'd been excised, along with a chunk of my hair, so it was just Theo and I posing as see no evil, hear no evil, our heads so shoved together that they both fit under the crown. On the back of the postcard, one sentence:

For smart people, how did we ever get so dumb?

23

"My heart hurts," I said.

"My heart's replaced with a stopwatch," Pat said. "Instead of a brain there's a calendar marked up with things to do."

On April 26th, we were slumped in a corner of Pat's empty bedroom. Vanessa was off on a farewell lunch with her father. All that was left was a box of cleaning equipment, a trash bag, two cans of lukewarm beer, and us.

"What took longest before you got here yesterday," Pat mused as she examined a half-empty Bic pen chewed at the end wrapped in a hairy dustball which we'd decided to leave on the floor as a gift for the next tenant, "was Nessie's room. They hide things, you know. She let me ditch her dolls, her party favors, but she kept an entire box full of used coloring books."

"Why?"

"Beats me. They're very obsessed with teeth at her age. I

swear Ness makes some connection between getting her feet strong
enough to stand on her toes for ballet and losing her baby teeth.
She's a mystery."

"So's Preston—he was so nostalgic."

"He's a sentimental bastard."

"I suppose he's allowed to cry over his own kid if three hours
ago you got to mourn twenty empty plastic containers of Rainbow sherbet."

"Great for freezing. What's left?"

"You got your key to your landlord, the table to your ex-
mother-in-law?"

"Yes."

"Then except for Jeff, whom you begged I shouldn't mention,
all we have to do is finish these beers, scrape tape off the refrigerator, and wait for Ness."

In less than two weeks, Pat had got a new job and a furnished
apartment in Boston near a good school and ballet class for Nessie,
tied up her projects at work, interviewed for a replacement, hired
one and minimally trained her, sublet her present house, had a
house sale with lemonade, packed, and moved boxes across the
street to the house she'd bought and now planned to sublet.
Amidst all this, she managed to have a birthday party for Nessie
and deliver house plants to friends with her hair clean, her face
cheerful and attentive.

"Why am I doing this?" Pat asked.

"Partly as obstacle course, but mostly because you got a more
interesting job that pays more, though personally I think the only
job challenging enough for you is the Presidency."

"You know I couldn't have done it without your help."

I checked to see if she was being sarcastic. She wasn't, though
for the past weeks I'd helped much less than I could have. If I
had a job, a husband, kids, I'd have an excuse, but I had only
self-pity over the lack of these things, and, temporarily, a car,
which I'd hoped would allow me to escape self-pity. Mobility
was at least distracting. I spent one morning at a small museum

about an hour away and that afternoon changing a tire on the Fiat that went flat on the expressway—luckily Theo had a spare. The next day was spent getting the tire patched. I looked at clothes and bought hot pink velvet to reupholster the seats of my dining-room chairs, then returned that and bought pine green. I stayed out of my apartment as much as possible, partly because being out saved me the agony of finding a legal parking space, but mostly because at least then I could pretend that Walter may have called while I was out. Pat's cheerfulness, self-control, vigor, and organization stood in such blinding contrast to my morose clutter that on an almost metabolic level she made me feel like a lost cause, but I didn't know how I could live in Philadelphia without her. She'd been so central a fixture to my emotional life for so long—a basic human right, like heat or hot water—that several times I'd imagined Walter wasn't the real loss. Pat was.

"God, Pat," I blurted out, "why can't we go back to Bath? Listen. Why not stick Nessie with someone and fly standby?"

Pat and I had escaped to Europe together on a day's notice nine years before. Our friendship had been new then; we'd devoted ourselves to it with the energy of youths who can leave behind unpaid rents and fret only that house plants would wither, records buckle from humidity. I hadn't yet started graduate school, Pat hadn't got married or divorced, and our futures had felt so exotic, so unexplored that Europe was tiny, dull by comparison.

"We had so much spirit then," I sighed. "So much faith."

"We made Gidget look scholarly," Pat added, removing her glasses to chew on one stem like a pipe-smoking expert on educational television. "I really appreciate your help, and I'm also very proud of you for handling the whole Walter mess so well."

"I've certainly had enough practice with messes."

"Haven't we all."

"I think I win the gold medal for monotone and monochrome."

"This time you haven't called there every five seconds or had Cortina heart attacks."

"I have too. Over every white car. I just haven't told anyone about it."

"That's something."

"Jesus, Pat, can't I go with you?"

I had volunteered to drive to Boston with her, help her set up, drive back with her when she returned to clear up the other house in May, her new house being the only snag in an otherwise smooth transition. With its fixed mortgage, new wiring and plumbing, and blessed structural soundness, it was a shame to part with the house, but it was too expensive to use as a tombstone commemorating her long and stultifying life in Philadelphia. My life was so embalmed that I was desperate to get out, if only briefly. I certainly couldn't justify a vacation after so much unemployment. Helping Pat would be a good excuse, with Theo as added attraction.

"I won't get in your hair. I'll stay at Theo's, watch Ness."

"Alex, please don't open this can of worms again."

She gave me the sidelong look we'd adopted in the past·two weeks—a glance solemn in its brevity, such as you need for sheet music you're trying to memorize. Our panic was much like the stage fright of kids at recitals. I got her face in measures, in phrases. Now I could only look at the hand on her knee with the strong, even fingernails I'd always envied, their ovals the same shape as the opal ring she'd worn since I met her and since five years before that. The ring was a gift from her first boyfriend, about whom I knew everything, right down to an unrivaled circular motion in lovemaking that always reminded Pat of the intense noise you get by running a wet finger delicately, yet with velocity, along the rim of a wineglass. Her hand moved to her eye, which was wet.

"I'm scared," she said. "Do you know that?"

"It's a lot better to be scared than to sit around waiting for something to change."

On the way to the refrigerator to scrape, we glanced out at the Packard, gleaming and sleek, incongruous as a spaceship on Beaumont Street.

"Jeff wanted the house, you know," Pat said. (Jeff was her journalist, whom she hadn't seen regularly in months.) "If I sold it, I wouldn't sell it to him. Jeff's a poor mill-town boy and I'm a poor steel-town girl, and here I was with a job and a house and silver options. Never mind that I hauled ass for it; I owed it to him as one of the brethren. Either that or he treated me like Katharine Hepburn in *Philadelphia Story*. I'm tired of being a mother to them. You get fathers; I get sons."

"Would you sell the house to me?"

"Sure. Use your lunch money."

"I could finish the work before I left for the Foreign Service and if I don't get the job, then I'll have somewhere to live."

"I can just see you hanging Sheetrock and grouting tile," Pat said. "You could get your own sit-com. 'Miss Fix-It'—burst pipes and broken hearts. You demonstrate the Freed method of changing the seal on a toilet, which ought to leave them laughing in the aisles, then Vivian drops by in a dither about Rich. Commercial. After station identification the toilet's shiny and you and Viv are having a heart-to-heart about interracial marriages. Next week: 'Handy Leatherwork.' "

"Okay, okay," I said, weaving a little fantasy of my own: Alex alone with the natives on an anthropological search, her tent surrounded by bears, bugs, and deathly silence. No phones, no department stores, no bath towels. Recently, my fantasy of independence had taken the form of acceptance into the Foreign Service. Pat's house was an attractive stopgap. Never mind that I'd criticized her about it only months before.

"You told me yourself the structural work's almost done," I urged. "Surely you don't think I'm incapable of painting without your supervision."

"Painting's the least of it. There's *carpentry* up there, Alex."

"But there's also wallpaper to come down, spackling, all of which I know how to do."

"You *are* serious, aren't you?"

"My lease runs out June fifteenth. You're paying the mortgage through May anyway. I could fool around there for a month, decide if I like it. If I do, I can either take over the mortgage or rent from you; if not, you're not much worse off."

We stared at the house for a while. "I'll give you the key," Pat said, placing it in my hand with a pantomime of surrender and, I think, an assumption that I'd never enter.

The sight of Preston and Nessie outside filled us both with dread. Not only had we developed a fairly strong distaste for Preston over the years, but his arrival signaled Pat's departure. His uncannily high forehead and dark, endless eyebrows gave him an accurately baleful look. He lifted Nessie on to the hood of the car and held her by the shoulders as if he were comforting her.

"Poor bastard," Pat said. "Somebody ought to love him. Ness doesn't know what a move means. She thinks it's a holiday. Maybe that's the sanest attitude. Let's just pretend I'm going away for a couple of weeks."

We cried, then sobered ourselves to get rid of Preston. I stood outside the Packard until Pat and Nessie were loaded and arranged, and Preston was done with goodbyes and instructions. Nessie gave me the triumphant smile of a child whose mother is taking her to the zoo while *your* mother makes you stay in your room.

"Alex," Pat said, "you keep the faith."

"In what?"

"In yourself."

"Too late."

"Don't cry anymore," Pat said, crying herself. "You'll kill yourself driving home."

"I should have such luck."

We hugged through the open window of the car, Nessie's imperious face indicating she was used to strange behavior from adults.

Soon I was home alone. Between staying at Walter's, working at Pat's, and generally fleeing the scene of the robbery, I hadn't really inhabited my apartment for months. The plants Pat had given me were like flowers in a hospital room. The order was stale and impersonal. In the mail: an electric bill, a ghastly phone bill, and a Xerox of the wedding invitation that Jessica had sent months ago with *Well?* written across it in red laundry marking pen.

I cried until the doorbell rang. I saw a flower truck outside and ran downstairs. The flowers were in fact for me.

> If all's on schedule you're home alone by now. I love you and will always love you. Thanks again and cheer up. Above all don't—*don't*— move toward that phone!
>
> XXOOXXOOXX
>
> PAT

Missing Pat too much to appreciate the flowers, I indulged in a long, soporific cry and put the flowers in water before I disobeyed Pat's instructions.

Judy answered Walter's phone.

Why hadn't I expected that?

Her "hello" was breezy and fearless.

I hung up, and would probably not have made it through the night were it not for thinking about Pat's house.

For six months I'd mostly been brushing my cheek against the hair on Walter Danner's chest after lovemaking as if, by tuning out everything except the exacting harmony of pore and follicle, I could knit a hammock for us that would make my suspension between past and future a bower and not an abyss. I had claimed to be thinking of my future, but my brain, like Stacey's camera on Halloween, had been set on automatic pilot. Now Judy had walked directly in front of the camera, forcing me to think about the future. If I didn't get into the Foreign Service, why stay in Philadelphia? Why, on the other hand, go anywhere, do anything? All around me people walked dogs, studied the mating patterns of insects, peddled Venetian blinds and political ideologies. I know a piano teacher who could never go professional because he'd broken all his fingers boxing. Philadelphia had a planning board that decided to fund a renovation of Fitler Square, tearing down the ginkgoes that someone must have decided to put there to begin with.

I was not without options. But I felt like the Scrabble player who considers until he's so addled he can't play a single word. Even to be a mailman you had to take a test, get on a waiting list. People return to medical school in middle age, skiers lose their legs—it wasn't over, but it wasn't just starting, either.

Walter got Margaret's olfactory sense, Judy got Walter, and when I thought of my future, all I could imagine was cleaning up after Pat with the mindless momentum of someone who has ten minutes to find an atom bomb planted in Grand Central Station.

The renovation could challenge not only my arm and back muscles, but my endurance and my aptitude for long-term planning. I imagined Pat's gratitude, Theo's grudging praise. My work could siphon off some of the corrosive energy I'd devoted to Walter and, before Walter, to other men. Walter aside, the routine work might have a calming effect. It would be the novocaine that allowed me to drill the cavity and stand at the edge of the excavation pit I was presently calling my life.

There was a small catch.

I knew nothing about renovation, hadn't the patience for it, and found it unbearable without Pat's encouragement and company.

The next day, I drove the Fiat to the half-finished house on Beaumont. Pat's furniture piled in the dining room, in the unfinished bathroom and kitchen, was worse than cadaverous. It's not that I expected to find beheaded bodies in the disconnected refrigerator, carnivorous rats in the attic. The house had only been untouched for a day. My life, at that late date, would not reward me with a closure as dramatic as a murder in an empty house. Indeed what was so terrifying was the knowledge that the house was just a pile of matter.

I scraped wallpaper for a couple of hours with the radio on and was fantastically, cosmically bored.

Assuring myself that it would be better the next day, I spent the evening with Stacey Easterlin, who had gossip about Walter. Stacey had missed most of my Walter fuss just as I'd missed her slow progress into love and probable marriage with her mathematician. At a party that Walter couldn't attend, Judy Gold had met Stacey, and having no way to place Stacey with Walter or with me, had discussed her reunion with Walter. Judy said that she should have stuck with Walter because your first choice on a multiple-choice test is usually correct. She'd talked about planning a pregnancy, arranging to meet Walter, then screwing her brains out. The questions raised by that gab session—was Judy telling the truth? Did Walter know any of this? Did Judy want this to get back to me?—restored the full pain of the loss, as did a letter from Theo the next morning in the awful scrawl that made it necessary for him to type even his index cards.

Dear Sob Sister:

Where have you been? I've called and called.

Excuse the handwriting but this is a flash bulletin and my typewriter, in an act of anthropomorphic defiance, has run off to the repair shop.

Now that Connie's invitation confession has hit the stands, I have a confession of my own. Yesterday I boxed all the clothes and shoes Judy left in my closet, all the books she left on my radiator and the hairdryer she left in my medicine cabinet, and gave them to the Salvation Army. I got a tax deduction slip made out in her name and mailed it to her at Walter's. This exorcism was unaccountably satisfying.

Judy called later in the evening asking sweetly if I might mail a few things. I said sure—let the slip surprise her—and no sooner had I'd finished some pacing than Keith Morgenstern called.

He sounded nice, smart, and misrepresented by Judy. He's out of the hospital, rebuilding his practice, and quite ready for the divorce. He wasn't surprised to hear about her and Walter, and neither, finally, should we have been surprised.

It was the first time I'd talked that long to a man in some time. I think I may look him up next time I'm in New York.

Last night I dreamed you were going out with him (Keith, I mean). Interested?

Joke.

My happiness with Judy, yours with Walter—they were kind and obliging to us because they knew it didn't matter. Anyone would have done for either of them.

Anger's fun, not to mention cleansing.

What haunts me most about all this is to what extent I myself am responsible. Much of the pain is the loss of self-respect inherent in having judged badly. To what degree does my fear of being manipulated render me an ideal victim for smooth operators? What if Freud's right after all and the jungle of the unconscious is really a city with mapped streets, like the New York subway system?

I hope you're proud of me for entertaining such abstract notions in such a cheerful tone.

For the first week or so, I holed up in my office, saw students, read too much. But recently I've been making all of the standard steps toward rehabilitation—seeing people, going to movies. Saw *North by Northwest* and wanted to be Cary Grant. Saw your friend Pat, who likes her job and misses you.

Judy hurt me more than I hurt Pam, a dynamic example of big fish eating little fish and a good education. I needed it. You didn't, having already been through this twenty too many times, but there's always the hope that the shock will be strong enough someday to cause a last replay of the Alexandrian dramas of the agony, the ecstasy.

Perhaps I'm being paranoid, but I've suspected one of the main reasons you haven't been in touch with me is that you feel my loss of Judy has overshadowed your loss of Walter. You're wrong. I do feel for you, and I'd like to talk with you about creative recovery.

Anyhow it's over and Connie is right, alas—we should be relieved. I am relieved. Do you believe that? If I can fool you, I'm more talented than I thought. I haven't fooled you yet. Then again you haven't fooled me yet. Pat thinks it's a definite step for you to talk so little about what you're going through, but I don't think it ever does any good to swallow misery. Not if you're going to be a martyr about it. So? So? Speak up.

Your Enchiridion brother,

What I assumed was the signature was in Chinese.

Theo, the person I most respected in the world—the man who leaped over stereotypes of masculinity into humanness, his eccentricities balanced by his capacity for kindness—was playing rebuffed lover with the same overexuberance he'd used in his performance of fiancé. He was *playing*. I should know; his performance of anger and strength was close to my own routine.

Stripped of my best friend and my lover, not to mention my stereo, my typewriter, my television, and my self-irony, I spent a quiet day at home, cleaning my apartment. I defrosted the refrigerator, polished my teapot, took the stove apart and cleaned under the burners. No one called. I packed winter clothes, fed plants. Hours later, in a mechanical trance, I balanced my checkbook, paid bills, sent the R.S.V.P. to Jessica informing her that I'd be in San Francisco for her wedding in June assuming I survived insanity and bankruptcy. Short of rearranging my books according to size or publisher, there was nothing left to do but eat, fantasize that San Francisco might change things, and respond to Theo's letter.

I fetched Stacey's extra television so I could watch it while designing a card for Theo that featured a paper-doll series of Christs on the cross cut out of the stock market pages. Inside I printed:

> Thanks for your concern. It's returned. Miss Freed is closed for remodeling, but will be in service soon.

I stared with clinical horror at this bit of snideness and hoped that numbness might, after all, be the most appropriate outfit to wear to the precipice of a gusty change.

But by the next day this glacial numbness would give way to a titanic flood. Viewed from the shores of a better mood, it would have been amusing that the event triggering the break was a toilet without enough water pressure to flush and the uncomfortable dampness between the legs caused by discovering, too late, that there was no more toilet paper.

Having just put in another excruciating two hours scraping
wallpaper at Pat's, I sat down on the filthy floor to smoke and
confront the inevitable fact that Beaumont Street was no Lourdes,
that literal renovation was not likely to effect the figurative cure.
As usual, I could chastise myself for having failed and add this
failure to a list of failures, which made a formidable, if perverse,
vita. The only things that progressed in a straight line in my life
were cigarettes and the aging unto death. In the house which
provided dusty stagnation as a *Doppelgänger* of my internal state,
I made an earnest, plodding, Phil-style attempt to assess the roots
in the past so as to predict future options, but there are no roots,
no first causes in a process so airtight, external, circular. Walter,
unemployment, smoking were as tangled as a hundred necklaces
in a jumbled jewelry box; all I could do was count randomly,
pull uselessly at one strand or another. Fourteen nights and fifteen
days or 360 hours since I saw Walter, 600 cigarettes since I saw
Walter, 174,700 cigarettes or thereabouts since I started smoking,
210 days of unemployment unless 1980 was a leap year—these
calculations took me a very long time, and by the time I had
completed them, I'd forgotten them. When the toilet didn't flush,
when there was no toilet paper and I shuffled from the bathroom
to my purse to retrieve a scrap of tissue with tobacco clinging to
it, it occurred to me that I was mad; that, as Judy had said,
madness was dull; that I wasn't going to slit my wrists vertically
or even butcher my nice dark hair with dull scissors, but would
instead be like this forever.

I didn't cry.

In what seemed at the time a very satisfying coincidence, I
had exactly the correct amount of change to make a three-minute
call from a phone booth a block away to Bethesda, Maryland.

"Where are you calling from that's so noisy?" Connie said.

"Mom."

Between the bad connection, the trolley sounds on Baltimore
Avenue, and a sudden migraine, my head got a conchlike echo
that recalled my auditory LSD hallucination twelve years before.
I wondered whether I could be having a flashback produced by

the exactly parallel situation of a friend leaving, as friends had left then; that was the last time I'd called my mother from a phone booth, and once more it was to ask her who I was, what I should be doing.

"Yes, Alex?"

"I was just thinking about when I called you tripping from college. Remember?"

"That and the crab lice are things I'd like to forget."

"You told me to take some tea and get some sleep."

"Sensible advice, it seems." She laughed. "I hope you're not tripping again."

"The way you responded was smart in a way. You'd figured out that the sex and drugs were a conflicted attention-getting device: I was rubbing your nose in my rebellion, and at the same time I was begging to be leashed. You forced me to fall back on my own resources."

"Alex, is anything wrong?"

"Don't you see that at eighteen I didn't *have* those resources? Actually, I've never gotten them. Do you understand?"

"I think so. You're calling me long-distance in the middle of the day to tell me once more that it's all my fault."

"Mom, please, don't be so defensive."

"You try raising kids. The part I want to see is the part where all you kids become parents. You've gone on about our neglect. They've taught you in college what our neglect does. You're all going to eat your hats. Your father and I have done a magnificent job—too good a job, dear. You're a spoiled brat."

"Let's not start on your hand-me-down shoes."

After some silence, the operator cut in to tell us our time was almost up.

After more silence, my mother talked, very fast: "I love you, Alex, but what *is* the matter? You're bright, you're attractive, you're Caucasian, you're well-educated. You've had every advantage. I feel very bad that you're unhappy but there's nothing I can do about it. *Nothing.* Not now. Maybe we should have picked you up and shaken you, and not rewarded your self-pity."

"Or you could have taught me how to be happy and rewarded me for that, rather than teaching me to sit under the table with my tail under my legs like fucking Sam."

"Shut up!" my mother shouted. "Get a job!"

I just had time to call her a bitch before the phone clicked, then disconnected.

When I got back to Pat's, I realized I'd locked myself out. My cigarettes, apartment and car keys, and wallet were in the house.

Luckily, though I'd locked the car door, I hadn't rolled up the window, so I was able to get into the car, but of course I couldn't go anywhere in it. For a long time, I sobbed with my head on the steering wheel.

Then I scrounged around on the floor of the Fiat, under the seats, and in the cracks of the upholstery, until among the paper clips, pen caps, crumbs, and cigarette butts I found the dime I needed to call Walter Danner.

24

Walter and I arranged to meet late the next morning at the bar of the Barclay Hotel. Why the stuffy Barclay I didn't question. I didn't ask Walter to help me break into Pat's. For fifty dollars, a locksmith who accepted credit cards jimmied the lock on the back door and lectured me about security as the police officer had on Waverly. The sight of my purse untouched on the floor where I'd left it made me feel almost as blessed as I had felt when Walter was home to answer the phone on the first ring—although in truth, and stupidly, I hadn't imagined him out.

If I couldn't imagine a rebirth of my relationship with Walter, it was only because for me it had never died. I could therefore justify a meeting as killing the poor thing off and enacting a proper burial. The ritual was as necessary as the last cigarette before the firing squad. Of course, having been through such reunions before, I was quite aware that the euphoria I felt about seeing Walter only mirrored the inevitable ensuing despair. But for a minute the reunion seemed logical. We'd finally come full circle: now I courted the rapist. While I should, as my mother was fond of saying, quit while I was ahead, Walter was too receptive to our getting together for me to feel rebuffed.

Despite having cycled many times, by many routes, through perplexity, anger, guilt, disbelief, and raw pain, I still didn't know what my position on Walter was, and I needed a position. I would use compassionate calm to draw him out on the events that reunited him with Judy. Had that been Judy on the phone the afternoon in March when I'd accused him of infidelity? Had their affair already started? Or had it started much earlier—as far back, perhaps, as Thanksgiving, when the sofa at Walter's was messy with extra sheets for the houseguest, perhaps just to fool me? I had a horrible picture of Walter and Judy in Atlantic City together the very morning of my surprise birthday party, conceiving their baby.

Walter, I guessed, would be cool and courtly by turns. He'd also be late. I therefore prepared the next morning as slowly as possible and strolled to the hotel knowing I'd still beat him. Though I was fortified with the newspaper and coffee, I'm sure Walter wasn't fooled by my absorption.

Bursting into such a quiet, industrious room, Walter seemed a kind of caricature: Superman leaving the phone booth. But perhaps that was my imagination, for the waiters treated him with full deference. It wasn't just because he was male—Theo would have got the same treatment I had. Nor, as my Aunt Carol would have speculated, were the waiters anti-Semitic. The waiters responded to fatigue. As Walter crossed the almost empty room to my corner table, his pace and gestures were those of the harassed businessman whose battened humanity had to be attended to even more efficiently than the knot in his tie.

Never had I seen Walter look so exhausted. He was puffy under the eyes. His neck was too pink from a recent haircut, his ears seemed to emerge from his head at too sharp an angle, and his chin was set too tightly, as if he'd been grinding his teeth in his sleep and had hurt his jaw. The bit of his upper lip revealed by his newly trimmed mustache looked prenatal, transparent, afraid of light.

"I know," he said, with a shrug of the folder he always carried. "We both need sun."

"At this time of year, I always feel like an insect under a rock."

He smiled and ordered coffee. Then we smiled at each other until the coffee arrived. "I've missed you," he said.

"I bet."

Entirely the wrong foot, though Walter looked braced for it. I lit a cigarette and asked him how everything was going, then waited for him to answer at too great length, which he did.

He'd been named executor of his mother's will, a messy job complicated by his sister and his father freaking out. Margaret had left a good deal of her estate to Zoll, who, it turned out, had been her lover for many years; Judy Stark and Jacob Danner were morally indignant that Margaret could have kept a gigolo and wanted to contest the will. In this they were united against Walter. In everything else they were at each other's throats. All of this was painful for Walter, made it harder for him to be shoved into the role of adult, and, he realized, only stalled his own confrontation with feelings about his mother's death.

He had picked up a packet of sugar and was kneading it assiduously. As he broke the packet into the ashtray where I'd just crushed my cigarette, he changed the subject to his smell and taste.

The return of his senses and his mother's death had coincided so exactly that it was impossible not to link the two. Margaret's death had liberated Walter. He couldn't deny it. He smelled, tasted relief. He also felt the guilt that relief entailed, so when his senses started deteriorating, which they did almost immediately, he couldn't help thinking that if smell and taste were her legacy, she was an Indian giver.

Their return was, the doctors believed, a temporary aberration almost certainly instigated by the LSD. A research team in the area was in fact working with acid in order to prompt subjects to a memory of their senses. The subjects were trained to harness their memories; if it was finely tuned enough, memory might in essence replace direct experience.

"That's disconcerting," I offered.

"I'm very pessimistic. I can understand how you can get the memory of flowers or coffee to happen at the right moment, but what good's a memory of something burning?"

"How many people are participating?"

Perhaps I wanted to stall the discussion of Judy, either because I couldn't bear it yet or because I wanted to prove Walter's cowardice and callousness in not bringing it up himself. At the time, though, I was mostly aware of how comfortable it was to be with him. I had not succeeded in hating him. The shame of missing him made me want to cry.

"There are forty, fifty people coming to sessions in this city, maybe another three hundred from other states for batteries of tests. Believe it or not, I'd never thought to ask how many people are in my predicament."

"Millions?"

"Thousands anyway. Most of them fat, a good number impotent, or frigid. The connection of odor and sex isn't just the stuff of poetry. There's a whole primeval level of awareness people have, even if they kill their senses with cigars and Big Macs. There's a new panic I've been feeling lately about being the last of a species—a homing pigeon that got amnesia. The last ant in one of those plastic ant farms."

"Do you think"—I stroked an imaginary goatee in a moment of missing Pat, who could do a psychiatrist imitation masterfully—"this feeling might be rooted in your mother's death?"

Walter smiled with eyebrows.

"I'm sorry," I said. "I didn't mean to make light."

He took his hand from his chin and grazed the hand quickly

along my face, down to my arm, to my wrist, which he squeezed—
not a terribly seductive gesture, but I hadn't been touched since
Pat left, and when he said again that he missed me I thought I
would self-combust.

"Hear from the Foreign Service?"

The question was startling, not only because it was out of
context but because I was surprised Walter remembered. I hadn't
discussed the Foreign Service with him much. Now I realized
he'd asked because there was nothing else to ask. I had no work,
no family deaths.

"The Foreign Service would clear up a lot for you, wouldn't
it?" he asked.

I crabbed the hand under his wrist toward my cigarettes.
"Too bad it didn't happen, say, on April fifteenth. Then you
wouldn't have to feel guilty—not that you do."

"I do."

"How guilty, as Phil would say, on a scale of one to ten?"

"Twenty, but I'm so guilty about everything—mostly
Margaret—that you haven't got top billing. I've reserved a room
upstairs."

I almost choked on exhaled smoke. "You're kidding."

"Facing the park."

"Tell me you're kidding."

"Just as somewhere quiet to talk."

"Somewhere Judy can't track you down?"

"You know, Alex, it's like playing hooky. Every day I didn't
call you made it harder to call the next day. I've been irresponsi-
ble, I know that, but it's complicated."

"Not at all complicated. You fucked me over."

"There are other ways to sum things up."

"Name three."

"Keep in mind none of this was intentional—"

"Theo was right. Only the conscious can be damned, but no
one claims consciousness. We can therefore no more be condemned
to hell than dogs who shit on the rug."

"Come on, Alex. I'm not trying to get out of having been a prick. I'm just saying we can talk better if you don't act like I did all this to be malicious. It only makes me defensive."

"You know what I hate? I hate this whole school of argument which says you should never accuse someone of doing something wrong, only of having hurt your feelings. You drop a bucket of tar on my head for no reason? Gee, I wonder if I might trouble you to understand how this might hurt me."

Walter grinned. "I've always loved your examples."

"Flattery, my dear—"

"Will get me to point two."

"I thought it'd never happen."

"It almost didn't."

"Do you realize," I gasped, "we're bantering as if nothing has happened?"

"Almost, except it's making me hoarse."

We'd unwittingly slipped into whispers as the room filled.

"If we don't eat lunch or leave," Walter said, "there'll be cops chalking the outlines of our bloody corpses out there. I was sort of looking forward to a hotel room. I get like a kid in them."

"Okay," I said. "But I suppose I'll hate myself for it in a while."

"But only for a while."

"That's the trouble."

When the elevator doors closed and Walter suavely drew a key from his pocket so he could provide a floor number for the operator, it hit me: my need for him was so transparent he hadn't even needed to see me to know I'd agree to this scheme. Walter and I stood in the elevator with our shoulders just touching.

"Hotels are neutral territory," Walter said, peering down the hall on the eighth floor. "They're a clean slate."

"Don't count on it. Bleck!"

I referred to the décor of the room, which was done up from floor to ceiling in hot pink and green, like a bilious Easter egg. "How could this happen?" I asked.

"The sixties," Walter said dolefully as I opened the curtains. "Psychedelic doesn't date well. I've got eyestrain."

"Come over here and look at the nice green park, then."

"First I'm going to piss to the side of the toilet seal."

I hoped he wouldn't be too long. I didn't want enough time for a nervous breakdown. I considered the state of my depression to be not only swallowing my anger and pride but enjoying his company. Though I'd promised myself this wouldn't happen, it did: Walter emerged from the bathroom and put his arms around me from behind, studying the view over my shoulder with his head pressed into my hair and his hands on my hips; I didn't even sound convincing to myself when I said, "We shouldn't."

There may be nothing more heavenly than physical contact with someone whose body you've missed. There's the excitement of the new plus the comfort of the old—a synthesis as intoxicating as the first cigarette after a stab at quitting, with that undulating sense of redemption and damnation. Rittenhouse Square, seen from above, was also familiar and strange. Walter pressed his pelvis into my back and moaned into my neck.

"See the fifth window from the top, second from the left?" Walter pointed to the building across the park as I moaned back. "Jacob's living room. He has a telescope mounted at his window. I spent a good part of my adolescence watching people screw in this hotel, maybe in this very room."

"That's terrible, Walter."

"I loved it. Did a lot for my sexual self-confidence to watch potbellied traveling salesmen huff with their whores."

"Let's close the blinds."

"Know what felt more private to watch than the sex?"

"People with food poisoning in their bathrooms?"

"People in the square. It's a public park but a lot of the time the faces look so withdrawn. My favorites were the single women up at dawn to walk their dogs."

"What were you doing up at dawn?"

"I had a lot of energy as a young man."

Thirty-year-old men always bemoan lost youth ironically to indicate that any boyish flightiness has been shed, so I was surprised to find myself feeling sympathy for Walter, who leaned against the wall in a posture of utterly unironic defeat. I leaned into him, kissed the spot protected by his collarbone, let him draw me closer until I was stereophonically hit by the treble of his deodorant, his sweat underneath like a bass, and the overriding melody that was pure Walter Danner smell. "You're right," I started to say, "smell must account for a lot," but Walter's touch on my hair distracted me with exactly the goose bumps I get when the lights dim and the symphony does its final tune-up, that chill of being plugged almost umbilically into the miracle of artistic creation; and just as at the symphony I always wish that moment of striking up were prolonged, before the first lush contrast between chatter and the true speech of music, my loudest thought now was: *Don't move*, let's stay, stop time, make it last so I don't have to recognize this as AM radio, our feelings false, our love as heavy and fleeting as Chinese food.

Through telepathy or a similar desire, Walter complied.

We stayed in this position by the window long enough to make me happily inarticulate, like a watered house plant.

"Alex?" Walter said.

If that was intended as an inquiry about how I wanted to proceed, my touch must have served as an answer, for very shortly we were undressed in bed—or, rather, on it, kneeling on the hot-pink spread in what struck me as overly bright light for a Western exposure at noon.

The speed with which we'd conformed to my worst predictions by jumping into bed instead of settling anything somehow didn't make me indignant, disgusted, snide, or tearful. We kissed, kneeling. My thoughts simply drained out of my head into my genitals until my brain was buoyant, liquid, and intercourse was a sweet urgency, a miracle I could expect patiently—the ship in the bottle.

Every touch must have promised recognition, return. With

Walter that afternoon I came almost upon penetration, something
that had happened to me before only in dreams, where my pleasure was often a Mobius strip, or concentric. Perhaps I was
imagining it? Sex is in the head anyway, I thought, as the pleasure dissolved into a series of fears: (1) (my eyes were closed, but
I still hid them behind Walter's shoulder, because every thrust
brought too much light from the window, and even through lids
it hurt like a lungful of water) I had no idea how Walter felt and
he had equally little connection with me, for in my surprise I'd
neglected to send up the expected flags of approach and arrival;
(2) I had, for the first time in thirteen years of intercourse, entirely
forgotten birth control. The moans of protest I made, Walter at
once misread as passion, my efforts to disengage as playful fric-
tion—was this, then, how unconscious wishes for pregnancy
were manifested? And I was ovulating. I'd heard the misty-eyed
tales of the moment of conception as one of great awareness. My
record-breaking sexual response heralded my child. In what must
be the sexual-death equivalent of life flashing before the eyes, it
was absolutely clear to me that I was pregnant, that I wouldn't
miscarry, that it was my own fault, that I wanted it to happen. I
surveyed my alternatives. Have the baby and keep it, have the
baby and give it away, don't have the baby, have it or don't with
or without Walter's support—all of this in rhythm to his thrusts;
let my baby play with Judy's baby, don't even tell my baby
about his or her half brother or half sister. It was decidedly the
thought of Judy Gold that wrenched me.

"Birth control," I said. "Stop." But Walter didn't. "Walter!"

I didn't scream. Instead I literally went for the jugular—my
hands and nails to his neck. He didn't have time to react. I was
shocked myself at the speed of the reflex.

He fell off me.

For less than a second I thought I'd killed him.

"Walter!"

He was crying. The shallow breaths he took were from tears,
not suffocation. He sobbed face down like an infant, his mouth
open, his wail high-pitched and tremulous.

"I don't want to lose you," I said; then I just held him, hardly breathing.

Walter stopped crying.

"Your face changes," he whispered after a while.

"What?"

"You look different from every angle. I can't tell you how many times I've looked at you as if I had a camera, wanting to freeze you, just keep you still for long enough to figure out how you really look. But you squirm out. I've never been able to get you in focus."

"Are you saying you can't control me?"

"It was exciting at first. But it isn't just your face. It's everything. There are knobs loose on you. You just don't tune in right."

I sat up. "What are you trying to say?"

"For a while I assumed it was me. It wasn't that I'd been having a great time with women. I'm not very trusting and we're so different. It's not that I wasn't drawn to you. Don't think I didn't want to crack the code."

Walter had sat up and was talking steadily. I had begun to shake, mostly from delayed horror at my own violence. Walter was holding me by the face; the proximity of our faces gave him the malevolent distortion of a fish-eye lens. I said, "You haven't even mentioned Judy."

"Judy doesn't have anything to do with it. It wouldn't have worked out between us anyway."

I pushed his hands away. "You're very good at coming up with these fakey romantic reasons to justify your amoral behavior, aren't you?"

He shifted to sit on the edge of the bed in the posture of a benched athlete from a losing team, so he didn't have to look at me as I talked with growing fury.

"No wonder you're going back to her. You know what your problem is? You have no imagination. You've been with her and inertia keeps you with her. She doesn't upstage you and she's so caught up in being Judy that she doesn't bother you, which is convenient, because you're so caught up in being Walter that you don't have much time for anything else. You're a fucking narcissist. I mean fucking literally. It's your only form of communication. I'm right, aren't I? I'm right."

"You're a little too fond of being right," he said quietly. "That's part of the problem."

"Subjective relativism is a fairy tale told by men in order to justify polygamy."

"You see? How am I supposed to deal with lines like that? I do feel bad to hurt you, but when you say I'm so stupid and mean, what am I supposed to think except how lucky for you that I'm leaving?"

"I could have predicted this. In fact, what's scariest is that I *did* predict this. I knew from the beginning you were a jerk—I didn't need Pat to tell me that. Yet I kept hoping. When you came over with the Doberman, I already knew you hated women, already knew you wouldn't keep up all that romance, and I told you so. You did precisely what I predicted you'd do. Still I was surprised, because I'd already begun to believe my reading of you, and my reading was wrong. I wanted you to be warm and smart and you're not. You're right—I *do* trust my judgments too much. You and Judy deserve each other."

"Fine," he said, standing.

I grabbed his wrist. "Why did you do this to me, then?"

"Let go."

"Why did you meet me and rent this room and put me through this?"

"Stop. That hurts!"

I released his wrist. It was red, with nailprints. Walter whipped on his underpants—our nakedness was an unbearable vulnerability. I began to cry convulsively. Walter just stared for a moment as you'd stare at a falling aerialist. Then he somehow managed to get his arms around me, stroke my back, feather kisses across my eyes to vacuum tears. While his touch was very gentle, the bittersweetness felt practiced. He touched me with the precision that someone who had just taken a Red Cross course would use in administering mouth-to-mouth resuscitation. He hadn't been crying for me. I would never know whether he was crying about his mother's death, or out of guilt for being unfaithful to Judy, or whether his tears had been just fatigue. I would never know if he'd loved me. Maybe he had never loved anyone, including Judy, but I'd never know. I was back where I started, wanting another man I hated: even now I could beg him to take me back, promise to be more good-natured, humbler, a more creative lover, more interested in his work, less critical. But I wasn't going to beg, because I didn't love him either.

For a good while I couldn't stop crying.

He held me until I calmed down.

"Are you okay now?" he soothed.

I nodded.

"I'll be right back," he said.

He went to the bathroom.

I walked to the window and looked numbly at the square. It was too busy. In a second, at least ten people finished bag lunches, looked at their watches, and rose to return to work. The ones who stayed were still, waiting for sunlight to warm their faces. A ghost of me rose to join them. I thought, I've had enough; from now on, I'm going to be tanned and happy and employed. I heard Walter flush the toilet, run tap water to cool his face. The bathroom door was closed, but I could imagine exactly the angle at which he leaned against the sink, examining his pale and tired face in the mirror.

While he hid from me in the bathroom, I dressed more quickly than I've ever dressed in my life, and fled.

FIVE

25

The Foreign Service letter was the only thing in the mail that afternoon, the ominous return address visible through the diamond-shaped cutouts in the box.

The envelope was too thin to be good news.

I had run home from the hotel, breathing through my mouth because my nose was blocked from crying, and I honestly didn't know if I could survive another rejection.

For a moment I felt dizzy the way you do sometimes when you stand up too fast; but the letter was an acceptance.

I was one of three hundred finalists whose names now went on a roster for a year for possible assignment.

I didn't jump up and down and yelp like a game-show contestant, because I couldn't believe that the acceptance wasn't an error.

At thirty, I'd never held down a steady job, none of my jobs had been government-related, and I was collecting unemployment at the time of my application. Naturally I hadn't told the State Department that—I'd said I was completing my dissertation—but it was nonetheless amazing that their computers hadn't uncovered the lie, that my ex-thesis adviser had corroborated the lie when he was asked, as he must have been, to address my character. The only reason I could have snuck past 2,700 other applications was that a computer mixed me up with some other Freed, or a secretary preoccupied with her boyfriend typed the wrong form letter.

I held the letter backward to the hall light to see if it was personally typed or typed by a computer, but I couldn't tell.

Upstairs I dialed the number at the top of the letterhead and asked the woman who answered if she was the signer's secretary. She wasn't. His secretary had quit without notice; the temporary who was filling in until they found a replacement was off Xeroxing, and wouldn't know anything anyway. I explained my situation. The woman suggested that if I got an acceptance I was probably accepted. I pleaded with her to verify. She managed to locate a roster of accepted applicants, and my name was on the list, but when I asked her to find my file just to double-check, she said that the files had left her office for the placement office and if the government had made a mistake, I could sue for psychological damages.

I called the placement office, where I was once again assured of being accepted if I'd got notice, and was told crossly not to get too excited—I didn't have a job; I was just on the roster.

Usually I can't tell what I think of news until I discuss it with Theo and Pat and my parents. Yet I'd just received the most important news of my year and didn't want to tell anyone. For a moment I couldn't remember why I'd applied. If I'm away from home for a night, I miss my coffeepot, my mail; I have to be at the station an hour ahead of time, and even standing at the gate with my ticket in hand, I still worry about missing the train. Emotionally, I wasn't the ideal Foreign Service candidate. I tended to overthink things and get nervous. That tendency was, of course, what I'd hoped to overcome: the Foreign Service might allow me to explore from the security of a government job the turbulent world I'd ignored for so long.

In a way it seemed perfect, but I knew it was too perfect.

Timed as it was, the acceptance could delude me that I was moving. The end of my unemployment compensation and lease were imminent; a Foreign Service assignment was not necessarily imminent. Being on the roster was another holding pattern, a halfway measure that could get me off track as Walter had. Furthermore, there was no compelling evidence that I'd like Foreign Service work even if I got it. The chances were good that this work would not be exotic, certainly not at first. If there was any pattern to my career failures, it was that I'd chosen fields like anthropology and film that promise glamour but deliver mostly drudge work.

There was no point in telling Theo or my parents. They'd say I was tilting at more windmills, and I wasn't sure that they were wrong.

Through a night of little sleep I traced my future: with or without an assignment, in Philadelphia or elsewhere (where?), employed (how?), alone or with a new man (tender, trustworthy), in a spacious new apartment (fireplace, bay, parquet). I thought about the man's sorrow when I broke my lease to leave for distant embassies. And I thought of the woman who interviewed me. Was she responsible for my getting on the roster? If so, why had she pushed my candidacy forward? Perhaps if I could see myself as she saw me, I'd fluctuate less between believing the Foreign Service a blessed foundation and a cursed pipedream. Until six in the morning, my mind weary and fast at once as from too much caffeine, I treadmilled scenarios of tracking her down. I'd catch her at two in the morning with her feet on the desk in her office, with cognac, her books boxed, savoring her last minutes as Assistant Ambassador. She'd remember me at once, greet me warmly: "I enjoyed the challenge of the work, but after a while it got to be too much. I'm getting married next month in San Francisco." "Great! I'll be there for a wedding myself," I'd say. "Let's meet for lunch." Over lunch she would tell me how well the Foreign Service prepared her for other work, would introduce me to her husband's best friend. Or she wouldn't remember me at all. Of course she'd remember. Not only would she remember, she'd arrange for me to be her right-hand woman in South Africa. "I respected your imagination. Don't see much of it in this line of work." "I hope I don't disappoint your faith in me," I'd say. At age ten, I acted out all roles in similar insomniac dramas: rock star, senator. Or she'd gasp and say they'd uncovered my résumé lies during security clearance, my appointment was a mistake, I should never have got past the interview, she was calling Washington before it was too late. I'd sue for psychological damages. "What did you do in '80?" "I sued the United States government."

I fell asleep somehow, woke at noon, and, to avoid more hair-pulling, watched television, although watching TV alone in the day seems more heinous to me than drinking alone before dinner.

On television, James Stewart got sent to Washington as a stoolie by corrupt politicians who mistook his simplicity for stupidity. Jimmy won over not only the Senate but Jean Arthur. "I wonder if it isn't a curse to go through life wised-up like you and me," the cynical working girl mused to a reporter, and moments later she was hooked. So was I. An overgrown Boy Scout's hope and trust might not hurt, at least for a while. But hope and trust gave way to more obsession as soon as the movie ended, and by three in the morning I was in such a state that I *had* to know, right at that moment, why I was chosen and what my likelihood was of getting an appointment.

Luckily, the working day had begun in Senegal, where the biography of the woman who had interviewed me indicated she was employed. The international operator thought there was nothing peculiar about someone wanting the number for the American Embassy in Senegal at three in the morning. I dialed direct.

"American Embassy," a cheerful American voice said, through less static than you'd expect.

Trembling, I asked for Marcia Taylor.

I was told to wait a moment. I waited.

"She isn't here. Is there something I can help you with?"

"When do you expect her?"

"One moment, please."

The call was transferred three times. Three people asked me cheerfully if they could help me. I suggested to the third that the call was long-distance, and asked if I might be told when Marcia Taylor would be in.

"She isn't employed at this embassy anymore," the man on the phone responded.

"Do you know where she is employed?"

"New Caledonia, I think."

"Could you confirm that?"

"I could try."

In the process I was disconnected. It took me a moment to figure out I'd been disconnected, because the noise wasn't the click-and-snow I was used to but an eerie progression of echoes.

I got the number for New Caledonia from an operator just as blasé as the first, dialed, and was once more transferred several times.

"May I ask who's calling?" said someone chewing.

"Alexandra Freed."

"And what is this call in reference to?"

"Are you screening Marcia Taylor's calls or is she not there?"

"The latter."

"When do you expect her?"

"If you'd like to leave your number, I'll have her—"

"Would you?"

"Certainly."

I gave her the number.

Then I sat by the phone for an hour, waiting for a call from New Caledonia.

At five, I enumerated all of the reasons that could delay Marcia Taylor from returning my call.

I began to call New Caledonia again to confirm my number with the secretary before I realized that the number I was dialing wasn't international at all. It was Walter Danner's.

Cut it, Freed, I told myself. *Just hang it up.*

I went for a walk.

Because I've only seen sunrises after all-nighters with too much nicotine and worry, dawns are always run-down rather than refreshing; the empty streets are discarded sets from Grade B movies; and the few mortals who creep around corners with lunch pails, briefcases, or dogs are distorted, furtive. But that morning I walked for a long time under a fuchsia sky, by more dewy greenery than cities usually have. My key was in my pocket; I carried nothing; I let my cold arms inscribe bold arcs. It was good to be outside.

26

Dear Pat,

Why am I writing you a letter? Why aren't you here?

You're probably lucky you're not. Few people make worse company than those going cold turkey off calories, liquor, love, or nicotine (I've quit smoking again). Even our moments of freedom from want are irritating, because we get the gleam of the born-again blind man at Lourdes, when all that's at stake is a Napoleon or a Bloody Mary. You know the symptoms. This time I decided not to inflict them on anyone. Of course silence from such a devoted chronicler of self can be perceived as an even more vociferous demand for attention, but there's nothing I can do about that. I've continued to convalesce mostly alone.

How are you?

Every time I think of you—which is often—a little voice asks, "Why isn't Pat here?" Because she moved. "Why did she move?" Because she got a job. Simple logic: you go from one city to another where there's a job waiting, an apartment, a new neighborhood place to buy milk. How did they know at the environmental coalition that they wanted you in particular? Only one per customer: one public-relations director, one wife, one mother. Everyone in a slot, but in a certain frame of mind it doesn't seem confining so much as magical—so many slots! A zillion rolls of film processed daily of children's birthday parties, days at the beach, and there's someone to linger over each frame.

It was a twisted blessing that you haven't been here to console me, because the isolation has forced me to think. I'm by no means thinking well, but at least I'm not hysterical. Following Theo's lead, I've been walking off the withdrawal. Last night I saw a prostitute so gorgeous I did a double take when I realized she was a man. Two local panhandlers with encrusted bare feet chatted philosophically on a stoop, while a couple pressed against the glass window of a store, talking softly. An attractive man in jogging clothes opened the door of his house to shake out a rug.

As I passed, he stopped shaking and smiled. I've taken to reading the newspaper in the park, hungry for elections, international incidents, inflation. The last time I'd read the paper seriously, people in the Philippines were crucifying themselves, as they do annually, to celebrate the Resurrection. "It used to make me nervous," confessed a man who had been crucified ten times, "but now I'm used to it." Then there's the wonder of the residential streets—the oblique views of intimate dinner parties, of record albums being changed, of a man drinking his glass of milk before bedtime, standing up, the refrigerator door open. Even to witness an old woman rising to shut off a television can seem a satisfying kind of modern drama, a testament to the miracle of even the smallest human act.

Was that what you were trying to tell me when we argued about the Beaumont renovation in the winter? It has taken me this long to admit the possibility. Bliss is a song and dance, but happiness is more like singing to yourself in the shower. Because it doesn't bowl you over, you needn't brace yourself for it with pessimism, with knock-on-woods and *kineboras*, with the dignified caution of the *I Ching* ("The superior man / Takes thought of misfortune / And arms himself against it in advance"). I've begun to try to enjoy the quieter shades of happiness. If the sky has a mauve tint with a little mystery in pink around its edges, it's sometimes enough to sit near a window and an unseasonable breeze.

Sad for someone who has accomplished as little as I have to need to learn not to push accomplishment, but I believe I need to get rid of my delusions of grandeur about what constitutes adequate progress. I may well be in exactly the same place this Halloween as I was last Halloween yet be there more happily. Tripping once in college, I walked around asking everyone, "This is it? This is *it? This?*" Yes, folks, it is. Things do tend to just roll along. When you read biographies of political activists or experimental artists from the sixties, they're always apologetic about having settled down, become middle-class and middle-aged. With the narcissism of youth, they believe they've *invented* aging. But non-baby-boomers have grown older too. After a while everyone seems to smooth out. Maybe my thirtieth birthday will turn out to have been a cause for celebration. Maybe ten years from now I'll be nostalgic for this very moment, even remember Walter Danner fondly.

In a funny way Walter helped me. His mother told me he had a narrow emotional range. I was indignant about that assessment at the time; now I believe it was a rave review that only a mother could have made. Walter was such a prick that I can know the disaster wasn't my fault. I don't regret having done or not done this or that. My only fault was having been attracted to him in the first place. Now I'm thinking about that attraction with more distance, less pain. In a way it's simple: I've wanted a man just like the woman who married dear old Dad. I've chosen men who, like my mother, are domestic, internal, and not very consistently nice to me. That these men are often stereotypically "male" as well as being passive is not contradictory at all—it's just smart camouflage, for me and for them. It's very hard for all of us, I think, to find the middle ground between Scarlett O'Hara and Popeye. Sometimes it feels like that humanness is impossible: there's one side of the fence and the other side of the fence, and in the middle you're sitting on pickets. But one of these days I'll no longer be impaled on the spikes of this particular conflict.

You know what I'd do with a man right now, if I had one? I'd spend a Sunday afternoon with him when it's raining and both of us have books to read. No mail to rush home to and the Sunday papers. I'd skip the paroxysms, go directly to peace. Of course I'm aware that the notion of peace may be another one of our generation's misconceptions. After one has given up on a better world, it's supposed to represent a dignified defeat to stay inside with one's subtle décor, body-building equipment, and gourmet food. I haven't quite yet given up on the world, or on myself. On both fronts, the only real bit of news I have is that I got on the roster for the Foreign Service. I haven't told my family yet because I don't want them to laugh at me. I've had to laugh at myself, to make this much of what is really just a job possibility, tracking down one of the interviewers in New Caledonia to ask her how or why I'd been chosen. By the time she returned my call yesterday, almost two weeks later, she only

confirmed what my diligent auto-brainwashing has begun to
help me believe: yes she voted for me, if she recalled, but I was
certainly qualified; I'd probably enjoy the work, at least for a
while, but there are no guarantees on an appointment; I'd better
not stake everything on getting one.

"When change is to be made," the *I Ching* says, "there are
two mistakes to be avoided. One lies in excessive haste and
ruthlessness, which bring disaster. The other lies in excessive
hesitation and conservatism, which are also dangerous." So I'm
trying to be balanced, though I should confess I think about the
Foreign Service far too much. As I walk, I find myself adopting
the buoyant detachment of the traveler who loves Philadelphia
as only someone who has a prospect of leaving could love it.
How sorely I've underestimated its tree-lined historical streets,
its ample parks, its friendly pace; how much I'd miss knowing my shoemaker, my Armenian tailor, the Pine Street phar-
macist and grocer! I soak up the skyline, the warmth of the cobble-
stone.

I miss you. I want to know how Boston is, how Nessie is
adjusting, how you're enjoying the job. I want to sit down and
have coffee with you from one of your clean white mugs.

Are you sure you don't want to give two weeks' notice and
travel around the world with me?

Love,

Alex

27

Better to have gnawing self-doubt about the Foreign Service than
about Walter Danner, whom I had by no means forgotten. Phan-
tom-limb recollections of his touch could make me ache enough
that I had to remind myself: You are recovering from a loss. It is
not an interesting loss but the recovery cannot be automatic.

Walking on Delancey Street on the way from buying Ellen

Mayer's birthday gift, I met Walter, Jacob Danner, and Judy Gold head-on.

"Alex?" Walter said.

I'd seen them coming, but hadn't registered them as more than attractive Philadelphians strolling center city at lunchtime. As we drew closer, I recognized Walter and saw that he and Judy were holding hands lightly, as if fingertips were all the contact they could take in the heat.

Both Walter and his father leaned forward from the waist, as if ready to bow. Both tucked in their chins and looked up, the expression at once brazen and abashed, the steadiness of their eyes announcing irrepressible interest. The same ruffled hair, Jacob's without the red; the same self-effacing shoulders. No wonder Margaret had been so down on her son—he looked far too much like Jacob Danner. They both wore suits. Walter's was a cream-colored linen, and he looked particularly compelling.

"Have you met Jacob?" Walter asked, pumping his father's shoulders in a way that indicated recent, and still uneasy, reconciliation.

Judy was visibly pregnant in a puffiness of the face and limbs. Jacob shook my hand. The very gallantry of his gesture indicated complete indifference. Walter may not have even mentioned me.

"What's the occasion?" I asked.

"My birthday," Walter admitted.

"Thirty-two!" I was almost tempted to pull out the wrapped present in my shopping bag. The realization that Walter would not have much personal use for a maternity dress made me smile. "I forgot," I said.

"He wishes he had," Judy said. "How are you?"

"Fine. You?" I asked, nodding toward her stomach.

"I'm going to be a blimp," she said, making a frog's face.

"How was Pat's interview for the job?" Walter asked, scratching his head in the comic-book way he always had when embarrassed—he'd got a new watchband. Until even a week before, I might have still found the inappropriateness of the question endearing. I realized he was staging a first encounter with me for

Judy's benefit. I deliberated whether to mention the Barclay or to play along. I played along.

"Fine. She got the job. She's in Boston."

"What did she do with the house?"

"Stacey Easterlin is buying it with an inheritance from a rich aunt. How's the old olfactory?"

Now it was Walter's turn to double-take. I watched him calibrate how to answer a question he'd already answered without betraying our Barclay meeting to Judy; I watched Judy squint, trying to spy whether Walter and I had been in touch.

"Almost gone," Walter said uncomfortably. "The LSD. Temporary."

"Nevertheless you both look quite fit. Are you settling in, Judy? How does it feel to be back?"

I was still smiling. Judy grimaced in an attempt to smile back. "Fine."

That my feigned calm was convincing enough to cause discomfort invigorated me, despite the strange fact that most of the intensity—albeit low voltage—was presently between Judy and me, not Walter and me.

So convincing was it that Jacob asked: "Do you and Judy know each other from school?"

"School of hard knocks," Judy said.

That flipness so distorted her face that I knew she was trying to tell me something. Then she looked as if she wanted to hug me. She looked a great deal sorrier about losing me than Walter did—a great deal sorrier about something.

We chatted a bit longer until Judy suggested that they'd be late for their lunch reservations, and we walked in opposite directions—my posture erect, no doubt, from pride at having endured the encounter.

A hand on my shoulder stopped me. It was Judy. Walter and Jacob were talking, arms crossed, farther down the block.

"Someday," Judy said, "I want to explain."

"Aw, that's okay."

"Please don't be mad at me."

"I wouldn't worry about it too much."

"Will you stay in touch?"

I grinned. "I doubt it."

"Why not?"

"I think you're an asshole."

We stood for a minute, considering that.

"I almost forgot," Judy said. "Give this to Theo, okay?"

She had to twist off the engagement ring, which was tight on her swelling finger.

"Tell him that I'll always care for him," she added, "and that I'm sorry."

She made a little whine like the one I'd heard on my parents' couch in April, and hugged me, quite hard. I was so startled that I hugged her back.

Walter was watching us. Before Judy disengaged, Walter widened his arms into a majestic arc, genuflected, blew a kiss, then made a gun with his forefinger and thumb and shot the gun into his mouth. I shrugged. He shrugged back.

"Bye," Judy said, her eyes moist, her facial muscles quivering with a surfeit of genuine emotion so large and mysterious that I had to think Walter was right about one thing, at least—I didn't know everything.

Jacob hadn't witnessed this exchange. He was concentrating on a woman up the street—a tall, pretty blonde who was hugely pregnant. Ellen Mayer, waddling back to her office. I laughed and waved. The diamond engagement ring flashed on my hand.

"Wasn't that Walter?" she said.

"Yes. What a coincidence. Happy birthday."

I gave her the present. She opened it, laughed with pleasure, hugged me. "My God," she said, noticing the ring, "are you and Walter engaged?"

"Lord, I haven't talked to you in a while, have I? We broke up, sort of, the night his Doberman got run over and his mother died. The Doberman was a gift from Walter the day we started seeing each other. It was his, because I'd given it back, but it was also ours in some sense, and its death so perfectly coincided with the death of the relationship that the symmetry was a tad harrowing. If it weren't for the Foreign Service acceptance, I'd probably be institutionalized. The woman who was just hugging me is Walter's ex-wife. They got back together after she managed to get pregnant by him. I'm surrounded by pregnant women. For a while she was engaged to my brother, but the kid isn't his. Theo's, that is. The ring is Theo's. She just returned it to me, that's all."

"Hmm," Ellen said.

"Sorry you asked?"

"Sounds like you've been hanging out with a bad crowd. Want to get coffee and talk about it?"

"You know, now that you mention it, I think I would. I think they're creeps. I think I'd like to talk about how awful they are and how wonderful I feel to be rid of them. Sound interesting?"

"More interesting than going back to the office. Shall we go to your place or duck in somewhere before it starts to rain?"

"It's not going to rain."

We studied the sky. I thought about the rendition of my relationship with Walter as I just gave it to Ellen, tight as a synopsis in *TV Guide*, and I realized I was just as happy to leave out my reunion with Walter at the Barclay Hotel and our strange little communication, just now, over Judy's head. Now I risked remembering things in this distorted form forever. But maybe that wasn't such a bad thing. Maybe it was important to forget the humiliation and the stomachaches and even the blankness, because then you could love again with less fear, just as a woman who forgets the pain of labor is more likely to have more children.

It started to rain.

We ducked under an awning and Ellen ran around the corner to her car for an umbrella, her half-boxed maternity dress trailing ribbon. By the time she returned, clutching her stomach, the rain was a squall and the umbrella hardly helped because passing cars splattered us no matter how far from the curb we walked. We walked laughing, wet, our arms linked.

28

"Your father and I would like to know what is this nonsense about the Foreign Service."

It was May 19th and I was out of breath, having just taken the steps with a pile of résumés. The slightly raised letters seemed still damp on the craggy surface of the bond.

Pat had told Theo, and Theo had told my parents.

"Well, I've gotten my résumé ready for dissemination to anyone and everyone, since I've decided to renew my lease on Waverly while awaiting an assignment. If I'm appointed, fine; if not, then I'll go on."

"With what?"

"We'll see."

"And why weren't we told?"

"I guess I assumed you wouldn't approve. First I needed to think it through."

"You and your brother." Connie sighed. "About everything you manage to act like you're sneaking out in the backyard to smoke dope. I keep thinking any second my children are going to grow up. Not for my sake. Believe me, the so-called empty nest is big and clean and quiet. How are you ever going to be happy?"

"A question to be asked."

"And your brother! He's seeing the Pat you knew with the daughter."

"Oh, Mom."

"He sure likes these surrogate mothers. What's he going to do with another older woman—and this one with a child!"

"What accounts for this latest paranoia?"

"I suppose I should pray he'll play this out, then marry some normal person his own age."

"Pat is more normal than any of us. It could be an old-fashioned marriage like yours and Dad's—but the heart'd be smart and the brain warm."

"Don't tease me."

"But, Mother, they're not even dating."

"He hasn't told you they're dating?"

"They've had drinks as friends."

"If you can think back to his last affair of the heart, I daresay the fact he hasn't told you is a bad sign. Well, your father wants to talk to you now."

"Is he going to nag me about the Foreign Service?"

"This is your father," Phil said, in his radio-announcer voice, and launched right into an attack on the inanity of my counting on, or wanting, an assignment. I listened to his reasons, all of which I'd identified myself, and told him rotely I'd think it over.

"What's to think about? The Foreign Service is an angel on a pinhead."

"Kind of hard to visualize, Dad."

My father was deciding on consulting work himself. While he told me about his offers, I tried not to be preoccupied with Theo, who hadn't called about the Foreign Service; he'd just passed the news to my parents. In the next two days, I tried to call him at home and at his office, but I couldn't reach him, and when I couldn't reach Pat either I didn't want to call either of them anymore. After all, why hadn't they called me with concern or congratulations?

With great energy I began to spread résumés around town— three PR agencies, a noise-control institute, TV and radio stations, an environmental consulting group, two newspapers. In each office I felt the happy detachment I'd basked in during my Foreign Service tests. People drinking coffee with their feet up; people as many-limbed as Hindu deities with phones balanced under their chins as they shuffled papers; the little plants that grow under fluorescents; the staplers and tape dispensers with names strapped to them—all the trivia and territoriality of working life—struck me as instantly recognizable native customs would strike a tourist. Each office was as claustrophobic as the tiniest medieval hamlet, and to me as quaint, for I could leave—I always had.

Despite my confidence, no one seemed to need me immediately. Just as I'd begun to worry, I got a telegram from Theo announcing that he and Pat would be in Philadelphia that evening to settle with Stacey Easterlin on the house, get things to Boston, and retrieve the Fiat.

He didn't say how long they intended to stay, whether or not Nessie was coming. The assumption was that I'd be utterly free to contort around their busy schedules. Houseguests couldn't have been more badly timed; I was finally getting mobilized, and I would have been more resentful if there wasn't so much simple joy in seeing them.

They were fully themselves: tired Theo (he'd driven most of the way) in his halo of smoke; bright and beautiful Pat, the most iridescent woman I know; Nessie with a premature look of impending sexuality as she moved her hair behind her oversized ears. Pat apologized immediately for barging in. With a smile and a hand on my arm, she managed to communicate both concern for me and confidence in me—my brain must have been mostly functioning, she seemed to say as she looked around my apartment, if I could have got dinner ready and the table set on such short notice. They were starved. As they sat down gratefully to eat, Pat picked out shrimp and scallops from Nessie's gumbo and talked (again, again) about real estate.

Pat wanted to buy a deserted Catholic boys' academy outside of Cambridge. It had an acre with 200 feet of frontage, 11,000 square feet each on four floors, a gym, an athletic office, a periodical room, a media center, a mess hall, a chapel, and 11,000 square feet of parking lot.

"I want the chapel," she said. "Even you'd die over the ceiling in there, Alex. The altar would make a great kitchen. A lot of the rooms have linoleum but under the linoleum is maple this thick, folks." She gestured, licked her lips, as if describing a steak.

"I want the parking lot," Theo said. "You can make a nice

little income off a parking lot. These days when I think about leaving academe, it's a toss-up between opening a parking lot and a fast-food chicken franchise."

"How much?" I asked.

"One million one hundred and fifty thousand," Pat admitted. "Even in Boston with good financing, it's no bargain. You know how they arrived at that figure?" She squinted at the air near the overhead and pounced up to swat an imaginary fly. "It's completely chimerical. I'm sure they'll come down. We'll have to see what a condo conversion would cost us per unit."

"Who's this 'we' who has one million one hundred and fifty thousand dollars?"

"Some hypothetical investors who need depreciation for tax purposes. As for my share, the Packard and the house on Beaumont ought to do it."

"You'd sell the car?"

"I hate it," Nessie scoffed.

"It gets six miles per gallon," Pat said. "It also gets stared at a lot. I feel like I need my hair done to pick up Ness at ballet."

"Not to mention license plates that say SUGAR or TIGER," Theo added.

I shook my head. "To think that poor cancerous old man helped fund you in these shenanigans."

"We write," Pat smiled. "He's lonely. I've been bribing Ness to write to him too."

Ness made a face.

"Touching," I said. "Maybe he'll leave you everything."

"He's wiped out."

"See? Why accumulate so much junk when there's no square footage in the afterlife?"

"That's the spirit," Theo said. "Get them scriptures down so you can indoctrinate your natives."

It was Theo's first reference to my Foreign Service acceptance. I thought he would elaborate when he blew out a ponderous cloud of after-dinner smoke, but what he announced was that he too planned to make an investment in the condo conversion of the boys' academy. I waited for Pat to scowl at him—after all, the idea of Theo affording a house in Boston on his salary was only slightly less ludicrous than the idea of my affording one on unemployment—but Pat's stage was usurped by Nessie, who had encountered a scallop, spat it out in my direction noisily and began to gag and bawl.

I got up to wash my arm.

"Vanessa," Theo said, taking the red-faced child into his lap. "If the Red Guards collect four wheelbarrows of night soil in the morning to serve the people of the commune and five wheelbarrows of night soil in the evening to serve the people of the commune, then how many wheelbarrows of night soil have they collected in all?"

"Nine."

"Good! Now a group of Red Guards raises four black pigs, then they raise six more. How many pigs have they raised in all?"

"Ten."

"Excellent! Now would you like some ice cream if Alex has some?"

Pat rushed up to get her some, but despite the sudden motion I caught her looking at my brother with the wonder and joy you'd reserve for the first redbreast of spring—a look of such exultant trust in him, such respect and pleasure, that even when she checked herself and gave equal time to smiling at me and her daughter, her love for my brother was muskily omnipresent. She said she was exhausted. It wasn't the drive. Pat hadn't got any sleep because she'd spent the night with my brother. It had probably been the first time they'd slept together too, after a period of unspoken and escalating fondness; they'd probably had a merry time discussing whether or not to tell me (in the car, with Nessie asleep); they were trying now not to look at each other too often, too intently.

Maybe I was as paranoid as my mother, but I doubted it. Pat and Theo!

Of course they wouldn't tell me. Even if they'd had time,

they would assume I'd be hurt, angry, jealous, and they were right. While Pat got Nessie ready for bed, Theo talked gravely of Pat's plans, which were basically to sell the house to Stacey and ship belongings to storage in Boston. I had a week of unemployment compensation left and no money to pay my June rent, which had gone up. (I was quite broke, my I.R.S. and robbery compensation checks having been poured into a ticket to San Francisco for Jessica's wedding and into debts.) I could therefore further resent Pat's logistics being so central. If the new Alex Freed could calmly entertain company amidst so many unknown variables, at least someone should notice. Pat and Theo didn't. Nessie, emerging from my bedroom in pajamas, rushed to tackle Theo's legs. Shortly thereafter, when I saw Theo's hand on the small of Pat's back, I had a lightness of head and of gut, both gleeful and dismayed, such as champagne might produce. Pat and Theo! *So you've gotten to know each other, after all,* was what came to mind, but before it got anywhere near my lips, Pat squinted to the left of me as if I were the small print on an eye chart and congratulated me on the Foreign Service.

"Thanks," I said.

"The Foreign Service," Theo groaned, slapping his forehead.

"No forehead-slapping permitted on the subject of my new vocation," I warned. "Why are you so set against this appointment?"

Pat did an imitation of buttoning her seat belt for a roller-coaster ride—troublemaker! Theo cocked his head. "I'm not against it," he said. "I just can't believe you got it. You don't know jack about government or politics."

"Evidently I knew enough to pass the test. What I don't know I can learn. Maybe my newness will make me particularly conscientious and energetic. Maybe I'll broaden my horizons."

"Your horizons couldn't be any broader. The only trouble with your horizons is that the paint on them is spread so thin. If you walked to the edge of your horizons, you'd fall off. So a year from now you'll know a little about Foreign Service bureaucracy, a little about the street layout of some malnutrition-laden nation.

You'll have screwed a native or two and will know some new recipes. Where'll that get you?"

"Same place China will get you—to wit, a year older."

Pat steered the conversation back to lightness: "*I'm* learning politics. We all come to the office each morning to be reminded that the air's going to kill us if the bomb doesn't get us first and there's little we can do about it. Makes me feel a bit schizophrenic: I'm paid to ring the environmental doomsday bells; then in my spare time I invest in real estate. Meanwhile there's so much backbiting and competition at the office that they'd personally drop the bomb, if they got personal credit for saving us from it. You know, I'm so tired that everything I say I'm reading off a sort of dot-point matrix in the back of my eyes. Know what? When I said 'matrix,' I saw the word, then I saw a wedge of Brie that looked like the piece economists take out of the National Budget pie."

"You *are* tired," Theo said.

"I get a Scrabble board when I'm tired," I said.

"When I'm exhausted," Theo said, "my sentences are justified like newspaper columns with a lot of space in between the words."

Nessie wailed, curtailing conversation. Pat got up to tuck her in, promising to remove her from my bed later. I turned to Theo. "Well?"

"Well what?"

"What's going on with you and Pat?"

"You mean our Groucho Marx nose-and-eyebrow sets didn't disguise it?" he asked, eyes lit.

"No, and Mom has already figured it out."

"No shit!"

"What are you hiding?"

"There hasn't been anything to tell yet," Theo whispered. "It just started. But what can happen? I leave for China in August. I'd love to invite her, but there's no context yet. Besides, there's a false clarity things get when there's an end in sight—what if we're only getting along so well because knowing I'll leave in

August removes the threat? I don't know what to do. We planned to come down here as friends before we slept together. Then we did, and still came down. We didn't even discuss it. Isn't that odd?"

Pat entered and announced that she'd disposed of Nessie and would love a shower. I got her towels.

Theo spoke, blushing, as soon as we heard water: "I feel so *stupid* nowadays. After Judy left, I was surprised my bladder still worked. How did I get involved so fast? Pat's so sweet, so pulled-together—then again, Judy seemed that way too."

"How involved are you?"

"Well, every time I see a couple walking arm in arm, I puff up. I feel this bond with them, almost a complicity."

"Theo, just answer my question."

"I don't know. I can't read her yet. Then there's Vanessa. I don't know what to make of *her* at all."

"She's a kid, which means she's got anyone's complexity, minus the vocabulary and the pubic hair."

"I mean I don't know how she figures into Pat's decisions."

"Heavily. It's probably easier to start your own family from scratch."

"I love the kid," Theo said.

Then he shrugged, gave the lover's puzzled sigh.

If I asked Pat how things were going, she'd answer in English, without the teenaged mysticism. I was on the floor, Theo slouched in the reading chair with his after-dinner brandy balanced on his stomach, his philosophical cigarette held in fingers that also tapped on his knee; his distant smile was exactly Phil Freed's. The whole posture, in fact, was my father's TV mode, with cigarette replacing cigar—were there dormant posture genes?

Shortly thereafter, when Pat came in and leaned against the radiator in my robe, drying her hair with a towel, Theo sat up straight and put his hands between his knees, told her she looked good, which she did, innocent and rosy as a child. The innocence was at least partly feigned. Theo had clearly never seen her post-shower before, and by picking this moment to treat him to the sight, Pat at once defused and detonated his desire: she could be casual, among friends, but since he couldn't touch, there was the thrill of abstinence.

Courtship suddenly seemed an absurd ritual that I'd been spared. Of course I knew I was jealous—of my brother's attention, my best friend's attention, love in general. Nevertheless I wasn't entirely sorry when Pat inquired about sleeping arrangements. I suggested that she and Nessie keep the bed; Theo and I would play with the remaining permutations of floor and sofa bed. Pat smiled with some relief, I imagine, about stalling the announcement of their new relationship. Theo scowled as if I were more oppressive than Connie Freed.

In fact, I felt like my mother. Forget passion; I wanted to play Scrabble.

I could also have used a dose of family feeling.

"Want to play Scrabble?" Theo asked when Pat went to bed.

"You read my mind."

We got more cognac and the Scrabble board. Theo was first. He stared at his letters for a long time. I nudged him.

"Sorry," he said. "I was thinking about Pat."

He put down a seven-letter word.

"Big shot," I said, putting down a word worth almost as much.

We played Scrabble for a while, without talking, heatedly.

"You know," Theo mused during my turn, "love and peace have very little in common. Love is, and always has been, death-defying. It's the flying trapeze—there's usually a net under you if you do it wrong."

"Are you trying to ruin my concentration?"

"I'm hoping that Pat'll come to China with me."

"Don't hold your breath."

"She probably won't go, it's true, but why not try?"

I shook my head. "Ellen Mayer told me the other day that two people don't go further than one. The myth is that one person goes to the bank and the other to the laundromat, so both have half as much to do, but in fact there's double to do—twice as much necessary cash, double the laundry, plus all of the phone calls to negotiate who gets the car and when you'll convene—"

"Is your point that I'm afraid to go to China alone? Rest assured that neither Pat nor I needs someone to take care of us. If anything, both of us are too suspicious of security. We view it as an opiate. That fear can be excessive. We've earned security. We deserve excitement. Why can't we have both?"

"Theo, I truly hope you get both, as soon as possible, but this soon is premature, as you must know yourself."

"How soon isn't premature?"

"When you understand the order of the relationship, its nuts and bolts. No matter how confusing things can seem, I still have faith that behind all the calico and stripe and polka dot of a life, there's an inexorable sense—not only rhyme and reason but an eternal sestina in iambic pentameter."

"You've always been a great Baptist believer in Order," Theo said.

"That's true. Hindsight does wonders for a cost-benefit study. Now that Walter's through, I have a better idea of what *might* work for me in a relationship. Only when something's settled do you get the bird's-eye view, get to see your present situation as a little acre, lighter or darker than the surrounding land."

Theo shifted in such a way that he upset the Scrabble board.

"It wasn't a good game anyway," I said.

"In fact"—he lit a cigarette and offered me one (I shook my head, wondering when he would notice my abstinence)—"the argument you just presented is an excellent case for jumping right in. Sometimes you've got to act on faith."

"You once made me promise I'd remind you of Judy Gold if you ever got swoony like this again."

"How long do I have to mourn that failure?"

"Long enough to figure out why it happened. Judy may have set the trap, but you took the bait."

"It's hard for me to take love and sanity lessons from someone whose life is in such shambles."

I could only gasp and say, "My daddy could beat up your

daddy, if it weren't the same daddy. Shall we compare my admittedly screwy relationship with Walter to yours with his charming ex-wife?"

"Screwy's right. Why do the people who hop into bed with anyone become the most self-righteous proponents of traditional courtship and marriage?"

That piece of viciousness actually made Theo look cross-eyed. I told him so. He leaned toward me with a minister's soulfulness—no, a teacher's. He'd shifted into Harvard gear. "Look, I know you think you're getting calmer and less morose, and you don't feel I've given you credit. You're blue in the face waiting for someone to compliment you—well, maybe I have been niggardly with the praise. Maybe I've gotten so used to you crying wolf on self-transformations that I'm not noticing the real ones. But if that's the case, then you have to admit Pat and I can be whole with each other in a way neither of us could be with you, and it isn't just sex. You've known us too long. Newness isn't just an airbrush. New knowledge can be sharper—more flattering but also truer. Things often just happen fast."

"Indeed, you and women are so consistently *Sturm und Drang* that I'm puzzled I'm the one who got the reputation for bed-hopping and hysteria. Don't get me wrong. I find your optimism about love quite endearing; unusual for a man to be so open about it. But please recognize the idealism for what it is and try to temper it with a little self-awareness. What would you say if a month after Walter I was madly in love with someone else?"

"During these months of 'pouting,' during all the months I was seeing Judy, I worked. My so-called idealism isn't my base. There's no threat of my crumbling if a relationship doesn't work out. I'd probably be thrilled if you showed the resilience to start dating again."

"In me it was repetition compulsion and cowardice. In you it's resilience?"

"I owe you an apology. I'm so excited about Pat that I've shoved your problems aside. What are you going to do with your life?"

"Why is it so crucial? I've done fine up to now as a failure."

"Alex—"

"You're not being fair to me about the Foreign Service. Half the time I'm an idiot and half the time I'm a savant, but never do you treat me like a nice, loving person with assets and deficits and some time to whittle away at before I die—more time, now that I've quit smoking."

"Not again."

"And why is my taking the chance on the Foreign Service any more absurd than your taking a chance on Pat? If all I've done is pace, then the Foreign Service is a giant step. It'd be getting *out* of myself, wouldn't it? How could attending to the world *not* be an antidote to so many years of self-involvement?"

Theo leered. "The born-again me-decader defending the rights of baby seals?"

"Things are interesting out there, Theo."

"I'm sorry," Theo said, dropping the match from yet another cigarette into an ashtray now so brimming that the match fell off onto the couch—I swooped for it, examined the damage (none). "Alex, there are so many roles and vocations that'd suit you. You'd make a great lawyer. You'd also make a great shrink. You have fire and wit—"

"You condescending bastard."

"But the Foreign Service? It's a fantasy—Clare Booth Luce among adoring natives. You need discipline for that work, and tact—neither your strong suit. Mostly you need a political sensibility, which is utterly alien to the way you think—"

"Gee, Professor, it would be futile for me to compete with you in that area, wouldn't it?"

Theo rolled his eyes and began to put away the Scrabble set.

"You're the politician, right, Theo? You who spin this China shit off the top of your crazy-quilt brain in your finest Ivy League pig Latin with no regard at all for the realities of Chinese politics or Chinese life—Christ, you talk about the Chinese as if they're adorable industrious little China dolls from 'It's a Small Small World'! That's 'political sensibility'?"

"That's cheap fighting," Theo said quietly.

"And you have the nerve to tell me I'm incapable of a goddamn government job? I'm overdoing the thrill of the job and I'm not smart enough for it all at once? Well, fuck you, Theo."

"Fuck you too. Once again I overestimated you. You're so jealous of Pat you can't see straight."

"Jealous? Not at all. I just think she could do better."

"How you have any friends at all is beyond me."

"Yeah? I haven't heard you complain about using me as a matchmaker. I don't see you introducing me to any eligible young men in Harvard Square."

"Who could stand you?"

"Who could stand *you*, you skinny, pompous little prick?"

We were screaming. The decibel level must have been high for some time, because our bodies had seen to it that we rose, to make room for expanding diaphragms. We stood, red-faced, with balled fists, on either side of a half-assembled Scrabble set. A piece of Theo's hair had unfurled from the rest of his hair at the angle of a unicorn's horn, casting a shadow down his face; when he looked up at it, he got an expression of saintly terror and martyrdom. At the same moment, I was having hair problems of my own. A piece was in my mouth. Theo tried to blow the hair off his forehead while I tried to spit the hair out of my mouth. Neither of us, for some reason, thought to enlist hands. We spluttered, loathing each other.

Pat was there in her nightgown when Theo and I regained enough composure to understand that we were thrashing about openmouthed like landed fish, to realize how poisonously we'd been going at it, and to react with the kind of laughter that's hard to stop. We collapsed on the floor, scattering the Scrabble tiles, upsetting the ashtray, clutching our bellies. Then we stopped laughing and just stared at each other, mystified.

Pat was back to her radiator. It was near the open window and she shivered from the bit of breeze.

"Did we keep you awake?" Theo asked.

In her translucent gown, wearily rubbing eyes and face, Pat

was consummately a parent. In the past, Theo's and my bedtime often crossed paths with my parents' rising time, and since it saddened them to see us up ("Do you plan to sleep all day?"), we tried to be as quiet as Jews hiding from the Gestapo. We would part the curtains and look at Phil, in his suit—redolent, no doubt, of aftershave—watching the dog sniff in the dew while he awaited his car pool. When Phil drove off, already telling a wide-gestured anecdote to his colleagues, Connie would do the breakfast dishes, come upstairs to dress, and, before setting off to help a friend or charity with something pressing, peek in on us. We'd pretend to be asleep, snoring mouths open, sheets tangled on the twin beds in the room we shared now that my childhood bedroom was a den. Falling asleep to the motor of Connie's car, it was almost as if we protected our humanity by sleeping through the business day. But now Pat's glowing adulthood, her rich responsibility, put us to shame.

Theo was red—from laughter, from embarrassment. He shuffled for a second, furiously avoiding eye contact, then squatted and replaced the butts in the ashtray, scooping off the rug what ashes he could get with the edge of a matchbook.

Pat, I could see, wasn't angry at all. She was amused. "So?" she said. "Who won?"

Theo stood. "Who do you think won?"

"The truth?" Pat said. "It doesn't surprise me to see you at each other's throats. I'm amazed you get along as well as you do. You both expect everyone to have the same feelings as you at exactly the same moment. You can get huffy or morose in reaction to what's often just somebody else having a different mood. You have contests to see who can be more self-controlled, less childish, but the very fact you have the contests belies the control. I guess it's because your family is so close-knit that you expect everyone to be like you. I have six brothers, and I couldn't have a discussion with one of them for more than six minutes on a topic more personal than inflation rates or the N.B.A. playoffs. A six-minute conversation on the weather would represent commingling of souls with some of them. One or two are sort

of like Martians. Well, not Martians. Catholics. One has eight
kids—"

"Ed?" I asked.

"Close. Fred. Ed's the reformed alcoholic now enrolled in a
seminary. The only thing we have in common is dirty-blond
hair. So if I'm in the mood for love with someone who's staring
into space with gritted teeth, I don't necessarily take it personally."

"That's why we love you," I said. "You're so grown-up and
self-contained and so able to bestow what is called 'space.' "

"Not really," Pat said. "The extreme side of being able to let
things slide is that they often slide right into the pits. They can
also get quite dull. Dull and muddy. That's why, of course, I
admire *you*. Your family has made you childish and demanding
at times, but it has also given you an appreciation of engagement.
You're both plugged in most of the time. Ain't nothing wrong
with giving off light."

"Except in the summer you're likely to attract flies," Theo
said.

Pat drooled and lolled her head.

"Sorry," Theo said. "The other thing our family has given
us—this is what we have to deal with, Alex—is a yearning for
serenity. We keep thinking that on the other side of the rainbow
there's somewhere dark and cool and soothing where we don't
have to perform anymore, don't have to worry anymore."

"No such country," Pat said.

"You live in it," Theo told her.

"Just looks like that to a tourist."

Theo took Pat's hand. "I'm sorry, Alex," he said.

"I'm sorry too."

"Good," Pat said. "Can I go to sleep, then?"

"The Foreign Service is fine," Theo said. "I approve of you
being in the Foreign Service."

"And I approve of you seeing Pat. Tell me how it happened,"
I said, sitting on her opposite side and taking her free hand.

"Do I have to?" Now it was Pat's turn to blush.

"Not yet," Theo said. "I'm out of cigarettes. Alex, come with me to get some?"

"Sure," I said.

"Wait up a little, Pat, and we'll tuck you in."

But when we got back from our silent walk, Pat was already asleep, sprawled face-down on the living-room floor. We looked at her lovingly for a minute, as parents look at a sleeping child. Then we put her into my bed next to Nessie, turned out the light, tiptoed into the kitchen, and pulled out the chairs to sit down for what was probably going to be a long night. We had a great deal to discuss.

29

On the floor of the living room with a throbbing coccyx and (martyred hostess) the worst pillow in the house, I listened to Theo's smoker's snore and tried to sedate myself by counting the passing cars whose headlights leaked through the Venetian blinds; but at that hour cars passed sporadically, so I counted time and money. Eight days left on unemployment and fifty-nine dollars in the bank: it was a simple equation. My insomnia got worse and the bottom line got clearer: I had to get a job at once. Right away I had to do anything at all, however deplorable: waitress, type, wear pasties and go-go dance. Anything. *Tomorrow.*

Even thus resolved, my stomach for further job-hunting was as weak as the light in the living room, by which I could just make out my microscope on the bookshelf—I could sell it. For a month's reprieve I could sell the microscope, the bike Walter had given me for my birthday (I had to stop thinking of it as Walter's gift), Walter's aunt's used sable coat, my several first editions, my cello, my gold bracelet—no. My life was depleted enough after the robbery without making a flea market of it. I could borrow money from Theo, Pat—no. I could call Zoll. Margaret Danner had said he badly needed a ghost writer. Zoll and I would talk of Margaret, kiss—no. *First thing in the morning.*

Either that, or I would kill myself. Suicide entered precisely as it always did—death itself bloodless, *pro forma*, the prelude to the child's revenge fantasies: how terribly sorry everyone would be! Suicide was out of the question. I didn't want to give Theo or my parents the satisfaction of seeing me defeated. If revenge were operative, better I should die in a junta coup in the Foreign Service, or in an old folks' home with the healthiest lungs in the family.

It was the suicide fantasies that reminded me of hospitals. Of course! Philadelphia has the second densest doctor-patient ratio in the country; some of its grant-rich research labs had to be illiterate. I'd floss my teeth and hit the hospitals with my résumés.

Pat's movers would come in the morning. Her closing was in the afternoon. I'd be called upon to lift boxes, keep Nessie entertained. The day would be hectic, especially since Pat and Theo insisted on leaving that night. Pat had a presentation for work first thing Monday morning that she had to prepare, Theo a heap of papers to grade and a dinner party at his chairman's house Saturday night; they both needed a day at home to unwind.

Well, screw them.

I couldn't help it. It didn't seem fair. They had work and money and love. I had nothing. They descended on me with suitcases and dolls and bags of crap, dumped them on my dining-room floor, ate my food, criticized me. I simply couldn't help tomorrow. They'd call me selfish and I'd probably cringe, believing them.

I'd leave Pat and Theo an apologetic note and sneak out before they woke up.

Determined to sleep, I suffered through the dream in which Walter and Judy are happy, ignoring me; my abandonment is so complete that I can justify smoking again. I smoke greedily.

Judy's hair in this dream is long. She wears it pulled back tight; her legs are long and tan.

> Dear Pat and Theo: I have some posthaste errands. Spare key to your left; Cocoa Puffs for Nessie to your right; brioches, eggs, jam, etc., in the fridge and I'll catch you later here or on Beaumont with hands over my face in remorse for having taken the Fiat hostage. Hugs & Kisses, Alexandra

I washed myself cautiously in the kitchen sink—that was a challenge. I felt surprisingly refreshed, not to mention proud that I'd got my clothes from the bedroom without waking Pat or Nessie.

My file cabinet full of clippings—a joke among friends—was in the hall, crammed with recipes for artichoke soup, features on transvestites in high-security prisons, one-paragraph traffic accidents. I got the folder labeled "Strange Science," triumphant that it was going to come in handy after all.

I had a cup of coffee at a coffee shop while I checked addresses. Then I spoke to a microbiologist who was about to prevent cavities with a vaccine. We arrived at his office at the same time, sharing an elevator. That made us affable. He was impressed that I'd heard of him—people all day blushed or swaggered or glowed in surprise that I'd heard of them, and I felt only slightly guilty when I flattered them with respect for their quiet work. Actually, the microbiologist said, speed-reading my résumé, he had a paper to present at an international conference in July; perhaps I'd check it now for grammar and clarity, then later work it into publication form? We shook hands. Next I dropped in on a man who was studying depression among the Amish. He didn't have anything right now, but a friend of his might. The friend, a psychopharmacologist with a wing of bright red hair behind each ear, had a huge tome that needed to be condensed into journal length. He'd in fact been sitting at his desk, masticating a pencil and wondering how on earth he'd do it, when his friend called to say I might drop by—"Santa's elf!" he greeted me, pumping my hand and immediately asking about my fee.

Could it be this easy? Cars vacated parking spaces as I pulled up. Everyone was in, everyone wanted to chat, and almost everyone seemed to need an editor, a writer.

On the crowded elevator in the next medical building I visited, I was shoved toward the back beside a young woman whom I noticed because she seemed so neat, so controlled, holding her purse and watching the floor numbers. The building had twenty-five stories. On the fourth floor, a lot of people got out of the elevator and the woman made a small sound, like clearing her throat; I didn't think anything of it. But on the fifth floor more people got out, and the next sound defined itself as a sob. Every subsequent stop took one person off the elevator and amplified the woman's sobs, until water was pouring through the hands she cupped to her face. No one said anything. We looked at one another sheepishly as if to say what can we do? By the sixteenth floor, it was just she and I on the elevator. Now she looked up every time the elevator stopped and cried when the doors closed. We both got off on the twenty-fourth floor.

"Um," I said. "Are you all right?"

She studied me with contempt. "Fine," she said.

We walked in opposite directions.

I took that as a sign not to get *too* cocky about my track record, and sure enough, the dermatologist who was next on my list had patients and wouldn't talk to me.

Next I spoke to an eye surgeon studying glaucoma, and another who was developing a new way to test chemicals, the present way requiring the eyes of live rabbits—my eyes opened wide at his impassioned talk of cruelty to animals. Neither man had immediate work, but both took my résumé with a look of considering where to stash it for handy reference. I spoke to a diabetes expert researching insulin at the cellular level and a wonder-drug R. & D. man with droopy, fleshy eyelids and an unhealthy look, as if he ate too much junk food; he not only had free-lance work for me, but he looked as if he'd ask me out to dinner eventually. I'd probably go.

How cheerful everyone was, how kind!

A biochemical corporation conducting a multimillion-dollar project to convert wood into ethanol had no free-lance work but would be happy to take an application for a full-time job. I politely refused. By now my briefcase was crammed with paper.

At a suburban cancer research center, I walked past cage after cage of mouse and dog and rat, remembered the crying woman in the elevator, and felt a little sad, but even there a secretary dreamily twirled in a chair, the phone tucked under her chin; people looking forward to being released for the weekend strutted the halls with hands in the pockets of their white gowns, thumbs sticking out, humming. In one cubicle, doctors had a birthday song and cake for a beaming lady doctor.

Maybe the California-like weather made everyone charitable. Maybe it was one of those days when my chameleon face changed for the better. Maybe too—I embraced the thought cautiously at first, then with abandon—I might be good at whatever I finally got around to doing, exuding confidence and competence. In any case, by three in the afternoon I had enough free-lance work to keep me fed and housed for at least two months.

I put down the top of the Fiat and cruised straight to Beaumont with tangled hair and fine spirits.

Theo and Nessie were playing hopscotch in the street between Pat's old house and her new house. Nessie, in pigtails and purple overalls, was probably slaughtering my brother. The squares were marked with packing tape rather than chalk. Theo's shirt-sleeves were rolled and he wore an expression of intense concentration as he stood on one foot, the other foot scratching an itch on the standing leg; one hand was on his waist, the other shielding his eyes from the sun. A peculiar posture to hold for any length of time, but then the Freeds have never specialized in grace.

"Look who saunters onto the scene too late to pick up any

heavy cartons," Theo said, with a grin that was, if not yet completely loving, at least conciliatory—what we didn't finish discussing tonight we'd discuss in two weeks, in D.C., when we convened for my parents' surprise anniversary celebration. "Don't think I didn't see that, Ness. Pat's still at the closing. Where've you been?"

"Your turn," Nessie said, poking my brother in the stomach. To me: "I'm winning. When Mom comes, we're going out for ice cream. *Go*, Theo!"

He went. I flopped on the curb to watch with the tired but floating sensation you often get on Friday after lunch at the end of a work week.

Pat soon arrived carrying a sixpack, her sandals, a signed contract on the house, and a check from Stacey for fifty thousand dollars—but no bottle opener.

"I don't care." She waved the sandals for emphasis in a way that made it clear she'd already had a beer or two after the closing. "Theo will open them with his teeth."

"Can we go for ice cream now?" Nessie asked.

"Soon, my patient darling. First we must briefly celebrate the end of an era."

Nessie returned, sighing deeply, to her hopscotch game. Theo's huge key chain had a penknife, small scissors, and several varieties of opener (an old gift from me, since he lost key rings so effortlessly). He opened the beers while Pat examined the check lovingly, then decided where to put it (back pocket). Pat and Theo sat on either side of me.

"Everything get done, no thanks to me?" I asked.

"Sure," Pat said. "What got *you* out so early?"

"A job. Three, to be exact, with the promise of more to come." I elaborated.

"Connie will love this," Theo said. "I see a Jewish doctor in your future."

"I hadn't thought of that," I confessed.

"How do you do it?" Pat asked. "I've always wondered. Never have I met anyone who gets work so effortlessly."

"Aw, shucks."

"Alex, you ought to run an international how-to-do-it workshop on job-hunting. Maybe that's your true calling."

"Double shucks," I said, shooting an eyebrow Theoward to see how he was taking Pat's praise of me. He looked puzzled, a bit sheepish.

"We're not really happy right now," Pat speculated. "We're just tired. Theo, let's stay the night. I mean, this is really it"— she opened her arms to indicate that she meant the street, the city, her life here. "Besides, you and your sister yapped all night. I haven't had a second with her. I just can't stand another minute of *motion*. I'm not moving for anything but food."

Theo offered to take Nessie out for ice cream, and Pat and I gazed after the noisy departing car, then laughed, hugged, shook our heads. "Well?" I said.

"Oh, God," Pat said.

She was crying.

"You're the second crying woman I've encountered today," I said. "Is it a trend?"

"Everything's wonderful!" she wailed.

"Could you elucidate?"

I may have found my brother childish and idealistic at times, but Pat thought he was energetic and generous and brilliant, and furthermore she had *always* had a crush on him, from the time they'd met six years ago. When we used to joke about how fine it'd be—given how well we got along—if one of us were a man, Pat had often had Theo in mind. But she'd never imagined they'd get to know each other well. Now she wondered if Theo hadn't been subliminally in mind when she applied for jobs in Boston, for there he was, right after the interview, bringing flowers to cheer things up and volunteering to baby-sit, taking her to the movies, listening to her go on about her new job. The sense of *déjà vu* they'd had right from the start wasn't merely a romantic illusion. They did know each other well. In understanding me, Pat already understood Theo. Ways he held his head, kinds of wry remarks, even how he smoked a cigarette—the gestures that are so hard to read when you first start a relationship—none of it was foreign to her. She trusted Theo's heart because she trusted mine; she could be open to him in a way she rarely was to a man. She felt blessed. She was so happy she thought she might float away. Other times the happiness made her feel heavy, as if she were drunk in the afternoon. I didn't mind, did I? I didn't think it was incestuous or bad or hopeless?

I didn't, though I was surprised. It looked as if Pat was about to get what she wanted, what all of us want: a man who saw her not as needy or limited, but in the lively self-sufficiency she had worked to cultivate. That Theo should assume her self-satisfaction to be innate was only fair. That, after all, was the promise: you leave the beauty salon after the make-over and are immediately accosted by a prince who marvels that a woman so amazing could be available for him to discover at such a late date. Maybe Pat and Theo's courtship would be the first I'd ever witnessed in which the inability to analyze didn't seem contrived or self-serving. The two people that I knew no one was good enough for, that no one deserved, had found each other.

"Will we be sisters-in-law?" I smiled.

"I know it's crazy. But I also know if I lived through Preston, I can live through anything. I have this feeling I can't lose."

"Could Nessie?"

"She lived through Preston too. My love for her is stable. Theo has been great with her."

"And China?"

"Don't. Don't make me think about that. I don't want to think at all."

She just stopped thinking out loud. I felt the humming motor of her thought in the arm she'd slipped through mine. We savored the beers. Like me, Pat was entertaining mental slides of her future with Theo: romantic dinners, Saturday nights by the TV with the flu. Though I'd never thought of it before, my brother and Pat had complementary improvisational styles: Pat moved furniture in the middle of the night, painted trim, arranged sprays of cattails and Queen Anne's lace, while Theo, who had a total lack of imagination for interior design, was a whiz at imagining activities and carrying them through—the museum, fishing trips, barbecues. He'd get Pat and Ness dressed to pose for interesting pictures in the snow on the roof; Pat would get the prints blown up and frame them. He'd wake them at dawn for a day at the Cape; Pat would remember suntan lotion. And I could even imagine Theo as a father. If he spent an hour teaching Ness how to use a camera, it wouldn't be because he wanted to be pedantic or paternal but because he wanted a picture of himself doing a headstand.

But I couldn't imagine Pat and Theo in bed. I didn't quite understand their attraction. Theo had a record of skinny blondes with large, wet eyes; Pat was big and direct. Pat was given to men with chests; Theo was skinny. Of course, before Walter I never pictured myself with a redhead. I momentarily panicked: Theo would leave her. I saw Theo with his sneer, his immaturity, his selfishness, Pat trying not to cry. But then Pat interrupted with her head on my shoulder and murmured, "It may work."

"Maybe," I said.

"Or it may not."

"One or the other."

"Or both. Will Theo bring us ice cream?"

"I hope."

Then I just couldn't think about Pat and Theo anymore.

Lately my attention span was short. I experienced huge, gnawing, vague impatience, wanting—as at my parents' house—to be anywhere else, doing anything else. Right then, I wanted to check my mail, repot my ficus, begin my medical editing.

"Alex," Pat said. "You want us to stay, don't you?"

"Of course I do."

I patted her knee. She patted mine. We crossed arms to knee-pat at the same time, then we slipped into a game of patsy, playing hard at top speed until our hands were red and numb. It was during this ten- or twenty-second interlude, with Pat and me carrying on like drunks or prepubescent girls, that Theo pulled up with—Pat and I noticed, pointed, and squealed at the same time—a flat on the tire I'd recently had patched, on the front end of the hopeless Fiat. Theo shrugged. The way the sun hit him in his cream shirt made him momentarily gorgeous as he fumbled for something in the trunk of the Packard. Nessie was carrying two double-scoop ice-cream cones, one for Pat and one for me. The ice cream was melting at an alarming rate and the scoops on both cones threatened to topple. "Come on," we said, "you can do it!" We clapped, Bronx-cheered, stamped our feet as she crossed the street with the cones. Never was a street so wide. Never did anyone walk in slower motion, with more care; and just as the gap between us and Nessie was about to close at last, our hands and the ice-cream cones in Nessie's hands as close as Adam's hand and God's in the Michelangelo Creation so often imitated in freeze frames, Theo was there—"Smile," he said—with a camera.

30

I want to be a great, kind woman, I told Theo, even better than Pat or Connie. Don't underestimate the human capacity for change, especially for complete reversal. Just as poor families often have the merriest Christmases and mean families often produce gentle and soft-spoken children, my years of failure and indecision may yet mount to ambition, resolve. Don't underestimate me. Mom and Dad have told us forever that nobody loves you like family, but nobody hates you like family, either. Get a pair of the rose-colored glasses they give you for 3-D movies and the distortion may give you a more focused picture. I have life in me yet. My brain isn't totally withered. See me as the Foreign Service interviewers must have seen me, as my thesis adviser and ex-employers did who recommended me, as the doctors did who trusted me with their research. When I walk down the street, men often smile at me. My figure isn't bad. I'm a pretty good cook. I'm only thirty, Theo.

"But why are you so upbeat about free-lancing?" Theo asked. "I know the pay's not bad, but you've always resented it before."

"Maybe because this time it feels so temporary. I believe I'll get a Foreign Service assignment. The free-lancing keeps me busy and it's challenging without being so demanding that it requires cigarettes—not a one for thirty-five days. I think thirty-five. Long enough to lose count. That's change. I'm not having nightmares anymore about Walter, plus I get the reward of a trip to San Francisco at the end of the month. I'm in the mood for winding, hilly streets and brightly painted little houses. How is it there? Can you believe I've never been?"

"Don't you think 'Go West, Young Woman' makes a goopy conclusion to a year of unemployment and dating a shithead?"

"It's an open-ended conclusion. Nothing's settled. I'm just taking a vacation on my MasterCard like normal folk. Know what's nicest? In the last weeks, between the free-lancing and friends, I wake up, then it's bedtime. It was just that kind of random busyness I was trying to overcome when I quit PR last October, but now it seems so airy, so light—a perfect soufflé. Of course, work gains a lot by the contrast to idleness. When you get over a cold, you're so astounded and grateful when the air power-steers straight through your nose to your vital organs. The year gave me an elementary and, I suppose, long-overdue lesson in point of view."

"I endured twenty-seven years of your encyclopedic vendettas to listen to you enjoin me to look on the bright side? Promise me this won't last."

"Probably not, but I'm hoping to have a longer than usual remission."

"So when are you going to finish your dissertation?" Theo snapped, in imitation of my father.

It was Friday, June 6th, the last day of my unemployment compensation, the day of my father's retirement after thirty years of government service, and my parents' thirty-second wedding anniversary. The time that Theo and Pat had been in Philadelphia had flown by, with free-lance work and new offers coming in at a good clip. I'd patched the Fiat's tire again and Theo had flown in to Philly the day before to drive to D.C. with me: inefficient, but more fun, and besides we had to get an anniversary gift for my parents. We'd planned a quiet surprise dinner for them and had enlisted Uncle Nate and Aunt Barbara to keep them out of the house for the afternoon. In the back seat were two bags of gourmet groceries, and china to complete my parents' second set—eight exorbitant pieces that Theo had paid for (my share would be forthcoming) with the sale, at a loss, of Judy Gold's engagement ring. Pat preferred emeralds and rubies; when it was time, Theo said, he'd get her something decadent, more ornate than a transparent rock on a prong. Much to my surprise, Pat was actually mulling over the possibility of accompanying Theo to Peking on August 23rd—either that or Theo would postpone the China trip until the spring so he and Pat could live together. "Isn't this premature?" I had asked her on the phone. "Terribly," she'd agreed, then launched into an ode on taking risks that was very similar to the one Theo had recited during our argument. Despite Pat's uncharacteristic willingness to be persuaded into a hasty decision of the heart, she couldn't be persuaded to accompany us to Washington. My parents, she said, were a jinx. Pat and Theo weren't prepared for the predictable disapprobation, and though I'd argued that Phil and Connie would love her, I admitted they couldn't deal with Vanessa. Not yet. It was better to wait. So it was just Theo and I on the road to Washington.

Because the geriatric Fiat had no shocks and because both of us were terrible drivers, the presence of the china and the perishables in the back seat gave our simple trip a quality of mission and a fragile feeling compounded by the promise that the mood at home would be more melancholy than celebratory: Sam had died two days before—or, rather, had been put to sleep. My parents' fourteen-year-old dog had been deteriorating for some months from prostate cancer, a distended liver, and a weak heart, and was presently being mourned with a vigor more appropriate for a spouse or an assassinated President.

"Do you think it's sick?" I asked Theo.

"You get attached to animals. It's sad to see them piss blood on your carpet, unable to walk."

"But have you ever heard Phil sob like that over anything before?"

"No one else has ever been as devoted to him as that dog, except Connie."

"You know what she told me? I asked if they'd get another dog and she said they couldn't find a dog like Sam. 'He was so dignified,' she said. 'If he had to take a crap, he never squatted on the lawn like other dogs. He went behind a bush. He was such a private person.' *Person!* I suppose the rude-reminder-of-mortality angle is especially oppressive on the heels of Phil's retirement. Do you think either of them could survive the other's death?"

"Every evening at six o'clock for fourteen years," Theo said, "Dad has come in, kissed Mom, thrown his jacket on the banister, and thrown out his arms to greet Sam while Mom sets down Sam's refilled water bowl with one hand, winding the clock with the other. Now every time she winds that clock there'll be a time warp where the bowl should be. Every familiar element is a link. You take one link out and the whole structure falls down."

"Do you think we'll ever have lives that ordered?"

"We already do. If you don't get your *New Yorker* on Friday, your whole weekend's shot."

"But I'm single. My best friend moved away. I don't have people in my life I'd die without day to day."

"What would you do if I died and you couldn't call me?"

"Kill myself," I admitted.

"I doubt that, but so much of love is habit. Less than a month of sleeping with Pat and she already knows a quick stroke to the nose will stop my snoring. I know she takes a long time to decide from menus, and if Nessie acts up it affects Pat's mood immediately—changes the way her face is set, the speed she moves at. That makes sense to me. What's stranger is the fact that when Picasso died, his mistress immediately killed herself. She'd seen him for fifteen years but she'd never lived with him, never once."

"I don't have any trouble understanding an elephantine passion. I'm more used to passion than to routine."

"Bull," Theo said. "That's the old scarcity-value argument."

"Certainly the Freed line is that passion is narcissism. The important thing is being good, and good means selfless. That's what upsets me so much about their reaction to the dog. We've always been made to feel like emotionally second-class citizens—we take rather than give. Their most violent commitment is to something that wags its tail when fed. On the most obvious level, I'm jealous of that unconditional affection."

"It's true that Sam never had to finish his dissertation."

"It makes me angry," I said.

"You, of course, have been a bad girl. You know, even when Pat's angry at Ness, which isn't often, she manages to communicate that the anger is over X event rather than casting a pall over Nessie's whole existence. On the other hand, Ness isn't spoiled. She feels guilt rather than deep insecurity. I've been watching very carefully, trying to figure out how Pat does it. It's very impressive."

The night before, in Chinatown, Theo had spoken a good deal about Nessie: what the child needed, possible conflicts between her needs and his. A year in China would be formative for a seven-year-old. I was beginning to suspect that Theo was, in his marrow, a family man. The suspicion was cheering—if Theo could rise to the occasion of family, so could I.

When we arrived in D.C., we bought flowers, moved everything into the laundry room, and parked the Fiat around the block to prolong my parents' surprise. It was quarter of four. This we knew because all four grandfather clocks played their songs for the quarter hour—as usual, out of sync. It didn't leave us much time to prepare. Still we took several minutes to unwind with our feet up, enjoying the air conditioning and shaking our heads at the absence of Sam. I might soon leave Philadelphia for who knew where and Theo might soon be in China with or without Pat and Nessie. The insecurity gave us a bond. Neither of us knew what we were doing and both of us were grateful for the simplicity of preparing a meal: veal saltimbocca, fettucini, and asparagus. Dessert we'd left for Phil, knowing that we shouldn't steal the show from his dessert ritual. By the time my parents pulled up at six, the preparation was finished, the cheese-board set up, the champagne chilled, and we were showered, poised to meet them at the door as some compensation for a lack of barking dog.

My mother opened the door, saw us, and burst into tears.

My father, already in tears, followed with a sack of take-out Chinese food. "No Sam," he said.

They looked terribly old. The mourning period was not as over as we'd anticipated.

"Happy anniversary," Theo and I said.

"That's why Barb and Nate kept us," Connie sobbed. "What a wonderful surprise. Oh, forgive us. We've been keeping to ourselves and out of each other's way, because every time we look at each other it's a faucet."

We all kissed. "You're eating Chinese take-out on your anniversary?" I asked, pointing.

"We don't have much appetite," Phil confessed. "Did you get a Foreign Service appointment yet?"

That he could instantly launch into his career litany, that my parents could play good Samaritans by feigning an appetite for their children's cooking, comforted me that the evening wouldn't be a lost cause so long as we kept off the subject of the dog.

That morning, they told us over the cheese, they'd booked tickets to Europe as a gesture toward celebrating their anniversary and my father's retirement—he would not start consulting work for a month—but mostly to get them out of the dogless house. Theo and I said we thought that was a great idea.

My parents didn't look well. Their eyes were swollen from

crying and lack of sleep. There was no avoiding the topic of Sam, because almost everything seemed to conjure up memories of him. Discussing death seemed both to alleviate and to aggravate the pain. "Every life owes a death," Phil said, several times to test the sound of his new aphorism, and Theo told the story about Chuang Tzu playing drums and singing at his wife's funeral; then, with his amazing memory, Theo quoted the Taoist master at length: "Heaven and earth were born at the same time I was, and the ten thousand things are at one with me. We have already become one, so how can I say anything? But I have just *said* that we are one, so how can I not be saying something? The one and what I said about it make two, and the two and the original one make three. If we go on this way, then even the cleverest mathematician can't tell where we'll end, much less an ordinary man."

"Zeno's paradox," I said.

My mother looked puzzled, but charmed.

"The Chinese are good folk," Phil said. "Very high mechanical, spatial, and mathematical aptitudes and very poor eyesight."

"That's more like the Phil we know and love," I said.

Red-eyed, Connie raised her glass bravely. "It's not so terrible to be sad every once in a while."

"No," I said. "It's not."

"Nicely put," Theo said, then shot me a look to see if I'd noticed it was a Judy Gold expression—I had. We both shuddered a bit.

"We didn't nickname Mom 'the Guru' for nothing," I said.

"The veal is delicious," Connie said. "Everything is. Isn't this delicious, Phil?"

"Yes. They don't have Italian food in China. I'm warning you, Theo."

Already we'd had too much champagne. We'd lit a candle despite Phil's reminder that he hated eating in the dark. The candle made the suburban kitchen vast and Gothic, made my sad parents as golden as Vermeers. Though it was dark, though the table was large, I could see a slight soft down on the side of my mother's face, near her ear, and was so moved by it that I reached out to stroke her cheek. She put a hand quickly to my forehead in response, as if I were a feverish child. My father leaned back in his chair and lit a cigar, as he had at the end of a meal since the beginning of time.

There was a moment in that light, after dinner, after my father's smoke had begun to swirl toward the window framing a formidable treetop dusk in the friendly purples, mauves, and evergreens of Monet's Giverny paintings, when we were all absolutely quiet, absolutely still. For a pulsebeat I was terrified. The picture was so pointillistic that I could almost see the dots breathing the illusion of life into the composition, and the scene threatened to disintegrate down to the molecular level the way the world sometimes does when you're tripping—that grisly LSD trick in which you can see the maggot-infested eye sockets beneath even the milkiest complexion; see, behind the silk of lip, the gums flaring away from the teeth as violently as a candle lit at both ends. But only for a pulsebeat. Then Theo and I smiled at each other. Theo was handsome, and on one level the smile was without complicity, the self-congratulatory smile of hosts that has been shared a million times. But on another level the smile implied not only the whole history of our alliance but the knowledge that Theo, too, sensed the tenuousness of the evening, more fragile than china or old photographs. It was as if in the space of that smile Pat and Nessie could vanish from Boston, my few remaining local friends vanish from Philadelphia, Walter and Judy die in the middle of whatever—dinner or taking childbirth classes; everyone, all plans falling off the earth, not even falling but just gone, explosive as a camera's flash or the tunnel that recedes to a blue dot when you turn off the TV. It was as if, if Theo reached for his cigarettes or I pushed back my chair to clear the table, our parents would at any moment cry again, dinner would be burned, we ourselves would vanish from Bethesda—or Theo would be in China, our parents in London, me at an embassy somewhere still trying not to smoke, still moping over this or that, or out of money with my furniture pawned and no phone, all lines dead, conference calls impossible. So we kept smiling. Theo didn't smoke and I—a miracle—didn't dream of smoking. We froze the camera-obscura smiles, the gritty grins of ceremonial masks, because for that moment, at least, we couldn't bear to be anywhere else.

A NOTE ON THE TYPE

This book was set in a film version of Janson, a redrawing of type
cast from matrices long thought to have been made by the Dutchman
Anton Janson, who was a practicing type founder in Leipzig
during the years 1668–87. However, it has been conclusively
demonstrated that these types are actually the work of Nicholas Kis
(1650–1702), a Hungarian, who most probably learned his trade
from the master Dutch type founder Dirk Voskens. The type is an
excellent example of the influential and sturdy Dutch types that
prevailed in England up to the time William Caslon developed his
own incomparable designs from them.

Composition by Centennial Graphics,
Ephrata, Pennsylvania.
Printing and binding by The Haddon Craftsmen,
Scranton, Pennsylvania.

Typography and binding design
by Virginia Tan